WE PAVED the WAY

WE PAVED the WAY

Black Women and the Charleston Hospital Workers' Campaign

O. Jennifer Dixon-McKnight

University Press of Mississippi / Jackson

The University Press of Mississippi is the scholarly publishing agency of the Mississippi Institutions of Higher Learning: Alcorn State University, Delta State University, Jackson State University, Mississippi State University, Mississippi University for Women, Mississippi Valley State University, University of Mississippi, and University of Southern Mississippi.

www.upress.state.ms.us

The University Press of Mississippi is a member of the Association of University Presses.

Any discriminatory or derogatory language or hate speech regarding race, ethnicity, religion, sex, gender, class, national origin, age, or disability that has been retained or appears in elided form is in no way an endorsement of the use of such language outside a scholarly context.

Copyright © 2025 by University Press of Mississippi
All rights reserved
Manufactured in the United States of America

∞

Publisher: University Press of Mississippi, Jackson, USA
Authorised GPSR Safety Representative: Easy Access System Europe – Mustamäe tee 50, 10621 Tallinn, Estonia, gpsr.requests@easproject.com

Library of Congress Cataloging-in-Publication Data available

LCCN 2025028712 (print)
ISBN 9781496860064 (hardback)
ISBN 9781496860071 (trade paperback)
ISBN 9781496860088 (EPUB single)
ISBN 9781496860040 (EPUB institutional)
ISBN 9781496860101 (PDF single)
ISBN 9781496860118 (PDF institutional)

British Library Cataloging-in-Publication Data available

CONTENTS

Acknowledgments vii

Introduction 3

Chapter 1—Charleston's Local Protest Tradition 9

Chapter 2—Hospital Workers and Health-Care Activism 22

Chapter 3—"Union Power" 37

Chapter 4—"Soul Power" 57

Chapter 5—Respectable and Disorderly 73

Chapter 6—"McNair Fiddles While Rome Burns" 88

Chapter 7—Resolution and Disillusion 107

Conclusion 121

Notes 125

Bibliography 157

Index 167

ACKNOWLEDGMENTS

I have been researching and writing on the 1969 Charleston hospital workers' campaign for more than a decade. Yet, there continue to be avenues to explore this rich local history. This is a project of inclusion. I appreciate the opportunity to be a part of the community of scholars who do the work of expanding our understanding of African American women's activism and their contributions to civil rights and labor movements, locally and nationally. Many thanks to the Charlestonians who shared their personal experiences and recollections of the city's civil rights and labor history. A special thanks to Rosetta Simmons. A quote from my 2008 interview with her inspired the title of this book. It has been an honor to have had the privilege to share time and space with individuals whose lives and work have pushed the Black freedom struggle forward.

I am grateful to be surrounded by scholars in and around the field who have and continue to provide guidance and support as I chart the journey of a scholar and educator. At various stages of this process, I have benefited from the scholarship, feedback, guidance, and support of key individuals. Jacquelyn D. Hall, thank you for being my forever adviser. Your willingness to offer insight and wisdom as I navigate the academy has been invaluable. Will Griffin, Brandon Winford, and Shannen Williams, I sincerely appreciate each of you for holding me accountable, giving me turn-by-turn guidance on the book writing and publishing process, and most importantly for your friendship. Kerry Taylor, I cannot thank you enough for always being the kind of friend and fellow scholar who wants to see everyone win. Your feedback on this project in its various stages has challenged me and enriched my approach to writing about this movement. Hester McFadden and Jerma Jackson, many thanks to you both for introducing me to African American history and African American women's history, respectively. Learning from the two of you changed the course of my life. To the scholars whose work blazed trails, created space, and laid foundation: Darlene Clark Hine, Deborah Grey White, Nell Irving Painter, Jacqueline Jones, Tera Hunter, Crystal Feimster, Chana Kai Lee, Thavolia Glymph, Jacquelyn D. Hall, Jennifer Morgan, and Barbara Ransby.

I taught United States history survey courses and African American studies courses at Tidewater Community College–Norfolk for five years. It was there that I learned the value of being a well-trained classroom teacher in addition to being a scholar. TCC–Norfolk students, faculty, and staff also taught me about the importance of making consistent and meaningful contributions to the campus community. Thank you to my TCC family for broadening my horizons as an educator. I joined the Department of History at Winthrop University in fall 2018, and it quickly became apparent that I had joined a campus community committed to collaboration, success, and excellence in and out of the classroom. Thank you to my Department of History colleagues for being a community of scholars that promote collaboration and comradery. I am grateful to be a part of the Winthrop community. It provides me with the space to teach the brightest students and work with the most amazing faculty and staff. Special thanks to Donald Rakestraw and Gregory Bell for being champions and amazing supporters. Heartfelt thanks to Adolphus Belk Jr., Takita Sumter, and Monique Constance-Huggins for being intentional in your guidance and support. I would be remiss if I did not acknowledge Gloria G. Jones, professor emeritus at Winthrop University. Thank you for being my accountability partner, developmental editor, and cheerleader as I made my way to completing this manuscript. There are not enough words to express how much your sharing this journey with me has meant.

I have been incredibly fortunate to get support through various avenues. Funding for research for this project has spanned from my work at the University of North Carolina at Chapel Hill through the present. Many thanks to the UNC–Chapel Hill Department of History, Graduate School, Folklore in the Department of American Studies, Center for the Study of the American South, the Oral History Association, and the Winthrop University Research Council. I am incredibly fortunate to have had the assistance and guidance of librarians, archivists, and support staff at the Avery Research Center for African American History and Culture (College of Charleston), Catherwood Library Kheel Center (Cornell University), Charleston County Library, Charleston, South Carolina Records Center, Perkins Library (Duke University), South Caroliniana Library (University of South Carolina), and Waring Historical Library (Medical University of South Carolina).

Finishing this book project has been an extraordinary experience. It has been another demonstration of God's grace in my life. Thank you to my village of family and friends for your unwavering love and support. There are too many to name, but you know exactly who you are and what your support has meant to me. Most importantly, thank you to my daughter Madison M. McKnight. Your presence gives me purpose. You are extraordinary, and that urges me to continue to strive for excellence.

WE PAVED the WAY

INTRODUCTION

> I didn't sit in an office behind a desk. When I went on strike,
> I had some shoes, but when the strike was over,
> there was a hole in the bottom of my shoes.
> —MARY MOULTRIE

My first encounter with African American women's history was as an undergraduate in the late 1990s at the University of North Carolina at Chapel Hill. In my first course on the subject, the professor introduced me to *To 'Joy My Freedom* by Dr. Tera Hunter and *For Freedom's Sake* by Dr. Chana Kai Lee. These groundbreaking books made critical contributions to the expanding field of Black women's history and set the course for what would become my scholarly endeavor to study the movements forged by working-class African American women. Both works shed light on the plight of Southern African American women to carve out spaces for themselves as citizens, wage earners, activists, and advocates, while blazing trails for the entire race to do the same. Each work explores their relentless dedication to economic and social justice. These authors offer a framework for exploring and discussing Black women's activism and movement-making, the ties between Black women's work and organizing, and the impact of placing African American women at the center of discussions on race, gender, class, and power.

Nearly a decade later, as a doctoral student, I worked as a field researcher in Charleston, South Carolina, for the UNC–Chapel Hill Southern Oral History Program and was tasked with conducting interviews that focused on the 1969 Charleston hospital workers' strike at Medical College Hospital and Charleston County Hospital. As I researched the strike, in preparation for the interviews, I realized that even though the historical accounts mentioned hundreds of African American working-class women at the center of the movement, their voices were largely absent from the narrative. In the summer of 2008, after spending two weeks in Charleston conducting interviews with several individuals who had been associated with the movement directly or the local protest community generally, I left the city with a topic that I would spend more than a decade unpacking.

I wrote this book to contribute to an ever-evolving discourse on African American women's history, particularly in the area of working-class African American women's activism. I wrote it with hopes of bringing the women who initiated the Charleston hospital workers' campaign to the foreground of Charleston's civil rights and labor movements. On the one hand, I felt a deep sense of responsibility to being a part of the work that sheds light on the hospital workers' experiences in and contributions to the strike. On the other hand, I realized that the reasons for the missing voices proved far more complicated than them being merely overlooked or left out of the historical narrative. Originally, I set out to build a narrative based on oral history and became painfully aware of the fact that my goal for conducting dozens of interviews with former hospital workers was optimistic and unattainable at that point. In some instances, their voices were missing from the narrative because that is what some of the women who had been involved preferred. What I later realized was that when I traveled to Charleston to conduct interviews in 2008 and again in 2009, it had only been a short time since former striking hospital workers had transitioned from agitators to heroines in public discourse. The hospital workers' strike had just begun to garner more positive attention and celebration. In the early 2000s, many of the former hospital workers were either no longer alive or had left that moment of activism in the past and had little interest in exploring their part in it. In the end, my interviews coupled with oral histories conducted by other scholars at least begin the process of elevating the voices of the working-class women who joined the ranks of African Americans who had been waging a dual assault against racial and economic injustice since the late nineteenth century by confronting Charleston's health-care system and threatened to bring the city to its knees.

Much of what has been written about the movement focuses on the strike and views it through an institutional lens. I expand the scope by including the more-than-yearlong grassroots process of organizing leading up to the strike and by tracing the aftermath of the conflict. I do so by exploring the protest community in which this movement was born, the complexities of the individual ideals that shape the movement, and the distinct experiences among the women at its center. I also refer to this moment as the hospital workers' campaign rather than the hospital workers' strike in an effort to highlight the agency and power of the women at the center and to encapsulate the depth and breadth of this moment.

I situate the hospital workers movement within a broad tradition of working-class African Americans activism in which civil rights and labor issues were organically intertwined. African Americans, in general, and African American women, in particular, who attempted to gain equality and access could make little use of their newfound freedoms without the economic means to do so. Many of the hospital workers who organized in 1969 earned $1.30 or less per hour, which as of February 1, 1969, was the federal minimum wage and meant they did not have enough income to adequately feed, clothe, and care for themselves and their families. According to the US Bureau of the Census, in 1969, up to 73 percent of African Americans in the South lived below the poverty line. Households headed by Black women subsisted at 68 percent below the poverty line. Black women in Charleston viewed securing a job at Medical College as a major step up from domestic or agricultural labor. Yet most found themselves relegated to the lowest rungs of the hierarchy within the hospital, where they received the lowest pay, were systematically denied promotions, and were assigned to segregated spaces based on their race not their position. Perhaps most important, they were subjected to countless acts of disrespect. These conditions account for the duality of their movement: their struggle for economic justice was inextricably linked to a demand for racial equality.[1]

Discussions of the "civil-rights unionism" that emerged in the 1930s and 1940s offer a framework for examining the complex cast of characters and organizations that converged in Charleston and shaped the hospital workers' campaign in 1969. Scholars argue that the Black working class, reinforced by leftwing unions, initiated the earliest phase of the civil rights movement. The post–World War II period became a "window of opportunity" for a labor movement addressing issues of race and poverty to emerge. The hospital strike demonstrates not only continuities in a struggle for jobs and freedom that wedded labor and civil rights but also the rise of a new wave of unionization among public sector employees into the mid-1970s.[2]

The hospital workers' campaign emerged in the aftermath of two of the city's key civil rights campaigns and drew on local movement leaders for support. The 1960 lunch counter sit-in in the heart of downtown to protest segregation in public spaces, and the 1963 ruling in the school desegregation case against the Charleston school board (South Carolina was the second-to-last state to maintain legally sanctioned school segregation) placed the modern civil rights movement front and center in the city. Framing the hospital workers' protest as a contribution to the city's Long Civil Rights Movement challenges the popular notion that the city never experienced any significant civil rights activism and that what little did occur came to a screeching halt in 1965. The hospital workers' campaign was a part of Charleston's long labor movement as well. The local tobacco workers' strike of 1945 provided organizing hospital workers with a "corridor" to unionize in the historically anti-union state. Unionized tobacco workers became a source of leadership and guidance as hospital workers grappled with how to utilize union representation to address their grievances. The support of the longshoremen's union was critical as well and created another connection to the city's labor history.[3]

Chapter 1 explores the local protest tradition and community of activists that served as the foundation and springboard for the 1969 hospital workers' campaign. This is the space where burgeoning local activists such as Mary Moultrie, Isaiah Bennett, and William Saunders found guidance, training, and support for their movement work in and around Charleston, South Carolina. This chapter also highlights the decades of protest and activism that preceded the late-1960s movement.

Chapter 2 offers a brief history of health care in Charleston, Medical College Hospital's founding, and the impact of racism and segregation on African Americans' access to health care. The chapter explores Medical College Hospital in the broader context of the national movement for equality in health care and the legally sanctioned racial discrimination inherent in the Hill-Burton Act. The hospital workers' campaign takes root in this chapter, sparked by the 1967 termination of five African American hospital workers from Medical College Hospital. African American and mostly female hospital workers from Medical College Hospital, eventually joined by Charleston County Hospital workers, began to organize informally around issues of low wages, poor working conditions, and disrespect.

Chapter 3 traces the evolution of hospital workers from informally organized to unionized. Organizing hospital workers, in general, and African American women hospital workers, in particular, was a relatively new endeavor for Local 1199 Hospital and Nursing Home Employees Union and the labor movement as a whole in the 1960s. This chapter explores Local 1199 from early years through its arrival in Charleston. The union's presence marked a shift in the visibility and autonomy of organizing workers in the movement. Local leaders worked both in tandem and in opposition to the

Northern union, but all parties were committed to supporting hospital workers, even if they couldn't agree on the most appropriate and effective approach. The more-than-yearlong organizing erupted into a strike in March 1969.

Chapter 4 explores the dramatic shift in the hospital workers' campaign after the arrival of the Southern Christian Leadership Conference (SCLC). Local 1199 recognized the need for additional support for striking hospital workers. The union's extensive experience with a civil rights–based approach to labor organizing, coupled with its past connections to SCLC, made the decision to call on the civil rights organization an easy one. The chapter explores SCLC's motivation for taking on the hospital workers' crusade as another attempt at the Poor People's Campaign after the assassination of Dr. Martin Luther King Jr. and the recent lackluster outcome of Resurrection City. SCLC mobilized support for workers locally and nationally while implementing traditional civil rights–style protest. This expanded the scale and reach of the hospital workers' campaign.

Chapter 5 concentrates on the various ways in which the hospital workers' campaign demonstrated the complexities of Black women's civil rights and labor activism in the mid-twentieth century. The women who forged the campaign became activists in the moment, largely motivated by a need to maintain a job that allowed them to support themselves and their families. Workers committed to being the boots on the ground during the movement, even when their presence, voices, and contributions were being overshadowed by the competing aims of the individuals and organizations that supported the campaign. The workers' approach to protest involved traditional civil rights nonviolent direct-action strategies and militant confrontation. The central focus of this chapter is to tease out the aspects of the hospital workers' activism that offer a window into the dynamic nature of Black women's activism.

Chapter 6 traces the evolution of the strike from a local campaign into a nationally recognized movement. The campaign experienced widespread support from national civil rights and labor organizations. Local 1199's presence in Charleston resulted in financial support from local and national labor organizations across the country. SCLC called on the full strength of the civil rights movement, mobilizing thousands of people in support of striking workers inside and outside the city. This shift in the scale of the campaign increased concern among local, state, and national leaders, which led to a stronger push toward resolution of the strike. As the movement reached its pinnacle, stakeholders began to explore strike resolution options.

Chapter 7 explores the resolution of the hospital workers' campaign at both Medical College and Charleston County Hospitals. Local 1199 and SCLC were running out of time and resources and needed the strike to end.

Hospital workers remained committed to the cause until the bitter end. This chapter examines the process of resolving the strike first at Medical College and then Charleston County. The strike reached an end without hospital workers at the resolution table.

Charleston's working-class women are a part of a long tradition of African American labor, activism, organizing, and leadership. Shedding light on the strategies that they employed to combat economic and racial injustice expands and adds complexity to the civil rights and labor narratives as they relate to the multidimensional experiences of Black women in history. It also helps to ensure that the legacy of their confrontation will not be forgotten and can serve as a resource in ongoing battles for economic justice and racial and gender equality.

Chapter 1

CHARLESTON'S LOCAL PROTEST TRADITION

The women involved in the hospital workers' campaign inadvertently stood at the crossroads of a waning confidence in a nonviolent direct-action approach to effect change and the rise of a militant, armed self-defense ideology. For African American women activists, being at the precipice of change was not foreign. The working-class Black women that banded together during the Charleston campaign, some transforming into activists only for the moment and others persisting in that role, galvanized a movement in the same spirit as those before and around them. Josephine St. Pierre Ruffin, a middle-class African American woman from Boston and founder of Boston's first Black women's organization, the Woman's Era Club, issued a call in the late nineteenth century that morphed into the founding of the National Association of Colored Women (NACW). The NACW built its legacy on the motto, "Lifting as We Climb" and the work of "uplifting the race generally and for the advancement of race women in particular." Black women founded one of the first nationally recognized organizations to focus on the plight of the African American community, setting the stage for Black women's contributions to movement building in the generations since. Charleston's hospital workers joined the ranks of these movement makers and change agents after being groomed and guided by a local protest community.

South Carolina—and particularly the city of Charleston, which is situated on a peninsula between the Cooper and Ashley Rivers—struggled to acknowledge the presence and proliferation of the local civil rights and labor movements through the middle of the twentieth century. This unwillingness to acknowledge the existence of a long-standing and ongoing protest tradition, however, did little to undermine its presence, persistence, and impact. The hospital workers' campaign emerged in the late 1960s as yet another moment in the trajectory of Charleston's vibrant movement history. While local and state leadership seemed to be jarred by the resistance of hospital workers, this moment was in keeping with the range of activism forged by working-class women. The movement history of Charleston, a port city with a great deal of historic charm, and the surrounding islands is illustrative of the convergence of several traditions of activism, demonstrating the very essence of the long civil rights and labor movements: community mobilization, community organizing, bridge leaders, church-based activism, militancy, and labor organizing. This local movement history grounds the 1960s hospital workers' campaign in a protest tradition among working-class African Americans that spans the twentieth century, stretches throughout South Carolina and across the nation.

Aldon Morris, in *The Origins of the Civil Rights Movement*, defines this "tradition of protest" as having been passed from generation to generation through familial ties, educational institutions, churches, and other community-based organizations. He argues that African Americans who seek social change and solutions to the issues that plague their communities find themselves drawn to a "protest community." The 1969 hospital workers' campaign emerged in the moment forged by a group of working-class Americans—all Black and mostly female—who largely did not identify as activists. However, it did not spontaneously materialize, and it did not exist in a vacuum. The movement emerged as an extension of and supported by generations of grassroots activism and movement building that defined and shaped the local, state, and national African American community. The hospital workers' activism bourgeoned within and had been influenced by an era of social movement undergirded by traditional civil rights strategies and replete with student-led resistance, antiwar sentiment, and the rise of Black Power.[1]

Despite efforts to diminish the existence and significance of the local civil rights movement in Charleston and the surrounding areas, the presence of a strong network of local Black leaders engaging in movement building and activist training made it impossible to overlook. Esau Jenkins, known to the local African American community as a "race man," epitomized the local civil rights movement of the early twentieth century. Jenkins, a longtime resident of Johns Island, became one of the most prominent local businessmen and renowned civil rights leaders with his activism centered on confronting and eradicating racial injustices within the African American community. Two incidents of racial violence, one in 1938 and the other in the 1940s, against Black men on Johns Island prompted Jenkins to begin the work of formally organizing around the issues plaguing their community. In the 1940s, a white man shot Sammy Grant, a Black Johns Island resident, for kicking his dog. After a ruling by a local judge that the dog owner was not liable, Jenkins and other members of the community raised money for an appeal, which they won. Subsequently, he and those who joined the effort to advocate for Grant, founded the Progressive Club in 1948 with the general aim to uplift "local African American islanders through education, voter registration and by making available opportunities that might otherwise be lost on people living in this isolated environment." More specifically, Progressive Club members set out to improve race relations, offer relief to victims of racial violence, and provide economic, political, and educational assistance to members of the community. In the late 1950s Jenkins expanded the reach of his activism beyond Johns Island by organizing the Citizen's Committee of Charleston County, which focused on "the economic, cultural and political improvement of local African Americans."[2]

Jenkins was also involved in the community more broadly. He joined the executive committee of the Charleston branch of the National Association for the Advancement of Colored People (NAACP) (Johns Island did not have a chapter), presided over the Johns Island Parent-Teacher Association, and managed the Sunday schools at Wesley United Methodist. He also became a member of the Progressive Democratic Party (formerly the South Carolina Colored Democratic Party), an all-Black political party founded in 1944 as the antithesis to the state's all-white Democratic Party. The organization worked closely with South Carolina NAACP branches to provide the state "with a two-party system always conducive to healthy government, the hope of a majority of white citizens, and the 'force' Negroes need to end many of the flagrant discriminations against them."[3]

Jenkins and his wife, Janie B. Jenkins, developed a dynamic approach to increasing Black voting through voter education. In the 1940s, he and his wife began to offer "free, reliable" transportation to Johns Island students and adults to schools and jobs in Charleston and the surrounding areas. Their only request for payment was that passengers registered to vote. Eventually, the couple purchased a Volkswagen Deluxe Station Wagon, also referred to as a "microbus," that they utilized as a family vehicle and to transport John Island residents. The bus, marked with the message "Love is Progress, Hate is Expensive," was indicative of the couple and their efforts to uplift the community. During a trip to Charleston, one of the female passengers requested assistance in learning how to register to vote. This sparked Jenkins's decision to pass out copies of the state laws regarding registration and voting to passengers on the bus. During stops within the city of Charleston, he would read and discuss sections of the state constitution with passengers on the bus. During a time when Black people were being deterred from the voting booths by policies, intimidation, and violence, Jenkins provided voter education to African Americans right in the middle of town in plain view. Developing a mobile voter registration school, one of his greatest accomplishments, became an important tool in increasing the number of registered voters on Johns Island and an enduring part of his legacy as a civil rights leader. While he possessed very little formal education, he has been characterized as a "brilliant man" and is remembered as an "enlightened man who dedicated his life to making the lives of islanders better." While Jenkins did not have direct involvement in the hospital workers' campaign, the legacy of his activism infused the fabric of the movement.[4]

Charleston and the surrounding areas maintained a long and rich civil right activist tradition often defined in scholarship and local memory by the contributions of local Black male leaders. Black women in the civil rights movement, locally and nationally, struggled with the significance of their contributions being overlooked and undermined. A shift in the scholarly treatment of Black women's activism has occurred in the last three decades. Scholars have begun to pay closer attention to the distinct nature of Black women's influence on the movement as trailblazers, torchbearers, bridge leaders, and purveyors of participatory leadership. Septima P. Clark emerged as a pillar of the "protest community" and as a key figure in the network of Black people in Charleston and the surrounding islands who involved themselves in improving the lives of local Black residents. Clark, a native Charlestonian born to a father who was a former slave and a mother who was a Haitian immigrant, began teaching on Johns Island in 1916 at the age of eighteen because the city of Charleston prohibited the employment of Black teachers in its segregated public schools. Clark began her career in a one-room schoolhouse, where she oversaw over one hundred students with just one other teacher. As her career as an educator evolved, so did her civic engagement. Early in her career she joined the NAACP in an effective crusade to end discriminatory hiring practices in Charleston City Schools. In the late 1940s, she worked alongside Jenkins to provide aid to migrant farm families on Johns Island. She began teaching in Charleston City Schools in 1947. Less than a decade later, the school board terminated Clark's employment. South Carolina passed a law in 1956 that prohibited city or state employees from belonging to civil rights organizations. Clark ignored the mandate and publicly persisted in her involvement with the local NAACP. Undaunted, she took her dismissal as an opportunity to devote herself full-time to eradicating the issues that she believed were most prevalent in the lives of African Americans such as "the need for better schools, better health care, better job opportunities and wages, and increased voter participation."[5]

In the early 1950s, Clark began to develop a "citizenship pedagogy" which empowered the Black community by making a connection between foundational education, literacy, and the ability to understand politics and the economy. By the mid-1950s she had become fully engaged in the role that Belinda Robnett refers to as a "professional bridge leader." Robnett defines Clark as "a grassroots leader who moved from one rural community to another teaching literacy and citizenship, a leader with the ability to connect the needs of the people with the goals and objectives of a movement." After she became involved with the Highlander Folk School, an interracial adult education center in Tennessee, Clark maintained her ties to the Johns Island community. During her early years at Highlander, she and Jenkins worked closely to address adult education, voter registration, women's and children's health, and the overall well-being of Black residents of Johns Island. She returned to the island in 1957 to conduct its first Citizenship School, which provided an adult education program, with a particular focus on voter literacy, to African American residents. Clark met with students two nights a week for six weeks. At the end of the course, eight out of the fourteen adult students became registered voters. Clark's work on the island in conjunction with her connection to Esau Jenkins ultimately created a corridor for Black leaders from the island and surrounding areas to take part in the work being carried out at Highlander, as students and teachers. Their collaborations exemplified the value of the protest community and how local leaders utilized it to build and maintain movement.[6]

Individuals like Jenkins and Clark provided a model for local grassroots organizing and its meaningful impact. Their contributions helped shape the activism and leadership of Mary Moultrie, a nurse's aide at Medical College Hospital. She had a personal interest in the discrimination and inequality workers confronted. Reared on Wadmalaw Island by a father who worked at the naval shipyard and a mother who worked as a domestic worker and a housewife, Moultrie closely identified with the plight of the Black working-class. Moultrie got her start in civic engagement as a teenager working with Jenkins on local voter registration drives and other community efforts. Her interest in activism and organizing flourished within this protest community. She began her training as an activist and organizer by assisting in adult education classes and participating in the Citizen's Committee community organizing. Jenkins invited her to travel with him to participate in community events and gatherings. Local leaders called on Moultrie, as a teenager, to give speeches at meetings of the NAACP and Citizen's Committee. This training served as the foundation of the leadership she would be called on to provide during the hospital workers' campaign.[7]

In 1960, Moultrie moved to New York after graduating from Burke High School, an all-Black industrial school on Charleston's peninsula, and got a job at Goldwater Memorial Hospital in Long Island, New York. According to her, many Black women in Charleston followed the same pattern: after you graduated from high school, if your family could not afford to send you to college or you could not find a job, the next step would be to move north for work. She began as a nurse's aide, and after taking what the hospital referred to as a "waiver course," she was promoted to a licensed practical nurse and quickly became involved with the hospital's American Federation of Labor and Congress of Industrial Organizations (AFL-CIO) affiliated Teamsters Union. She recalled, at that particular hospital, joining a union was a part of being employed: "I knew that a union was for the good of the people. It was new to me, but it was almost an automatic thing." Moultrie returned to Charleston in 1967, just before the moment that sparked the hospital workers' campaign.[8]

Returning to Charleston, Moultrie immediately encountered the stark differences between Southern and Northern race and labor relations in the late 1960s. In New York, she had grown accustomed to the amicable nature of race relations: "In New York everybody, Black, white, Puerto Rican, everybody got along well." Back in Charleston as a hospital worker at Medical College, she experienced the precarious position of being Black within the Charleston workforce firsthand. She now faced the racism and segregation she remembered from her youth and witnessed how it translated into the work environment. She recalled, "When I came here I could see the separatism. Blacks didn't sit in the same lounge. They had a lounge, we had a locker room." She even faced demotion when she returned to Charleston. The hospital would not accept the training Moultrie received in New York, but knowing she needed work, she accepted the job as a nurse's assistant. Even with the challenges, working at the hospital was considered a good job for Black women in Charleston and a sizable step up from domestic labor. Within Southern Black communities, the "nonprofessional" hospital jobs gave the persons in those positions higher status. The steadiness of the work was more important than the type of work. Having that kind of employment gave workers more stability to the extent that many could enter realms of American society previously outside of their reach, such as home ownership.[9]

Precarity characterized the condition of employment among African American members of the working-class in the late 1960s. Charleston is no exception. Five Black female nurse's aides and licensed practical nurses (LPN) reported for work at Medical College Hospital during the holiday season of

December 1967. Anticipating that the workday would be like countless others, the hospital workers requested patient updates from their supervisor—a white registered nurse (RN)—in preparation for the shift change. The supervisor refused to follow the normal procedure and demanded that the women either get to work without the patient reports or leave. Defying the directive to operate against protocol, the women declined to proceed, and as instructed, they left. As a result of their defiance, hospital administrators fired the workers.[10]

As this moment unfolded, the presence of a viable and active protest community emboldened Moultrie to act in defense of herself and her coworkers. Moultrie quickly realized that Black nonprofessional workers, most of whom were Black women, faced a number of problems as employees of Medical College. In addition to a lack of job security, there was the matter of earned income. At the time, she earned $1.30 per hour, the same amount that many other Black workers made after a decade of employment. For hospital administrators, the fact that workers were making more than a dollar an hour was a major step in the right direction. According to John E. Wise, then the vice president and treasurer of Medical College, workers made fifty cents an hour in 1967. He argued that by 1969, the pay had been raised to $1.30 per hour. That amount was the federal minimum wage, but according to workers, it was not enough for them to adequately support their families.[11]

Equally if not more important than the issue of low wages was the matter of human dignity. According to historian Stephen O'Neill's assessment of the situation at Medical College, "the condescension with which most white supervisors at the hospital traditionally viewed blacks increasingly came in conflict with the rising expectations of Black workers." Workers' memories corroborate O'Neill's assertion. Moultrie recalled, "It was just a really bad situation. They didn't have any respect for us whatsoever. They would call some people out of their names. Call them monkey grunts, things like that. The treatment is what motivated people to want to change things. The discrimination, the prejudice sort of blew the top off the bottle." According to Claire Brown, an obstetrical technician at Medical College, "There was a lot of lack of respect. Basically, it was a Black-white issue. I don't think whites [in similar nonprofessional positions] felt it. Of course there wasn't too many whites that was in the positions we were—unlicensed, nurses' aides-type positions." Naomi White, a member of the OBGYN nursing staff at Medical College and quick to demand respect for herself and her coworkers, contended, "I could talk for myself and defend the other people's affairs because several times they tell me, 'Ms. White, you should mind your business. This doesn't concern you.' I said, 'It does concern me. You see the color of her skin and the color of mine? That's where the concern come in, and you don't be talking to her like that.'" Workers began to discover the commonalities in their complaints: the financial struggles they faced, instances of discrimination and the overall feeling of disrespect that they experienced personally or witnessed among other Black hospital workers.[12]

When Moultrie contacted William Saunders—a personal friend and prominent Black leader in the Charleston community—regarding the matter of the five terminated hospital workers, she brought attention to the broader issue of workers' grievances. Saunders, a self-proclaimed militant, worked as a foreman at the local mattress factory and had established himself as a powerful activist and organizing force in the community. Deeply involved in local voter registration and integration issues, the Johns Island resident believed that the concerns over discrimination and segregation within the hospital reflected larger issues in Charleston and the state in general. According to Saunders, when Moultrie approached him about the five terminated workers, he and three local ministers had been waiting for the opportunity to instigate a civil rights campaign in Charleston. He recalled, "What we did is that we waited for a very good case. Now, when I say case, not as it relates to legal terms because that's why I'm not concerned with the law, is whether or not we got power or not to enforce laws, but laws doesn't faze me that much. But we waited for the right time. . . ." According to Saunders, this moment happened to be a nice fit for a plan that was already taking shape among the city's Black leadership. He reasoned that organizing hospital workers presented as a natural progression in the broader civil rights struggle to bring an end to racism, injustice, and inequality.[13]

A working-class upbringing marred by racism and discrimination motivated his involvement in and commitment to matters of injustice and equal rights. In 1936, before his second birthday, Saunders's mother sent him by train unaccompanied from New York to Johns Island to live with her parents. His grandparents, like most Black people on the island, were Gullah, and they raised Saunders fully immersed in the language and culture. Gullah ancestry originated in West Africa and Gullah peoples are largely concentrated in the port cities and sea islands of North Carolina, South Carolina, Georgia, and Florida. The Gullah are notable for preserving aspects of their African heritage through language, handcrafts, and cuisine. They speak a language that the National Park Service of the United States Department of the Interior recognizes as "the only officially designated African-American Creole language in the United States." The language, a product of the communication that developed between Africans and British slave traders along the West African coast during the slave trade, stands out as one of the most distinctive aspects of the culture. In later years, numerous individuals and organizations, including those at the local and national level, initiated efforts to highlight the culture and preserve its history. But according to Saunders, the attitudes toward Gullah culture in the 1960s were far from positive. He remembered the stigma attached to being Gullah and the ostracism he suffered due to his heritage, "And [I] was treated so bad, being from the country and speaking a language called Gullah and folks making fun. There was a feeling in folk that if you spoke Gullah that you're stupid. The Blacks in the city of Charleston would just treat folk from the country just real, real bad."[14]

Saunders's grandparents, unlike most Black people on the island, owned the eighteen acres of land where they lived and farmed. White farmers sold Black people land they deemed undesirable, but Johns Island's Black residents took advantage of the swampy areas by growing rice. Saunders's grandparents produced sugar cane, peanuts, sweet potatoes, and sesame seeds in addition to raising livestock. His grandfather, William Pickney, also supervised a plantation for a white absentee landowner on the island. Despite their landownership, Saunders's grandparents were poor, and his formative years were bittersweet. His grandfather died when Saunders was seven, a devastating blow. He considered his grandfather a "remarkable person" who, even though he lacked education and literacy, was highly skilled and incredibly astute.[15]

Saunders's activist spirit was nurtured in the same protest community as Moultrie's. According to his recollection, he was involved in the Progressive Club from the beginning and even takes some credit for its origination. Saunders was only in his early teens when the organization was founded, and it is debatable whether he actually had a serious role in its development—though he did eventually serve as the organization's business manager. It is clear, however, that his civic engagement had roots in a community of grassroots organizers. Saunders fondly recalled his introduction to the local protest tradition, as he discussed two women from his childhood: "There were a couple of old ladies where I lived that used to take me for a walk and, you know, that used to talk to me and stuff like that. They were really good to me. They had no background, education, they had no children or anything, but they were just good people." These women, along with his grandmother, were among the original members of the Progressive Club. Saunders and his family also attended the same church as Esau Jenkins.[16]

Like Moultrie, Saunders attended Burke High School, arriving every day by bus because Black students were not allowed to attend high school on Johns Island. The unpleasant nature of his high school experience, filled with ridicule due to his poverty and Gullah accent, made it an easy decision for Saunders to leave school in 1951 at the age of sixteen to join the United

States Army. In spite of the fact that the United States was at war with Korea, Saunders saw his enlistment as an opportunity to escape poverty. He did not, however, anticipate that the racism he faced as an enlisted soldier would be far worse than anything he had endured in his hometown and surrounding areas. After basic training in Hawaii, he was sent straight to the front lines in Korea, along with only a handful of other Black soldiers. According to Saunders, "They took us in on that LST. I don't know if you're familiar with what that is, but it's the Navy ship that drops the front down and lets you run up on the beach with a gun to shoot people. That's how they did us. So it's been a hell of an experience." Ironically, even though Saunders found himself shoved out on the front line, he fondly remembered, "the only place that I've ever felt like an American was in Japan and Korea. The only place I ever was treated like an American was in Japan and Korea."[17]

Shortly after his return to the United States, he faced the brunt of that reality. During combat, Saunders suffered an injury to the foot and had to be hospitalized for three months in Japan. The Army honorably discharged Saunders at the rank of Staff Sergeant when he was nineteen years old. He returned to Fort Jackson in Columbia, South Carolina, collected his pay, and, along with several white soldiers, rushed to the local Greyhound bus station to get a ticket home. A white police officer approached him with his gun drawn asking, "Boy what's wrong with you?" Saunders expressed his confusion, and the officer responded, "You know you don't belong in here." Saunders, who had apparently forgotten the rules of racial etiquette in the South, responded, "Officer, no, I did not know I didn't belong in here. Where do I belong?" The officer directed him back outside to the back of the bus station where he could purchase his ticket. Saunders, expecting support from his fellow soldiers, was unprepared for their reaction. The men he stood with on the front line, looked the other way, refusing to offer a helping hand or speak up in his defense. As he sat down at the back of the bus headed home, he gazed forward at the white soldiers seated at the front of the bus and experienced an epiphany that would ultimately guide the course of his life and work, "You got to be a damn fool. You're in Korea fighting for freedom for Koreans and you ain't free yourself."[18]

After his return from war, Saunders quickly became involved in the local civil rights movement. But while he believed in its general aims, he openly contested its nonviolent ideology. "I consider myself a militant because I consider Blacks—if we believe in certain things, both for our family and our community, then we are militants." While he never adopted Islam as his personal faith, he subscribed to many of its teachings and philosophies: "I started watching Malcolm . . . [and] the Honorable Elijah Muhammad, because some of the stuff that he said was teaching, like: first know thyself and second know thy enemy, and if you know that nobody can do you any real harm. So if you begin to study yourself, your limitations, your strength, and those kind of stuff but also study your enemy, you can do it." His philosophies and approach to mobilizing and organizing provided hospital workers with support that became critical to their developing movement.[19]

Moultrie and Saunders began working closely with Isaiah Bennett to organize the workers who had already come forward and to figure out next steps. Bennett, a prominent figure in Charleston's labor movement, was born and raised less than forty miles up the South Carolina coast in McClellanville. He moved to Charleston in 1942, when he took a job at the American Tobacco Company's cigar factory. During his first years at the company, he joined the Tobacco Workers Union Local 15A of the Food, Tobacco, Agriculture and Allied Workers and Congress of Industrial Organizations (FTA-CIO) and participated in the organizing that led to the 1945 Charleston Cigar Factory Strike, one of Charleston's most extensive and impactful labor struggles. He was drafted to serve in the United States Army during World War II. Once the war and his military service ended, he returned to his job and the organizing efforts. Years later, Bennett's considerable union and labor organizing experience would prove to be a valuable asset to other local leaders and workers alike in both organizing and executing the hospital workers' strike.[20]

The cigar factory operated in Charleston from 1903 until 1973. When workers walked out on October 22, 1945, it was the city's largest employer. Workers in the cigar factory were separated by race and gender. African Americans worked on separate floors from white workers and found it almost impossible to obtain higher-ranking positions as foremen, mechanics, or oilers. Both Black and white women made cigar labels, but they did so on different floors of the factory. To further demonstrate the attention to maintaining separate spaces based on race, the factory provided separate water fountains and restrooms for Black and white workers.[21]

Two key events led to resistance among workers and ultimately to their strike: the cigar factory's refusal to honor their agreement to give unionized workers back pay after the war ended and the termination of a Black male employee due to allegations that he was "taking familiarities with Black female workers." After the war ended in late September 1945, workers developed and submitted a new union contract to the American Tobacco Company that included a request for wage increase and the back pay they had been promised. Responding to the union's appeal, the National War Labor Relations Board weighed in on the matter and mandated that the agreement be honored, including workers receiving the pay that the company withheld from December 1944 until October 1945. The factory's executives ignored the order and refused to negotiate with Local 15A president, Reuel Stanfield.[22]

The final blow hit on October 1, 1945, when Harold F. McGinnis, the factory manager, fired a Black male worker after allegations submitted by his white female supervisor that he was dallying with his Black female coworkers. The accused employee, a married man, was subsequently fired without warning. In response to what they believed was an unjustified termination, on October 3, Local 15A union stewards initiated an all-day sit-in in which approximately one hundred workers arrived, reported to their stations but refused to work. On October 4, when workers realized that the employee whom they believed had been wrongly terminated would not be reinstated, nearly a thousand workers walked out. In an attempt to quickly resolve the issue and get workers back to their machines, McGinnis agreed to meet with Local 15A representatives, address workers' grievances, and issue the retroactive pay. But the plans that McGinnis offered to handle their concerns were vague, and he was slow in issuing the retroactive pay. Workers felt that their employer continued to disregard their concerns and that the pervasiveness of discrimination and unfair treatment would persist.[23]

On October 22, 1945, approximately twelve hundred workers walked out of the cigar factory. They offered the following demands: back pay and a twenty-five-cent raise, implementation of nondiscrimination clauses in the company's hiring and firing processes, medical insurance and a closed union shop with membership as a stipulation of employment. The vast majority of striking workers were Black women, but there were a few Black men. Some white workers, both men and women, also participated. The union typically held segregated meetings, but this strike ushered in a new era of unionism in this branch of the Congress of Industrial Organizations (CIO). On the day they walked out, both Black and white workers met at the "Negro" United Service Organizations (USO) and decided that all future meetings would be integrated. The first of these integrated union meetings was held on October 26, 1945.[24]

The strike ended during the last week of March in 1946. Three things drove the resolution of the strike in the workers' favor. First, the solidarity of workers throughout the nation became problematic for the tobacco industry. In addition to Charleston workers, American Tobacco Company workers in Philadelphia, Pennsylvania, and Trenton, New Jersey, also staged strikes. Fellow workers refused to buy or smoke Lucky Strike and Pall Mall cigarettes. The National Maritime Union removed these two brands of cigarettes from their ships. Organizations across the country joined in the boycott of these products. The reduction in cigarette sales heavily impacted American Tobacco's bottom line. In addition to these boycotts, workers received financial assistance from a number of different sources, ranging from large national political organizations to individuals who just wanted to show their support. Even though there was not an abundance of funding, the fact that workers realized they had support provided a sizable boost in their morale. Most important was the "women's own determination and courage." In the six months that workers faced the perils of walking the picket line, they only had one negotiation meeting and that was the meeting that ultimately settled the strike. Workers had to possess a great deal of strength, a willingness to be patient, and a sense of hope in those months filled with both protest and uncertainty.[25]

At the end of the negotiations between the union and the American Tobacco Company, workers received a raise of eight cents per hour, a fraction of what they demanded. However, they achieved a number of intangible gains as a result of the strike. The mere fact that this group of working-class citizens, comprised of mainly women, faced off with one of the country's largest and most formidable companies and made substantial strides in the direction of equality and economic justice was a major feat. In addition to their personal and collective accomplishments, organizing as a racially unified Southern group set an example for the city of Charleston specifically and the South generally. Their movement offered a new approach to unionizing and organizing. Moreover, the success of the campaign cannot be measured only in terms of gains and losses because it opened the door for future movements and its legacy continues to endure. Considering the similarities and connections between the cigar factory workers' strike and the hospital workers' strike that emerged more than twenty years later, it becomes clear that the earlier campaign set the stage and provided a movement model for the campaign in 1969.[26]

Hundreds of Black, mostly female, hospital workers challenged Charleston's white power structure by going on strike from Medical College of South Carolina and Charleston County Hospital in 1969. Hospital workers spent more than a year orchestrating a civil rights–based labor movement in which they informally and formally organized around issues of low pay, racial discrimination, disrespect, and the unwillingness to acknowledge union representation. These efforts climaxed on March 20, 1969, and hospital workers joined the ranks of African Americans who had been waging a dual assault against racial and economic injustice since the 1930s.

Chapter 2

HOSPITAL WORKERS AND HEALTH-CARE ACTIVISM

From the end of the Civil War through the late 1960s, the demand for access to and equality in health care became one of the most critical and complex aspects of the African American freedom struggle. The African American community, particularly in the South, grappled with limited access, or no access, to health care, which often meant that the most routine issues could lead to long-term ailments and even death. African American students faced the challenge of being barred from local medical schools and medical training facilities, forcing them to seek and obtain training outside the South or to choose other fields. Southern cities and towns offered limited options for African American medical practitioners pursuing jobs and requesting access to health-care facilities for themselves and their patients. The complicated nature of race-based inequality and discrimination in health care resulted in a multifaceted resistance that galvanized the African American community, patients, and practitioners.

Exploring the history of Charleston's public health-care system and its connection to evolving resistance to discrimination and exclusion in health care serves two important purposes: It offers a window into what unfurled at the intersection of the civil rights movement and health care in the South. It also contextualizes the 1969 hospital workers' campaign by illuminating the pivotal moments that emerged alongside and in response to the evolution of Charleston's local health-care system. Prior to the late 1960s, local health-care policies and guidelines strictly adhered to the ideals and expectations of the racially segregated South. Charleston's approach to public health, albeit reluctantly and slowly, arose in response to and amid the national debate around the issue of "separate but equal." The history of health care in the city reveals the progression of nineteenth- and twentieth-century health care, the impact of race on access to local health care for patients and practitioners, and how the African American community experienced it. Exploring that history proves critical to understanding the late 1960s rift between African American hospital workers and two local Charleston hospitals, Medical College Hospital and Charleston County Hospital. The struggle for access to and equality in health care for African Americans helped galvanize community support for the hospital workers' campaign. This chapter frames the evolution of Charleston's health-care system as the backdrop for the 1969 campaign which emerged at the intersection of the civil rights and labor movements as well as at the core of struggles in civil rights and health care.

Due to poor sanitary conditions, Charleston residents from the mid-eighteenth century through the early nineteenth century experienced frequent cases of yellow fever, malaria, smallpox, and dysentery. Making matters worse, the city had limited health-care facilities and lacked a formal organization for medical professionals. An organization began to take shape during a meeting of local scholars and physicians who "desired to act as a Committee to consider such matters as will tend to improve the Science of Medicine, promoting liberality in the Profession, and Harmony amongst the Practitioners in this City." On December 24, 1789, the group unanimously voted to form a medical society. The Medical Society of South Carolina became the first major organization of medical professionals in the area. Comprised of fourteen members of the local medical community, the society guided the city toward a healthier citizenry by improving sanitation practices and establishing dispensaries for the "sick poor." By the early nineteenth century, in an effort to build a stronger public health-care system, City Hospital and St. Philip's Hospital became the main medical facilities available for white citizens, while a few small private hospitals were established in the city to treat Charlestonians of African descent.[1]

In 1821, the society developed the idea of building the first medical school in the South, as the majority of them were concentrated in the northeastern region of the nation. The society petitioned the state legislature for a charter and funding to establish the school. The South Carolina General Assembly granted the charter through an act passed on January 1, 1824, but rejected the plea for funds. Consequently, the seven original members of the faculty provided the financial backing for the project. Medical College of South Carolina opened on November 24, 1824, with thirty students. The institution experienced steady growth and by the academic year 1827–1828,

129 students were enrolled, the vast majority of whom came from areas within the state. By the end of 1831, the faculty expressed resistance toward the society's authoritarian approach to governing the college. Consequently, they petitioned the state legislature with a proposal to change the governing body of the institution, and the society countered with a proposal of their own. The society refused to concede control, and as a result the entire faculty resigned and formed the Medical College of the State of South Carolina. The new Medical College, incorporated in 1832, opened its doors in the heart of Charleston using the Old Theatre at the west end of Broad Street. The new Medical College, beginning with 105 students, 80 percent of whom from within the state, thrived causing the original Medical College to decline and close in 1838. The new medical school offered a limited health-care option for the Black community as it established an infirmary in 1840 that provided free health care for African Americans with "surgical diseases for the purpose of furnishing instruction at the bedside of the sick for medical students." It operated as a private institution until 1913, when it was recognized as a state institution to educate only white students.[2]

Access to health care remained limited, and health-care training facilities ceased to exist for African Americans in Charleston until the mid-1800s. Thomas Roper, a local merchant, pioneered the integration of health care in Charleston. In 1845, his last will and testament endowed the Medical Society of South Carolina with all of his property on East Bay and Queen Streets with instructions to take any income earned from rent or sale to build a hospital in Charleston "for the permanent reception or occasional relief of all such sick, maimed and diseased paupers as need surgical or medical aid, and whom without regard to complexion, religion or nation." Roper Hospital opened in 1856 with a separate ward to serve Black patients. In the years after the Civil War, the city underwent significant growth in the number of its health-care facilities. However, except for one ward at Roper Hospital, the majority of Black patients were still treated at underfunded private hospitals, dispensaries, and the local health department. Surprisingly, between 1850 and 1880 mortality rates among African Americans spiked from 21 to 41 percent. There could be a few explanations for the increase in deaths within the African American community despite the increased access to health care: First, an increase in the reporting of deaths among African Americans could be, at least in part, an explanation for the significant increase in the community's mortality rate. Second, was the reality that while the city's health-care system burgeoned, the African American community continued to be underserved and at-risk.[3]

By the early twentieth century, Charleston, like most of the South, persisted in its tradition of disenfranchisement and racial segregation. The Medical College remained wholly segregated; Black students had to leave the region for medical training. In 1938, the Supreme Court moved the needle toward integration in its ruling in *Gaines v. Missouri* (1938), mandating that states had to admit Black students to white graduate schools or provide them with equal facilities and programs, laying the groundwork for what would prove to be the NAACP's successful challenge to educational segregation. The city of Charleston moved slowly and reluctantly in the direction of offering greater access to the field of medicine for African Americans. By the mid-1950s, African American women in Charleston could receive nursing training at Roper Hospital. Medical College admitted its first African American student in 1965, nearly thirty years after *Gaines v. Missouri*. By 1976, eleven years later, the medical school only had nineteen African American students. Medical College remained the only medical school in the state until 1977 when the University of South Carolina School of Medicine admitted its first class. The limited number of medical training facilities coupled with restricted access to said facilities, meant African Americans left either the state or region for medical education or training.[4]

In August 1946, Congress passed the Hospital Survey and Construction Act, most often referred to as the Hill-Burton Act, which provided funds for the construction and modernization of hospitals. The legislation mandated that states designate an agency that would implement the program and develop a plan for administering the funds to local health-care facilities. The Surgeon General of the United States, in addition to vetting and approving funding applications, had the responsibility of ensuring that each facility provided care to all patients regardless of "race, creed, or color." Despite the anti-discrimination language, the act included a "separate but equal" clause that allowed facilities in areas where segregated health care had been customary to maintain those practices and receive federal funding. While the act significantly improved the South's abysmal health-care system, it left segregation and its inherit inequities largely intact.[5]

Parallel to the persistence of racial disparities and discrimination in health care, buttressed by the Hill-Burton Act, resistance brewed with the direct aim of confronting and eradicating this racial injustice and its impact. Beginning in 1954, the United States Supreme Court handed down a series of rulings that challenged the constitutionality of the act's "separate but equal" clause. By the early 1960s, health-care activists were focused on racial segregation and inequality as the root cause of disparities in both health care and medical education. According to John Dittmer, a significant number of those activists emerged in the mid-1960s as medical and nursing students, "influenced by the egalitarian platform of the Students for a Democratic Society (SDS)." Organizations such as the Medical Committee for Human Rights (MCHR)— founded in 1964 and led by health-care professionals—"provided medical care for civil rights workers in the South, desegregated area hospitals, and picketed at conventions of the American Medical Association (AMA) to protest the AMA's refusal to require its Southern affiliates to admit black physicians." This aspect of the Black freedom struggle, often overshadowed by the more sensational confrontations that focused on schools and voting, was buttressed by "legislative action and court decision" taking place "primarily in the pages of medical journals, at professional meetings, and in firm but fairly friendly talks between Black and white physicians and hospital administrators."[6]

Greensboro, North Carolina, already lauded as a beacon for civil rights activism in the wake of the 1960 student-led sit-ins, emerged as a key battleground in the struggle for justice and equality in health care. Dr. George Simkins Jr., a local African American dentist, led a group of African American physicians, dentists, and patients in initiating a lawsuit against two local hospitals—Moses H. Cone Memorial Hospital and L. Richardson Hospital. Both hospitals were private and received funding provided by the Hill-Burton Act. Neither hospital provided care for Black patients, and both barred Black physicians from practicing medicine within the facilities. African American North Carolinians struggled with limited access to health-care resources as there were only nine hospitals in the state designated specifically for the care of African Americans. The majority of hospitals across the state provided limited health care to Black patients or excluded them completely. African Americans in North Carolina in need of health care faced a grim reality: either find the means and time to make it to the nearest African American hospital or deal with the issue independently with little resources and no training. After having one of his patients turned away from Moses H. Cone Memorial Hospital in 1962, Dr. Simkins, operating both as a member of the local Black community and the president of the Greensboro chapter of the NAACP, initiated a lawsuit asserting that the two hospitals violated the Fourteenth Amendment rights of the African American physicians, dentists, and patients who were barred from hospital privileges and facilities. The lawsuit challenged the private status of the hospitals because they received funding through the Hill-Burton Act. The case garnered national attention prompting the United States Department of Justice to intervene on behalf of Simkins with a request to deem the "separate but equal" clause unconstitutional. Despite these efforts, in December 1962, the District Court of North Carolina ruled that funding from the Hill-Burton Act did not change the status of private, for-profit hospitals. In November 1963, the US Fourth Circuit Court of Appeals handed down a decision that deemed the separate-but-equal clause of the Hill-Burton Act unconstitutional, which prohibited segregated hospitals from receiving federal funds for construction. The US Supreme Court upheld the decision the following spring. Subsequently, the Public Health Service, an agency within the Department of Health, Education, and Welfare (HEW) that handled the disbursement of federal aid for hospitals, responded by refusing to accept applications for funding from segregated hospitals and rescinded all pending applications.[7]

Title VI of the Civil Rights Act of 1964, which prohibited federal funding for institutions with racially discriminatory practices, applied more pressure on segregated hospitals that relied on Hill-Burton support. By 1965, HEW, the federal department charged with enforcing regulations to implement Title VI guidelines, had been inundated with three hundred complaints against Southern hospitals, but no funds had been allocated for investigations and the agency was uncertain about how to proceed. The following year, MCHR partnered with the Legal Defense and Educational Fund of the NAACP and submitted seventy cases against Southern hospitals to HEW asserting noncompliance with Title VI of the Civil Rights Act of 1964. HEW had been tasked with an enormous responsibility for which it was unequipped, a fact that made it easy for segregationists to find ways to evade the mandates or ignore them completely. HEW's first effort to enforce the legislation in October 1965 involved a decision to impede federal funding to Chicago Public Schools pending an investigation of a complaint by a local civil rights organization. The matter ended with President Lyndon Johnson overriding the decision and firing the person who executed it. Consequently, others believed that they could suffer the same fate in attempts to enforce Title VI in health-care contexts. In that same year, Dr. William McCord, who had served as a professor and head of the chemistry department for twenty years, became the Medical College of the State of South Carolina president. Shortly after his tenure began, HEW granted the college $12 million for "physical expansion and research," despite the Title VI complaints that had been filed against the hospital. In early 1966, HEW began developing strategies for putting real teeth into the law. For example, it established a separate office to handle Title VI compliance for Medicare. However, it only had a staff of six individuals who were responsible for reviewing and certifying compliance for approximately six thousand hospitals.[8]

The 1967 dismissal of the five hospital workers at Medical College set off a chain of events that revealed that the systematic perpetuation of segregation and discrimination endured. In July 1968, just months after the workers were reinstated, HEW followed up with a routine investigation of the hospital. An initial report to Dr. William McCord, president of Medical College, dated September 19, 1968, and issued by Hugh A. Brimm, the chief of the Contract Compliance Branch of the Office for Civil Rights and leader of the inquiry, concentrated on equal education, health, and employment opportunities. According to Brimm's report, Medical College violated several of the mandates set forth by Executive Order 11246, which prohibited federal contractors and subcontractors from discriminating against employees based on race, color, religion, sex, or national origin and required employers to maintain an affirmative action program that ensured equal opportunity within the workplace. Many of the hospital's standard practices demonstrated an egregious disregard for the equal opportunity clause included in all of the government contracts it maintained.[9]

Brimm cited several infractions within the educational facility, which illuminated Medical College's conflict with the directives set forth by the Office of Federal Contract Compliance within the US Department of Labor. The college had no recruitment programs targeting Black students. The School of Nursing, for example, had never enrolled a minority student. The institution maintained racially segregated on-campus housing for the few Black students who did attend. Neither those students nor potential students were supplied with adequate information regarding financial assistance. For its on-the-job training program, the college partnered with racially prejudiced physicians. Brimm also reported that Black doctors were systematically kept out of Medical College classrooms and medical facilities citing, "Physicians at the hospital have faculty status—all are white. In order to practice medicine in the hospital physicians must be members of a specialty board. No Negro physicians in Charleston County are members of a special board."[10]

Racial discrimination and segregation permeated the health-care facilities. Medical College opened Medical College Hospital in 1955 with 500 beds. The hospital categorized patients as either service (nonpaying) or private, with the majority of private patients being white. The level of care that patients received varied based on whether they were private or service. Senior, more experienced, medical students attended to private patients, while lower-level medical students cared for service patients. Spatially, staff managed patient care along racial lines. Black and white patients occupied separate waiting rooms and received treatment in different areas of the facility. According to Brimm's report, there were allegations that the admittance clerk routinely contacted the floor nurse with information about a patient's race in order to get the appropriate room assignment. A letter from McCord to South Carolina State Attorney General Daniel R. McLeod substantiated these claims of racial segregation. In the letter dated November 26, 1965, the Medical College Hospital president expressed concerns regarding issues with Title VI compliance, asserting that "attempts are made to force me to break the law by assigning people on the basis of color, i.e., to specifically place a white patient and a colored patient in the same room in the hospital." Members of the surrounding community claimed that, in preparation for the HEW visit, hospital staff rearranged patients to create a more racially balanced appearance. In several areas of the hospital, Brimm found that restroom facilities were still segregated. John E. Wise, who began working at Medical College in 1967 as the vice president for administration and finance, recalled in an interview years later, "In those days they still had black and white toilets, black and white restrooms." When Brimm arrived in 1968, the "colored" and "white" signs had been removed, but it was clear from the outlines above the doors that it had been done so recently that there had been no time to repaint.[11]

Brimm's report also provided concrete evidence of the inequalities that Black workers faced. The hospital's outdated personnel policies and procedures did not include a federally mandated affirmative action plan, which meant that workers were not guaranteed equal employment opportunities. Each employment application required a photo, highlighting the importance of determining race in the hiring process. Many of the available positions required in-house experience, which in most cases, few Black workers could acquire. According to Brimm's report, "Employment patterns clearly suggest a stratification of employees with regard to race, i.e., administrative and professional positions are occupied by whites; non-whites are concentrated in service and non-skilled categories." Relegated to these "service and non-skilled" positions, African Americans earned as little as $1.30 or less per hour. This was the federal minimum wage for hospital workers after the 1966 amendment of the Fair Labor Standards Act, but it was below the $1.60 minimum wage afforded to workers in other industries. Exclusions from training, promotion, and higher-level positions ensured that African American workers would remain in low-paying positions.[12]

The HEW investigation findings underscored the fact that equal employment legislation emerged during a time when white business owners viewed their "habits and hierarchies as the natural order of things." Employers were unwilling and unprepared to implement the inclusion of African Americans that the Civil Rights Act of 1964 mandated. Laurie Green's study of the Black freedom struggle in Memphis, Tennessee explores the persistence of the "plantation mentality" as the root cause of that unwillingness and lack of preparedness. She defines the plantation mentality as "white racist attitudes that promoted white domination and black subservience" which had roots in both slavery and sharecropping. Sally Turner's experience as a Black woman employed at Farber Brothers, an auto accessories manufacturing plant in Memphis, provided an example of what Black workers in the South understood as "symbols of unfreedom." After she began working at the plant in 1962, Turner and her coworkers, suffering in high summer temperatures, complained about the lack of water fountains and the inadequate number of fans that management provided for workers to try to stay cool in the plant. Instead of installing water fountains, the plant manager brought in a bucket and dipper. For these workers, "being pressured to use what they perceived as a representation of an older plantation regime led Turner and her coworkers to similarly interpret other labor practices as symbols of the rural South they had struggled to leave behind." The bucket and dipper was the final blow that set their union organizing in motion.[13]

Black women working at Medical College in Charleston in the mid- to late 1960s faced similar struggles in confronting the "plantation mentality." According to one worker, those in positions of power viewed Black women as the servants who "have on an apron, washing dishes, cooking their food, and taking care of their little ones." She contended that white Charlestonians opposed the idea of Black women moving beyond the lowest socioeconomic circumstances: "If you want to move from that area to another area, they don't feel you need to go there." Mary Moultrie explicitly linked the plantation and Black women's experiences as hospital workers by asserting that, "Everybody saw McCord as a slave driver. Somebody who saw us as more or less as slaves, had no respect for us." Medical College's "nonprofessional" workers struggled to attain equality and access in hospital policy, procedure, and practice. The racial attitudes that relegated the Farber Brothers workers to a bucket and dipper in Memphis, spurred the accusations that Medical College Hospital workers had been barred from having access to the regular staff dining area and were being forced to eat in the hospital's boiler room. In a November 1965 letter to the attorney general, McCord highlighted the issue around dining asserting that, "Attempts were made to force me to require people to eat in certain dining rooms on the basis of color. I was required to require white individuals on staff to eat in the free dining room which at that time furnished meals at no cost to the wage-earning group, which are, for the large part, negroes." The racism and discrimination that Black hospital workers endured had become systemically normalized.[14]

In early 1968, a group of Charleston hospital workers, all Black and the vast majority women, found themselves at the crossroads of two important moments in American movement history: the burgeoning aspect of the civil rights movement that focused on eradicating racism, discrimination, and inequality in health care and the efforts to acknowledge and position hospital workers as critical contributors to the labor movement. In the 1950s and 1960s, labor unions regarded hospital workers as unfavorable targets for organization, in part because hospital workers often worked in facilities exempt from collective bargaining mandates. According to Moe Foner, a Local 1199 Hospital and Nursing Home Employees Union leader, the primary demographic of hospital workers—minority women who earned low wages—was unattractive to unions, who believed the constituency would yield "a low return in dues and a new kind of membership that most union were unaccustomed—or even unwilling—to deal with." By 1960, labor organizations began to demonstrate interest in these "forgotten workers," but more importantly, growing numbers of hospital workers constructed paths toward organizing for themselves. Charleston hospital workers joined the struggle for social and economic justice in the late 1960s by forging a movement that, according to them, aimed to "change the whole system."[15]

In the aftermath of the termination and reinstatement of the five Black female Medical College Hospital workers in the late 1960s, a movement emerged. The local protest community, led by Mary Moultrie, William Saunders, and Isaiah Bennett, shifted its gaze to the issues that plagued the experiences of working-class Black women in Charleston's hospitals: racial discrimination, low wages, and disrespect. Medical College Hospital workers initiated the organizing by hosting clandestine weekly meetings in small groups of only seven or eight people. Each week, everyone who attended had the responsibility to bring at least one new person whom they trusted to keep the meetings a secret. Not long after the meetings began, Isaiah Bennett offered Charleston County Hospital workers the opportunity to join the effort by sharing information with an acquaintance, Rosetta Simmons, a licensed practical nurse at Charleston County Hospital. Simmons jumped at the opportunity to get involved and began distributing information about the meetings to her coworkers and organizing their inclusion in the weekly meetings. Meeting attendance, while low at the start, swelled into the hundreds within just a few months as more workers from both hospitals joined their ranks. Together Medical College and Charleston County employed several hundred service workers, most of whom were African American and fewer than twenty of whom were male. The number of Black hospital workers—many of whom with little to no activist experience—that joined the efforts to organize around these grievances sheds light on the dire nature of their circumstances.[16]

The vast majority of the workers who forged and sustained the movement exist as a collective in the narrative of the movement rather than as named individuals. They are many, and their contributions countless, making it impossible to call them all by name or document their individual efforts in this work. Strategically highlighting specific individuals offers a window into the evolution of the hospital workers' campaign from its inception to its conclusion. Simmons served as the conduit for introducing Charleston County Hospital workers to the movement. Born in Mt. Pleasant, South Carolina, but raised in Charleston, Simmons attended the same all-Black high school as Moultrie and Saunders but lived in an integrated neighborhood. After high school, she began working as a domestic laborer in the home of a white family and eventually moved on to the housekeeping department at St. Francis Hospital. In a short time, the supervising staff saw her potential and recommended her to the administrator at the Roper Hospital School of Practical Nursing. Driven by a disdain for domestic work—"I did not want to be cleaning nobody's floor other than my own"—Simmons finished nursing school, passed the state board exams, and began working as an LPN at Roper Hospital in what she characterized as the "Black area." She worked at Roper until the area where she worked closed permanently in 1959. She then worked at Medical College until 1965 and began working at Charleston County Hospital in 1966. Her extensive work history in the city's hospitals provided a broad perspective on Black women's work in the local health-care system. That made her especially well-equipped for the activism and organizing she embarked upon. Simmons realized that her personal experience with discrimination and disrespect reflected the working conditions of many other Black workers throughout Charleston County Hospital. Soon after getting involved with the organization efforts started by Medical College Hospital workers, Simmons emerged as a leader, offering a unique perspective and demonstrating strong organizing skills.[17]

Simmons's motivation for getting involved stemmed from her opposition to white Charlestonians' view of Black women as perpetual servants—a feeling that was fed by her experience in the health system as well as by her resentment of the time she spent as a domestic worker. Characterizing herself as "fiery" and "aggressive," she resisted the relegation of Black women to positions of subservience both as citizens and employees. When asked why she and women like her decided to take on Charleston's hospital industry, she responded:

You talk about independent women. We have to be that way. You made us to be this way. We would fall through the crack. We would end up being nothing. I guess it was inbred and then what my aunt was teaching me to stand up for what I believed in. And I did that. I am so glad that I didn't slicker back. Well, I wasn't going to. I would fight first. I don't like people being taken advantage of. That is my real concern. That's in my everyday living.

Driven by a longing for something greater for herself and women like her, Simmons dedicated her time and energy to a movement she believed would not only generate change in the working lives of Charleston's Black female labor force but would also support their insistence on being treated with respect and human dignity in society at large.[18]

As information about the informal organizing of workers continued to spread throughout both hospitals, critical changes occurred in the organizing efforts that shaped the course of the movement. Once the number of organized workers swelled to the hundreds, Bennett secured the Distributive, Processing, Office Workers of America (DPO) union hall—the tobacco workers' meeting space and a much larger location—for their weekly meetings. Workers met every Thursday to discuss their grievances and share stories about their on-the-job experiences. They implemented a hierarchy of leadership by electing officers: Moultrie, president; Jack Bradford, first vice president; Simmons, second vice president; Ernestine Grimes, recording secretary; and Sadie Brown, financial secretary. Saunders called in speakers, including local ministers, community leaders, and business owners, to motivate and inspire the workers. According to one observer, the workers seemed to be highly motivated: "What impressed me was the tremendous spirit of the people there—the determination to do something to improve themselves."[19]

Early in the organizing effort, three white women who worked at the hospitals attended the weekly meetings. Even though they had "very few grievances, they were sympathetic" to how Black workers were being treated. The low number of white workers attending meetings reflected the small number of white workers in the hospital's nonprofessional positions. Black workers expressed gratitude for their support but made it clear that their movement would be just as powerful without their presence. As one worker put it: "We want your support, we feel we need your support, but we intend to win whether or not—whether or not you support us." Prior to the workers striking, the three white workers mysteriously got new jobs at other hospitals. Two were hired to work at the local Veterans Affairs Hospital, and the third got a job somewhere else. One of the white workers attended a meeting to report, "Look, I never applied to the VA for a job, you know, they just call and gave me a job." Mary Moultrie asserted that Medical College Hospital administrators orchestrated these job transfers in an effort to remove the white workers from the fray. More importantly, those changes in employment morphed their organizing into an all-Black movement.[20]

After about a year of clandestine organizing, workers felt it was time to take their grievances and organizing public. Moultrie set things in motion, with the help of Cigar Factory Strike veteran, Lillie Doster. Together they drafted a letter to Medical College president, Dr. William McCord. Doster worked at the cigar factory from 1943 until she retired in 1972 due to the loss of her eyesight. She worked on the fifth floor of the factory, the "box shop," where they assembled cigar boxes. Originally, she labeled boxes and eventually moved on to operating the machine that wrapped the boxes. Soon after she began working at the cigar factory, she found out about an earlier failed attempt to start a workers' union there. She was among those who organized the workers that voted to have FTA establish Local 15. Doster seemed to have had a talent for leadership. She served as a shop steward and picket captain during the Cigar Factory Strike and boasted that she only missed one day from the line. Still, looking back, Doster modestly downplayed her contribution. According to her, she happened to be in the DPO hall, which the hospital workers shared with members of Local 15, the day that Moultrie began working on the letter, and Doster said Moultrie "wrote it up, but I helped her word it." Despite her humble nature, Doster possessed a great deal of knowledge and courage, a legacy of the cigar factory workers' strike that would benefit the hospital workers.[21]

The letter that Moultrie and Doster eventually produced focused on a list of grievances, addressing relatively standard work-related issues such as job descriptions, shift differentials, leave, workers compensation, and on-the-job training. Three items on the grievance list became the workers' fundamental demands: "wages, discrimination and respect." It is not surprising that, in 1960s South Carolina, hospital workers would request higher wages and challenge discrimination based on "race, color, creed or union membership." However, the call for respect within the "List of Grievances" pushes for a reframing of how we think about what this civil rights–based labor movement meant to the women at the center of it. On the one hand, their involvement stemmed from their economic needs and desires to achieve equality within the workplace. On the other hand, the request for respect signifies a much deeper, more personal response to on-the-job treatment that Black workers believed denigrated their humanity and undermined their dignity. Simmons's assessment of what motivated workers to band together suggests that the lack of respect was central: "They all came together and saw that the need was that something needs to be done, because people weren't treated fairly and weren't treated as human beings, without respect."

Among the many grievances that working-class Black women had in white-dominated workplaces, respect was one, even when unspoken, they seemed most unwilling to concede.[22]

Moreover, the issues concerning wages included in the grievance document suggests that what workers faced was a bit more complex than Black workers merely wanting a living wage. In their grievances, workers asked the hospital to raise the salaries of employees making less than two dollars per hour raised to at least that and to provide a raise of twenty-five cents per hour for those making above that amount. Announcing a church rally in honor of Dr. Martin Luther King Jr. and in support of striking workers, Mary Moultrie referred to their struggle against "poverty wages and discrimination." It is clear that workers made a direct connection between racial discrimination and their inability to earn enough money to take adequate care of themselves and their families. Therefore, workers took issue with the amount of money they earned and the limits they believed were placed on their earning potential due to their race.[23]

Organizing workers used the grievance document to list their concerns but also to openly discuss the discrimination and inequality they encountered on a regular basis. For example, the document points to the issue of seniority: "Whereas a clause to be worked out based on the Principle that Seniority be respected." When the time came to provide pay raises, supervisors overlooked Black workers who had dedicated years of service. According to Moultrie, there were workers who had been at Medical College Hospital for over ten years and made the same wage—$1.30 per hour—she earned when she was first hired.[24]

Shortly after Moultrie sent the letter to McCord on behalf of the organized workers, McCord distributed a memo to all hospital employees. He assumed that most workers would not be interested in affiliating themselves with a union and argued that it would not be in their best interest. However, in case there was any confusion regarding the hospital's stance on unionization he declared, "WE DO NOT WANT A UNION HERE AT MEDICAL COLLEGE." McCord attached two cartoons to the letter to solidify his point. One depicted a union organizer holding the dues beside two individuals labeled "management" and "employee" fighting over job-related issues. The other image depicted a line of men placing money in a box labeled "union dues" while a man labeled "union boss" pulls the money out with one hand while seated at a table having cocktails with a woman. He argued that the union only wanted the workers' money and offered little benefit in return. Moultrie bristled at the assertion, retorting that it was an "insult because if you are making a dollar thirty an hour, you don't have any money." McCord's response angered other Black workers as well, including both those who had been a part of the organizing and some who had not, and it motivated a number of those workers who had not been involved to begin attending meetings. McCord refused to meet with representatives from the group, asserting that he could not negotiate with a union.[25]

After McCord's rebuttal, organizing workers approached Isaiah Bennett about the possibility of joining Local 15A. Bennett took their concerns and questions to Arthur Osman, international vice president of the Retail, Wholesale, and Department Store Union (RWDSU), who suggested that they contact Local 1199 Hospital and Nursing Home Employees Union, a hospital workers union based in New York. At this point, tensions began to surface between Saunders and Bennett. Bennett, a long-standing member of Local 15A and a Cigar Factory Strike veteran, believed in the necessity and power of unionization. Saunders understood the importance of collective action, but he was not convinced of the benefits of unions. He proposed that there should be an organization that helped people to confront racism and discrimination in the hospital. Saunders believed in the importance of hospital workers standing up for themselves and demanding equality. He stressed the importance of nonprofessional workers having a forum through which to organize like the professional associations to which doctors and nurses belonged. Despite Saunders's concerns, in the fall of 1968, Mary Moultrie drafted a letter to Local 1199 Hospital and Nursing Home Employees Union requesting its assistance. Her request for aid catapulted this grassroots movement into the national discourse on the struggle for equality and justice at the intersection of health care, the civil rights movement, and the labor movement.[26]

Early accounts of the modern civil rights movement have often centered on large-scale moments of protest, such as sit-ins and marches. Much of the narrative explores the evolution of the struggle for social justice that broadened to include a fight for economic justice. The push for equality and access in health care has been ever-present and equally as important. Charleston's health-care history in general and the hospital workers' campaign in particular offer insight into this particular component of the freedom struggle and how, like other aspects of the movement, the press to eradicate discrimination and exclusion in health care ebbed and flowed between a steady hum and a mighty roar at the local, state, and national levels.

Chapter 3

"UNION POWER"

The Charleston hospital workers' campaign sheds light on the complex nature of grassroots activism forged by African American women at the intersection of civil rights and labor organizing in the late 1960s. By that time, African American women already had an extensive history of grassroots civil rights activism, for which they have more recently been lauded as "trailblazers" and "torchbearers." If organizing hospital workers in general lagged in comparison to the organization of other laborers, organizing women in the healthcare industry, particularly women of color, was an even slower process. The Charleston hospital workers' campaign brought together a host of key contributors whose concerted and competing actions in the name of social and economic justice highlighted the strides and failures associated with the fledgling efforts to organize African American women hospital workers. Exploring the span of time from the arrival of Local 1199 through the resolution of the strike reveals the complexities of the relationship between organizing hospital workers who forged the movement and the groups and individuals that provided essential support to the movement. The Charleston hospital workers' campaign was not unique in its aims to eradicate social and economic injustice. It is, however, critical to the broader movement narrative, as it offers a window into the unique circumstances of this burgeoning sector of organizing in which working-class African American women forged a civil rights–based labor movement and grappled with precarious circumstances as they endeavored to provoke systemic change. The retelling of the hospital workers' campaign that crippled Charleston in 1969 offers an important example of the complexities of Black women's activism and organizing that played out at the local level but often became obscured and even absent from the historical narrative.

Mary Moultrie's request for Local 1199 Hospital and Nursing Home Employees Union to formally unionize the independently organized hospital workers shifted the trajectory and energy of the movement. Moultrie claimed that, without the union, "we would not have been successful at all because when they came in, they came in with experience. They knew about fundraising. They had PR people that could pull the press together so that we could get the coverage that we got. We certainly would never have made it without 1199." Local 1199 began organizing hospital workers in New York a decade prior to the Charleston hospital workers' campaign. The late 1950s and early 1960s marked a transition for the union from early efforts to organize the drugstore industry to a focus on organizing hospitals. Early organizing principles set the stage for the union's new direction. Local 1199 recognized that in order for the organization to continue to be effective and successful it would have to create a link between labor organizing and larger struggles for social change.

A focus on interracial and interethnic solidarity, which originated in the union's early years, helped the union to align itself with local civil rights organizations. These relationships helped expand the union's reach and strengthen its organizing abilities. Local 1199 identified its efforts as bigger than unionism. It saw itself as a part of the larger freedom struggle. Concentrating their efforts within the state, they operated with three key premises: an authentic mobilization of hospital workers, training for a militant strike with no regard for duration, and campaigning that solicited the support of the surrounding community and public officials. Local 1199 aimed to catapult labor organizing to the next level by linking its approach to the tenets of the civil rights movement under the banner of "union power, soul power."[1]

Local 1199's early leaders, motivated by radical ideology and a progressive vision of unionism, set a precedent early in its founding for the union's relationship to civil rights issues and the freedom struggle. In 1932, the Pharmacists Union of Greater New York and the New York Drug Clerks Association merged to form Local 1199 Retail Drug Employees Union. Leon Davis, a Russia-born immigrant that worked as a drug clerk, was among its founders and served as the union's president from 1934 until his retirement in 1982. In response to the political and economic precariousness of the Polish–Soviet War period, his parents sent him to the US in the early 1920s to finish high school. He moved to New York several years later to attend Columbia's School of Pharmacy. During this period, Davis joined a local debating society, which served as his introduction to the political arena. In addition to his political awakening, he got a peek at the world of labor unionism through a local strike of upholsterers. Davis walked away from pharmacy school and dove headfirst into labor organizing. By the late 1920s, Davis had situated himself firmly in a radical labor organizing ideology. In 1927, he aligned himself with the labor organizing affiliate of the Communist Party, the Trade Union Unity League (TUUL). As a supporter of the Pharmacists' Union of Greater New York, he played an active role in the daring efforts to organize "all workers in the pharmaceutical industry." Years earlier, as a student working in Harlem drugstores, Davis had begun to develop a commitment to interracialism. Bolstered by his experience, he joined the union in efforts to institute chapters in drugstores and hospitals all over the state. In their efforts to expand, the pharmacists' union took notice of a seemingly like-minded organization, the New York Drug Clerks Association (NYDCA). The NYDCA's focus on organizing and improving working conditions through a "militant spirit of struggle against wage cutting, speed-ups, and unsanitary conditions" paralleled much of what the pharmacists' union believed. Local 1199 had emerged from a collection of Jewish- and Communist-led New York City retail trade unions in the early 1930s. During the Second Red Scare, the US government and leaders of organized labor, the AFL and the CIO, targeted it and other Communist-led unions. Davis, nevertheless, ushered the union through the precarious decades leading into the modern civil rights era. Moving past the challenges, he began to set his sights on stretching Local 1199's reach into new arenas.[2]

In the late 1950s, Local 1199 began to expand its purview to grapple with issues of gender and race as additional strands in the struggle for economic justice. Historically, the sentiment among unionists was that women were "traditionally very difficult to organize and that money spent in attempting to unionize women was money wasted." Unionists argued that women "are more emotional than men and they simply lack the necessary staying power to build effective unions." Unions also resisted efforts to organize workers who were minority women due to the precarious nature of their employment, which led union organizers to believe that these groups of workers would have little leverage for collective bargaining. The unionization efforts of hospital workers faced additional obstacles, including exclusion from New Deal legislation such as unemployment insurance, disability benefits, minimum-wage protection, and the National Labor Relations Act. In addition, hospital workers were regarded as having committed the greatest of offenses if they "desert[ed] his or her calling" and left their patients to strike against hospitals. In 1959, Local 1199 began to organize workers at voluntary hospitals, which were privately owned nonprofit hospitals, in New York City. The vast majority of the workers were Black and Puerto Rican women. By the late 1970s, Local 1199 would be deemed the "most aggressive organizer among women workers" with more than 70 percent of its members being female and the majority of them being Black or Hispanic. In the late 1960s, the New York–based union pushed the envelope even further by expanding its reach to include other parts of the nation.³

In July 1968, Local 1199 formed a national organizing committee with Elliott Godoff as its leader and Henry Nicholas as his right-hand man. Godoff embodied the resources and ability that Local 1199 needed to invigorate hospital unionism in New York. Like Davis, Godoff had immigrated to the US from Russia as a teenager. He and his older brother were raised by a wealthy uncle in Patchogue on Long Island. He began his college education at Cornell University but later transferred to the Columbia School of Pharmacy at his uncle's request. He finished in 1934 and moved directly into a job that his uncle arranged for him at Israel Zion Hospital. As a trustee and generous donor, Godoff's uncle arranged for him to work in the hospital's pharmacy. The following year, Godoff accepted a promotion to director of the pharmacy. As he began to establish himself as financially independent of his uncle, he also divorced himself from his conservative Republican politics.⁴

Godoff has been dubbed the "father of present-day hospital unionism." Like Davis, Godoff firmly situated himself within the Communist Party's labor organizing efforts. His full-time position as the hospital organizer for Local 444 of the United Public Workers of America (UPWA) in 1945 jump-started his career within the labor movement. The Communist-led union organized several thousands of hospital workers in city-run institutions. Still, the strain of uncertainty and instability created tension among its organizers, and the anti-union sentiments challenged the organization's progress. In the mid-1950s, the union began to falter as it faced intensifying adversity: investigations of union leaders, on-the-job harassment, and shunning by once supportive community organizations. Godoff sought refuge within another union, Teamster Local 237, but would eventually find himself ousted after members took issue with the idea of "the Reds hiding within the Teamster organization." An unemployed Godoff ended up in the halls of Local 1199 and eventually across the table from Leon Davis being offered a job as an organizer.⁵

Local 1199 saw the Charleston conflict as an opportunity to test their "union power, soul power" campaign in a Southern city. Ideas for a national campaign to organize hospital workers emerged after their successful 1968 campaign to raise the living wage for hospital workers in New York. The rhetoric associated with the 1968 movement evolved from a discussion about wages to one that made a clear connection between earnings and human and civil rights. Local 1199 established a national committee and named Coretta

Scott King as the honorary chair. A victory would be a game-changer in the effort to eradicate economic injustice based on race. Local 1199 President Leon Davis sent David White, Brooklyn area director of the union, to Charleston to assess the situation and determine whether Charleston would indeed be Local 1199's newest campaign.[6]

White joined Local 1199 in 1966, first as an organizer, then as an area director. He would eventually serve as the elected area representative for Charleston. When he arrived at the union hall on his first day in town, he encountered over a hundred workers. They shared with him a summary of what had brought them together and fueled their organizing. Impressed by their spirit and determination, David took what he learned about the movement already in motion, presented a "favorable report" to Local 1199 leaders, and indicated that Charleston would be a good test case for the union. Several months later, in October 1968, Henry Nicholas chartered Charleston's Local 1199B. The union's newly chartered members elected Mary Moultrie as the local union's president to serve alongside co-vice presidents Jack Bradford and Rosetta Simmons.[7]

The arrival of Local 1199 and subsequent formal unionization marked a shift in the visibility, agency, and autonomy of Charleston's hospital workers. Two key factors sparked the changes in the nature of their protest and activism: the hospitals' state-supported resistance to collective bargaining and the eclipse of workers' efforts by institutional presence. As the national union took center stage, organizing workers were increasingly remanded to the DPO Hall and eventually the picket line, largely losing the ability to engage directly with those in power. Whereas they had previously been able to speak for themselves, hospital workers were becoming foot soldiers for a campaign that now served the interests of the union as an organization rather than the needs of its members.

Years later, Moultrie recollected the shifts in her own visibility and power as the leader of the local union: "I was strictly union. I was not one of the people on the outside pulling all these strings and stuff. I found out later that there were a lot of meetings that I knew nothing about. A lot of stuff that went on." She asserted that her focus dealt mainly with the concerns and efforts of fellow workers, whereas the union was "probably supposed to be trying to settle the strike and this thing and that thing. I was a rank in power although I was a leader. I stayed with the people. . . . . A lot of things, like the meetings they had behind closed doors, those doors were closed. I wouldn't know anything about them till later."[8]

Moultrie's ruminations highlight gender as a key aspect of and even an obstacle to women's civil rights and labor activism in the late 1960s. Even in movements that centered on women, men tended to be in positions of power while women provided the less visible labor. Charles Payne grapples with the role of women in the civil rights movement in his essay, "Men Led, but Women Organized: Movement Participation of Women in the Mississippi Delta." His research shows that, among 1960s civil rights activists, male and female, the resounding assertion was that "young people and women led organizationally." He argues that activism among African Americans in the decade prior was dominated by men. Payne also points to Karen Sacks's analysis of working-class Black women in Southern hospitals and the varying styles of leadership that emerged among men and women as another way to unpack this discussion. Payne highlights Sacks's claim that "women are organizers, men are leaders. That is, 'women created the organization, made people feel a part of it, as well as doing the everyday work upon which most things depended, while men made public announcements, confronted and negotiated with management.'"9

Sally Ward Maggard's gender analysis of the Pikesville, Kentucky, Methodist Hospital workers' strike in the early 1970s sheds light on the mindset that created some of the challenges that the Charleston workers experienced in response to their protest in particular and women's labor activism in general. In a study of unionized working-class white women, Maggard observes that they stood against one of the area's major employers for many of the same reasons that prompted the Charleston strike: "lengthy and erratic work schedules, heavy overtime duty, difficulty collecting overtime pay, harsh and discriminatory supervision, lack of job security, and discharges imposed without proper cause." When the hospital's nonprofessional workers walked out, the Communications Workers of America (CWA), the union representing the striking workers, urged them to "behave in pleasant, 'ladylike' ways" on the picket line. So, it became commonplace to find women on the picket line knitting, waving, reading, and cooking. Men, on the other hand, chopped wood for striking workers and stood in for them on the picket line at night to "save the women from being out on the picket from eleven to seven." Even in the midst of the labor dispute, the roles of men and women remained distinct, and the Pike County women seemingly stayed in their place.[10]

Initially, workers involved in the Charleston hospital workers' campaign expanded the bounds of women's activism by simultaneously building the movement and personally negotiating with state and local leaders as well as hospital administrators. For example, unionized workers, Moultrie, Claire Brown, and Jack Bradford, were front and center in a December 1968 meeting (not long after Local 1199 formally organized hospital workers) that included local leaders and hospital administrators. The workers raised concerns about threats of termination from their supervisors, low wages, racial discrimination, and disrespect. A meeting held in early March 1969 involved nonunionized hospital workers, the president of Medical College Hospital, and local Black leaders speaking on behalf of unionized workers. Hospital administrators, by this point in the movement, had become increasingly resistant to engaging in anything that remotely resembled negotiating with a union. They invited local Black leaders on behalf of organized workers even though those workers had union affiliation and representation. Nonunionized workers who attended this meeting asserted that they had no complaints about their experiences at Medical College, which was used to debunk the claims of unionized workers. The arrival of Local 1199 instigated a sharp turn in hospital workers' organizing tactics and its presence in critical moments that impacted the trajectory of the movement.[11]

There are several key individuals and groups whose contributions highlight the progress of the movement and the ebb and flow of organizing hospital workers' voices and agency. Isaiah Bennett played a key role in helping workers transition from the structure of their early organizing to unionization. Bennett, a trade unionist and notable local African American community leader, had strong ties to the local protest community. While some argued that Bennett had "little real influence" in Charleston—which for some invalidated his contributions to the movement—the sources suggest that his role in guiding workers in their efforts to organize was essential. From the outset, he was a proponent of the workers central to the movement, playing a key role in communicating their expectations and grievances. As Bennett had become so involved in the hospital workers' campaign that his union, Tobacco Workers' Union Local 15A, loaned him to Local 1199B as a full-time organizer. The locals were affiliated with the same international, RWDSU. His job was to steer the direction of workers organizing; maintain a line of communication between the workers and hospital administration; and make it clear that hospital workers wanted to be unionized. In winter 1968, acting as the "S.C. Area Director for Hospital Workers," Bennett quickly began making inroads for unionized workers to meet with McCord. In a memo sent to Reginald Barrett shortly after the union established Local 1199B, he requested that the local leader use his connections with HEW to orchestrate a meeting between McCord and the workers. According to Bennett, the workers wanted to meet with the hospital administrator to discuss "recognition and grievances." He listed five workers, including Mary Moultrie, and added that even though he wanted to attend the meeting, he would be willing to sit out if McCord would agree to at least meet with the workers.[12]

As Bennett continued to work on getting a meeting with Dr. McCord, he began to reach out to both the local and national community in an effort to garner support, wisely tying the plight of hospital workers to a broader struggle for freedom within the Black community. On behalf of the workers, Bennett sent out letters to "all Charleston physicians" explaining the aims of the hospital workers' campaign and requesting that they contact Dr. McCord to share words of support for their cause. A month prior to the strike, Bennett contacted members of local government requesting a meeting between the Charleston County Legislative Delegation to the General Assembly and hospital workers and expressing his hope that the legislators would help with resolving the situation. After the strike began, he reached out to the local chapter of the NAACP, requesting their assistance: "Your help is urgently needed if the Black people of Charleston are ever to be free." He even called on then Congresswoman Shirley Chisholm from Brooklyn, New York, asserting, "National attention is utmost necessity to allow these workers their right to union representation and an end to poverty wages and discriminatory practices in the hospital."[13]

Unmoved by Bennett's effort, McCord refused to meet with or even communicate with the workers. His resistance was buttressed by the fact that state law did not require negotiations with unions in addition to ongoing support from the hospital's board of trustees, nonstriking workers, individuals affiliated with the hospital and members of the community who supported the hospital administrator's stance. The prevailing assertion contended that nonprofessional workers did not experience disrespectful treatment or discrimination in their positions within the hospital.

In response, they reached out to members of the Charleston County Legislative Delegation to share their grievances firsthand in hopes of getting some additional support in their efforts to communicate with Medical College administration. In late February 1969, a group of approximately fifty workers, accompanied by Bennett and other Black leaders, traveled to Columbia, South Carolina, to meet with local legislators in the state's House of Representatives. While workers expected to meet only with members of the Charleston delegation, they arrived to find that many other members of the South Carolina General Assembly would sit in on the meeting. The workers presented a petition that included 3,700 signatures in support of their efforts to meet with Dr. McCord. Some explained that they had even attempted to meet with the administrator on an individual basis to no avail. Several of those present shared examples of the grievances they wanted the opportunity to air with the hospital administrator. Bennett offered as an example of inadequate wages and wage increases a worker whose annual pay had only increased by $6.80 over fourteen years. One nurse revealed that hospital administrators threatened Black workers with termination when they felt that they were being "sassy or uppity." Grace Evans, a nurse, expressed what seemed to be the collective sentiment when she said, "We're overworked, underpaid, and no one will listen to our grievances. This crisis for us will eventually get worse." According to Bennett, that worsening "crisis" for workers was a "potentially explosive" situation for Charleston.[14]

The all-white delegation did not offer workers any solutions. Representative Robert N. Turner, a member of the South Carolina General Assembly and ex officio member of the hospital's board of trustees, informed them that the delegation did not have the power to force hospital administrators to change their positions. In fact, local lawmakers had been having behind-the-scenes discussions regarding the hospital administration's behavior and had gone as far as to reach out to them hoping to help find a solution. Ultimately, their efforts had little impact because the hospital's president answered only to the hospital's board of trustees. In the meeting with workers, Turner suggested developing a bill that would force state institutions to come under the National Labor Relations Board and negotiate with unions, but he cautioned that that would only happen with the support of the General Assembly. His caveat suggested that getting such a law passed would not be easy. He explained that the state had already begun to address issues of race-based pay inequality by proposing a classification system that would result in equal pay for equal work. However, local legislators understood that the workers had no interest in waiting several years to see an increase in their pay. At the end of the meeting, the delegation assured the workers that they would continue to discuss the matter. While the meeting did not result in an immediate resolution for workers, legislators were clear about a few things: Even though they strongly believed that "regardless of who is right or wrong, the dispute could have been handled more tactfully by the administration," they questioned whether "any state institution would be handling the situation any better."[15]

Foremost in the delegation's concerns was the possibility of this dispute being the impetus for Medical College becoming a part of the University of South Carolina system, a fate that the legislators hoped to avoid. Just months before, a number of powerful local leaders began publicly questioning whether there needed to be some changes at Medical College, from the top down, including the board of trustees. The HEW investigation of the hospital and subsequent recommendations was also a cause for concern. The confrontation between Black hospital workers and administrators garnered additional negative attention. McCord's dismissive response to the workers' grievances reflected poorly on the hospital. These factors combined fueled the argument that the hospital was unstable and thus needed to become a part of the University of South Carolina system. Both House Speaker Solomon Blatt (Democrat) and Governor Robert E. McNair (Democrat) supported the idea, which would give Columbia a second medical college. Local legislators knew that the loss of Medical College would be devastating to Charleston's economy and community. For this reason, they ultimately refused to have any further involvement in the matter. After a meeting with hospital administrators and Governor McNair, the delegation denied the unionized workers' request for a public hearing in Charleston and declared that they had "done all within their power on the controversy at the Medical College of South Carolina." They finalized their involvement by stating, "We have gone as far as we can go unless there is new information."[16]

In an effort to solicit additional community support, a group of hospital workers, led by Mary Moultrie and supported by union representatives Godoff and Bennett, presented their grievances to the Community Relations Committee. The workers framed their concerns as impacting the entire community. Father Henry Grant, an African American priest at St. Stephen's Episcopal Church and relative newcomer to Charleston, empathized with the workers' plight. He had been a patient at Medical College not long before and recalled that workers there "were not treated with any kind of respect. No kind of dignity. They were treated like dogs." He also shared his own experience, recalling being referred to the hospital for two hip replacements and being treated like a second-class citizen who didn't belong there. He vehemently recalled his encounter, "You know, I was a taxpaying citizen who was legitimately referred and they treated me like I was a dog." When the group of hospital workers sought assistance from the committee, Grant was well aware of the kinds of issues that plagued their employment.[17]

As a community leader, Grant viewed the hospital workers' organizing in the context of the "general social revolution" of that era. He had close ties to both William Saunders and the city's most influential white leaders. He believed that Saunders and his followers had the same aims as the city's white leaders—"the same tranquility, the same economic growth of the community"—but neither side would communicate with the other. While many questioned Grant's motives and doubted his ability to maintain a relationship both with the city's most militant organizer and its most conservative leaders, he used his affiliations to attempt to resolve the issues between hospital administrators and frustrated workers. He and Saunders shared a suspicious attitude toward unionizing in general and the arrival of Local 1199 in particular. Saunders made it clear from the onset that he did not see a need for a union. Grant, for his part, took issue with Local 1199 more specifically. He did not trust Godoff, and he questioned whether the union had the workers' best interest in mind. He conducted research to find out how unions worked in other hospitals and found that the level of care in one Philadelphia hospital declined after its workers unionized.[18]

Motivated by his concerns regarding the union's presence and realizing that a strike could be imminent, Grant led the committee in devising a strategy to quickly resolve the matter before that could happen, thereby making the union unnecessary. The committee began by attempting to work with Charleston's legislative delegation, hoping that their influence on the hospital would help. It worked to remain neutral by gathering the facts and proposing a solution that benefited both sides. The hospital refused to negotiate, reiterating that, as a state agency, it could not bargain with a union. Grant eventually found himself forced to literally go between the hospital and Local 1199 in an attempt to resolve the situation. He recalled being at the Harding Inn on Calhoun Street in the heart of Charleston, where representatives from Medical College were on the first floor and union representatives had a suite on the top floor of the inn. According to Grant, "one night from nine o'clock until three in the morning I was on the elevator between the two. They were not going to bargain with them. Damned if they ain't. Under one roof . . . You wouldn't believe how . . . About that time, I said the hell with both of you. I'm going home and get some sleep."[19]

When Godoff got wind of what the committee attempted to do, "he became very furious about that." The union leader argued that this was a matter for the union to handle, not the local leadership. Grant responded that he was neither pro- nor anti-union and that his main concern was to get the situation resolved quickly and successfully before it escalated into full-blown protest. Ultimately, his concern that the union would take advantage of the workers weighed as heavily as them being disrespected and treated unfairly by the hospital.[20]

On Monday, March 3, 1969, the *Charleston News and Courier* reported that hospital workers had requested that HEW conduct a second investigation of Medical College based on allegations of "discriminatory practices, wages and working conditions." It seemed that the prospect of being investigated twice in one year lit a fire under the hospital administration. On Tuesday, March 4, the *News and Courier* reported that McCord had announced a plan to conduct monthly grievance meetings with groups of six or more randomly selected employees. The plan was the result of a two-and-a-half-hour meeting that included hospital administrators, legislators, and local Black leaders. McCord conferred with his administrative staff and Representative

Turner before he made the announcement about the grievance meetings. He maintained his position regarding his refusal to communicate with any union representative. McCord claimed that he had been advised by legal counsel that state law barred state institutions from acknowledging a union and that if he met with a union representative that would "constitute recognition and negotiation." However, there were no state laws against collective bargaining with public-sector unions. Hospital administrators and lawmakers made the argument that they could not recognize or bargain collectively with unions because South Carolina did not have a law that gave them the right to do so.[21]

His ongoing refusal to correspond with the union helps to explain why the Black leaders Esau Jenkins, Reverend John T. Enwright, and Herber U. Fielding had been invited to attend the meeting. Jenkins, Enwright, and Fielding traveled with workers to Columbia and supported them in their meeting with the Charleston delegation, so they would have had insight. They supported the movement and understood the plight of Black hospital workers. However, they did not represent the hospital workers and made that point abundantly clear, explaining that "they came to the meeting at Turner's invitation but could not really speak for the employees." They emphasized that they had not been chosen to represent workers and that "their involvement was not from a union standpoint but out of concern for the employees and the community." In the meeting, the group of leaders mainly reiterated what workers had already shared with the Charleston delegation in their Columbia meeting in February regarding wages, wrongful terminations, and their growing discontent. In addition, they expressed their support for the idea that collective action was important to effect change.[22]

In response, McCord offered his side of the story. Since he began leading Medical College in 1965, he had made a concerted effort to address complaints "brought to him by Negro leaders." He expressed disappointment and confusion as to where the controversy was coming from, as he claimed to have been "leaning over backwards to give everyone a fair shake." McCord made it a point to address the grievances regarding racial discrimination and low wages. He claimed that if any cases of racial discrimination were brought to him, he would take immediate action. He had an air of indignation, but what seemed like a staunch position against racial discrimination was muddied by the fact that, as late as 1968, Black and white patients were not housed in the same sections of the hospital, Black and white workers did not share a break room, and the outlines of the recently removed "Colored" and "White" signs were still visible over the bathroom doors. When questioned about the allegations that Black workers were being paid as little as $1.30 an hour, he responded that the minimum wage was $1.35 and that only a few dozen workers received the lower wage due to their on-the-job performance and would have the opportunity to increase their pay based on their improvement. At the end of the meeting, McCord maintained his refusal to negotiate with the union. He argued that he could "give the employees a fairer shake than the union" and restated his position on the grievance plan, his willingness to see any employee, and his openness to correcting the issues at Medical College.[23]

Workers quickly rejected McCord's proposal for a grievance procedure. They felt that they needed representation at these meetings to ensure that their concerns were being fully and fairly addressed. Despite the unionized workers' refusal to engage in McCord's grievance procedure, he proceeded with the plan to have the monthly meetings. On March 7, he conducted the first meeting under his new grievance policy. Only three of the preselected eight employees attended the meeting; the other five boycotted. According to McCord, the meeting "went very smoothly" and no grievances were presented. Instead, the main topic of discussion was how to structure future grievance meetings. While McCord was meeting with workers who seemingly had no grievances, a group of aggravated workers met with Mayor J. Palmer Gaillard regarding the dispute between the hospital and the workers. Mayor Gaillard would not disclose the details of what was discussed during the meeting, but he did share that he had given workers a few suggestions.[24]

Within a few weeks, McCord finally agreed to meet with a small group of organized workers. He sent interoffice memos to twelve workers telling them when and where to meet. The meeting was scheduled for March 17, 1969, at ten or ten-thirty in the morning in the hospital's auditorium and was supposed to include the twelve workers, McCord, and members of McCord's staff. On the morning of the meeting, unionized workers walked into the auditorium at the scheduled time to find thirty to forty Black and white workers who were challenging the allegations of poor working conditions at the hospital put forth by the now unionized workers. McCord was nowhere in sight. He did not attend and sent a representative in his place. Mary Moultrie, who was among the twelve workers invited to the meeting, refused to stay because McCord did not attend. She returned to work, but once workers heard about what happened in the auditorium many decided to confront McCord in his office. Moultrie joined them. Several workers, including all twelve who were originally invited to the meeting, stormed McCord's office and refused to leave, resulting in an impromptu sit-in. According to Moultrie, it emerged organically as their first demonstration. In response, the staff called Police Chief John Conroy, who demanded that the protesters return to work. All twelve of the unionized workers returned to their respective stations and worked until they were scheduled to leave. At the end of their shifts, each was called down to the nurses' service office and informed that they had been terminated. The Medical College Board of Trustees prompted hospital administrators to execute the terminations after issuing specific instructions in an August 1968 meeting that stated, "Due to the highly sensitive and delicate nature of the operations in this College and Hospital, any person or group that engages in any action of violent nature, or of a nonviolent nature which interrupts the customary operation of the institution and its function and which fails to desist on request of the Administration, shall be subject to immediate dismissal from the College and thereafter be treated as trespassers." That evening, Bennett reached out to both Mayor Gaillard and Governor McNair requesting assistance in getting the twelve workers reinstated. When workers and the union realized that reinstatement was not an option, they quickly planned a full protest. On the morning of March 20, 1969, hundreds of hospital workers, all Black and mostly women, joined together to form a picket line.[25]

When the picket lines went up on Thursday morning, the hospital already had a plan in place to deal with what it viewed as a nuisance and a threat to its authority. At 7:24 that evening, a local law enforcement officer read a temporary injunction issued by Ninth Judicial Circuit Judge Clarence E. Singletary on behalf of Medical College mandating the cessation of all striking and picketing at any of the hospital's facilities.[26]

Singletary, who had been a circuit judge in Charleston since 1961, suggested the injunction when hospital attorneys approached him approximately a week before the strike erupted. They requested an order against organizing workers to prevent them from impeding the daily operations of the hospital. Based on his past experiences with race-based issues in Charleston, he believed that the injunction would be necessary. He recalled the civil rights struggles that emerged during the early years of his career in Charleston, and he worried that the hospital administrators did not understand the full breadth of what they faced. He framed the hospital workers' campaign as a continuation of local nonviolent direct action that began with a lunch counter sit-in in 1960. He pointed to the sit-in as the model for the 1969 movement and asserted that it prepared him to handle the hospital workers' resistance.[27]

To ensure that the hospital administrators understood exactly what they were facing, he urged them to meet with state and local officials regarding the organizing hospital workers. He held a meeting in his office with a representative from the mayor's office, a member of the South Carolina Law Enforcement Division, and the city's new police chief, John F. Conroy. He then issued the temporary injunction, which specified that individuals on the picket line "conspired to picket and harass" and endangered the safety and care of patients. It also claimed that striking workers used "obscenities and acts of intimidation." According to the judge, he issued the order with two things in mind: The hospital would not be able to operate without police "containing and controlling the crowds at the entrance," and the organizers "at least had the right to picket in a peaceful fashion and be permitted to petition as any citizens would have the right aside from the merits of the labor issue." After Judge Singletary issued the injunction, Dr. William McCord, president of Medical College, held a news conference during which he refused to rehire the twelve workers and charged them with "deserting their patients and their duties."[28]

While Singletary wanted the hospital administrators to understand the strike in the context of a broader civil rights movement, the Charleston campaign also emerged in the broader context of a national and local labor movement already in full swing. Locally, just weeks before the hospital workers refused to report to work, more than three hundred members of the International Longshoreman's Association Local 1422-A staged a work stoppage, which resulted in a complete shutdown of the ports. The longshoremen demanded union recognition and negotiations for a labor contract. Hospital workers spoke out in support of the striking longshoreman because they believed they faced the same adversary: South Carolina and its strict anti-union attitude.[29]

Many people on both sides of the movement believed that the voices of local ministers would be critical to its success. Churches served as the bedrock of the Charleston community. The city boasted hundreds of places of worship, including an extensive list of historic churches that represented an array of different faiths and denominations. Workers reached out to a number of churches and ministers seeking assistance and guidance in the early stages of their organizing prior to Local 1199's arrival, and many members of the clergy participated in their meetings and offered their support. In the months after Local 1199 arrived and chartered Local 1199B, the union called on local clergy to speak out for disgruntled workers. Union organizers understood the culture of the area and realized that they would have to go through the churches to access community support. Henry Nicholas, a Local 1199 organizer, gathered information on the striking workers' church affiliations and had them meet with their ministers to garner support.[30]

Once the strike began, local clergy unified, at the behest of hospital workers, to support their efforts. On Friday, March 21, 1969, Reverends John T. Wainwright and Z. L. Grady organized and cochaired a meeting with seventeen of Charleston's ministers. They developed a plan to invite all local clergy to a meeting in support of the striking workers. Several dozen ministers, mostly Black, answered the call. On March 22, two days after the strike began, several of Charleston's local clergy met with Charleston Mayor J. Palmer Gaillard, the state attorney general, and representatives for the unionized workers and the hospital in an attempt to resolve the situation. Meeting attendees formed the Concerned Clergy Committee and developed a "Peace with Justice Proposal" in an effort to develop a bilateral solution. Their main goal was to "obtain a peaceful and just solution" after meeting with representatives from all involved parties.[31]

The proposal called on the hospital administration to acknowledge a group of workers—not necessarily union-affiliated—elected by an impartial party that would serve as the spokesperson for striking workers. This group would have the power to negotiate with management in order to address their grievances. Further, the Concerned Clergy Committee urged hospital leadership to "make a bold gesture of peace" by allowing workers to return to work and absolve them of any charges. The clergy advised striking workers to return to work without incident or agitation once they reached an agreement with hospital administration. They framed this return to work as a necessity for the community, not the hospital. "Our community needs the dedication of their service to the sick," they wrote. In an effort to affirm their neutrality in the situation, the clergy clarified their position, "We do not pass judgment on the actions of the employees who have been discharged or who have charges against them. Such is beyond our competence. But we do think these times call for aggressive action for the restoration of peace and a return to the noble vocation of tending to the sick."[32]

Based on references to the workers' responsibilities to their patients, it seemed that local clergy and hospital administrators operated with the same stream of thought in regard to the impact that the strike had on patients and patient care. However, beyond that, their thinking diverged. Hospital administrators submitted a document to the governor's office, and Dr. McCord spoke out publicly in a local news conference criticizing the proposal and the clergy who drafted it. The hospital administration supposed that the proposal called on them to "accept violence and patient neglect as a means to resolve the present strife." McCord rebuffed the clergy's suggestion to drop all charges against striking workers and rehire the twelve workers whose termination fueled the strike's start, charging that several striking workers either did bodily harm to or threatened employees who decided to remain at work. The hospital's president refused to consider any of what the clergy suggested, asserting, "We will not abandon our employees to lawless people. If our employees are willing to come to this hospital and take care of patients, we most certainly will not turn around and give in to acts of violence and intimidation against these employees." He argued that the twelve fired workers forfeited their rights to employment when they abandoned their patients for more than an hour. According to McCord, those workers had been assigned to the seventh floor, which housed some of the hospital's most critical patients who required constant care. Essentially, he claimed that the twelve workers were fired as a result of their failure to do their jobs.[33]

Representatives from the Concerned Clergy Committee responded to McCord in a news conference at Morris Brown AME church. They questioned how South Carolina as a whole had handled the issue of labor unions. They referred to earlier reports from state lawmakers confirming that there were no laws on the books barring state agencies from dealing with unionized workers. They pointed to the belief that "workers do have the God-given right to organize." While members of the committee dealt with the McCord's comments diplomatically, Mary Moultrie, who was among the twelve fired workers, took a direct approach. Leaving nothing open for deduction or assumption, she brought the conversation back to the key issues and offered a few important details when she said that "Shedding crocodile tears over the plight of patients will never cover up the exploitation, the horrors of poverty, the $1.30 wage and his refusal to provide a procedure for handling grievances and problems affecting the welfare of workers. By this time," she continued, "everyone knows that he dismissed twelve employees whom he invited to his office for a conference, because he later became displeased with the contents of their remarks." This moment affirms that, even though a number of groups and individuals spoke out on behalf of striking workers, the workers could effectively speak out for themselves.[34]

The Concerned Clergy Committee, despite their support for the striking workers, maintained a middle-of-the-road approach and a timid reticence to challenge either side. Their proposal called for a peaceful resolution and for workers to return to their jobs, but at what cost? The document failed to mention the history of degradation and disrespect that fueled the workers' movement. The committee, an all-Black group of ministers, avoided any discussion of the racial discrimination that defined the hospital's working environments and led to the strike. Black leaders, the bulk of whom were members of the clergy, placed more emphasis on resolving the strike than they did on resolving the problems that triggered the strike.[35]

Local 1199 recognized that, even with some community support, they still faced the challenge of negotiating with the hospital. The initial injunction, which halted all picketing around Medical College, and the amended injunction, which only allowed ten individuals with at least twenty yards between them to picket "in a peaceful manner," made it clear that both the hospital and state stood as obstacles to workers getting the resolution they needed. In order to prevail, the union would have to fight this battle on several fronts and through various means.[36]

Workers pushed the strike at full throttle, showing up to the picket lines by the dozens while surrounded by hundreds of supporters who joined the demonstration in spite of the parameters of the amended injunction. As workers carried out the movement on the ground, Local 1199 challenged local and state authorities on the workers' behalf, going head-to-head with the city of Charleston and the state of South Carolina over what they viewed as anti-union tactics. In response to the legal action taken by the hospital, the union filed a petition with the United States District Court for the District of South Carolina, Charleston Division to have "all legal proceedings involving the union and Medical College" moved from the Court of Common Pleas and General Sessions to the US District Court at Charleston with hopes of also having the injunction lifted. Medical College attorneys responded by submitting a motion to have the legal proceedings remain at the state level. As a result, US District Court Judge Charles E. Simons issued a restraining order on behalf of the hospital against the union that included Judge Singletary's amended injunction. Simons ultimately ruled that the case would remain in the state court. His ruling also mandated that the injunction continue and refused the union's plea to have the restraining order rescinded. Judge Singletary set a hearing in the state court for April 3 during which the union would be required to "show cause" as to why they should not be held in contempt of court for violating the injunction. Singletary postponed the hearing until April 10 and then issued an order that it would be postponed indefinitely because the state's attorney general became the attorney of record for the Medical College.[37]

Meanwhile, State Attorney General Daniel R. McLeod confirmed that the state could not prohibit employees from joining a union, but he reiterated that the state and its agencies could not confer with them. However, he revealed, "there's no law actually specifying this." He further explained, "At the same time there is no authority delegated, and in the absence of this authority the agencies of the state have no power to bargain with union." In this moment, South Carolina's staunch resistance to unionization simultaneously came into focus and became more complicated. Even though the state did not have a law against unionization on the books, the state essentially said that since no one has been given the authority to deal with the issue of union recognition, it would ignore it entirely. This convoluted legislative response to unionization highlighted the anti-union sentiments that existed at the core of the hospital and state's strategy to resolve the strike. Unlike in other local labor campaigns, such as the tobacco workers' strike and the port walkout, the hospital workers' union was unable to achieve recognition by the offending party, much less enter into negotiations. The anti-union state of South Carolina supported Medical College in that decision.[38]

The 1945 tobacco workers' strike with Local 15 and the Longshoremen's Association Local 1422A port walkout in 1969 provide proof of the fact that, in spite of the state's stance on unionism, the city of Charleston had not been able to avoid union presence or completely impede its growth. Encouraged by this history, Local 1199B continued to increase the pressure by implementing strategies to strengthen the number of unionized workers and to spread the movement beyond Medical College to five other local hospitals. While they garnered only mild interest from workers at most of the hospitals, Rosetta Simmons, Local 1199B vice president and a Charleston County Hospital employee on strike, had connected many workers from Charleston County Hospital to the movement even before the union arrived. This made it easier for the union to convince those workers to join their ranks. Much like McCord, Dr. V. W. H. Campbell, Charleston County Hospital administrator, refused to meet with union representatives, citing the state's ambiguous law regarding state agencies negotiating with unions. He did, however, claim to be open to setting up a meeting with workers to hear grievances and concerns. Campbell quickly specified that only selected workers would be able to attend without a union representative present. In response, on Thursday, March 27, "a group of workers estimated at between 50 and 90 marched to the administrator's office." While Campbell declined to meet with the large group, he suggested that they elect a few representatives to attend a meeting scheduled for the following evening. Later that evening "between 90 and 100 persons attended a meeting at union hall" with Local 1199B and decided to go on strike the following day. Charleston County Hospital workers started a picket line on the morning of Friday, March 28.[39]

The hospital workers' strike, a last resort, was the culmination of a chain of events that spanned the better part of a year. Hundreds of hospital workers, all Black and mostly women, framed their resistance to racial discrimination, economic injustice, and disrespect of human dignity as much more than a dispute between them and the hospitals they challenged. They created conditions in which their resistance would ultimately have to be addressed by the hospital, the city of Charleston, the state of South Carolina, and the United States Government. The Charleston hospital workers' campaign was not the first of its kind, but it certainly offers a window into the intricacies of grassroots civil rights–based labor organizing forged by

African American women and supported by men. This first phase of the strike raises questions about leadership, autonomy, and power within the context of Black women's activism.

Striking workers, backed by Local 1199 and eventually Local 1199B, readily took on the city of Charleston and confronted the racist and sexist ideologies that impeded Black working-class women. However, union leaders realized that as a Northern union campaigning in an anti-union Southern city and state, they faced unfamiliar obstacles. They understood the obvious challenge of dealing with the racial discrimination workers faced on jobs in a recently integrated South. The union also understood how critical support from churches and the African American community would be for hospital workers' efforts. Also, the union recognized the movement as being driven by converging civil rights and labor issues. As the union worked to figure out how to navigate the complicated and multilayered situation, recognizing that it would require a sophisticated and multidimensional approach, hospital workers continued to urge the movement forward. Local 1199 knew that it would take some heavy artillery to effect change in a city like Charleston and in the state of South Carolina. The Southern Christian Leadership Conference (SCLC) would be their weapon of choice.

Chapter 4

"SOUL POWER"

Striking workers endured in the movement, motivated by what seemed like simple ideals: equality, a decent wage, and an end to discrimination and disrespect. But multiple layers of expectation, ideology, approach and contribution gave way to a complex campaign. The second phase of the 1969 hospital workers' strike involved a dramatic shift due to the arrival of the Southern Christian Leadership Conference. The presence of the national civil rights organization impacted the campaign in three important ways: it galvanized local and national support for the striking workers; it launched the local civil rights–based labor struggle to a national stage; and it provided another mediator between the workers and the hospital. Workers needed allies to support them in their efforts to resolve their issues with Medical College and later Charleston County Hospital. Local leaders, Local 1199, and SCLC all stepped in to support them in their movement by amplifying the complaints that sparked the strike while simultaneously strategizing to help resolve the dispute.

Early in the strike, local Black leaders such as William Saunders expressed little to no support of the union and local clergy made it difficult to discern where their allegiances lay. For that reason, it quickly became clear that Local 1199, as a Northern labor union, needed endorsement from an entity with which Charleston's Black community could identify if they were to generate widespread local support for the striking workers. Keenly aware of the reality that a large portion of the workers they represented were African American, Local 1199 had forged strong ties to the civil rights movement and witnessed the benefits of that kind of collaboration long before the Charleston campaign. In June 1962, Leon Davis, Local 1199 president, was jailed for thirty days for refusing to call off strikes at Beth-El Hospital and Manhattan Eye, Ear and Throat Hospital, both in New York. In response to Davis being jailed, approximately fifty African American and Puerto Rican community and religious leaders joined forces to form the Committee for Justice to Hospital Workers to support striking workers at both hospitals. A. Philip Randolph, founder and president of the Brotherhood of Sleeping Car Porters, an African American labor organization, and Joseph Monserrat, national director of the Migration Division of the Puerto Rican Department of Labor, cochaired the organization. The committee boasted over two hundred members including key leaders from the Puerto Rican community such as Judge Emilio Nunez as well as representatives from all of the major national civil rights organizations: the NAACP, Congress of Racial Equality (CORE), National Urban League, and SCLC. In a letter to *The New York Times*, the committee charged that the hospitals aimed to "perpetuate involuntary servitude among the minority group workers at the bottom of the economic ladder." Their assertion had a striking resemblance to that made by organizing Charleston hospital workers in the late 1960s who charged Dr. William McCord at Medical College with being a "slave driver." In addition to their committee's support of striking workers at the two New York hospitals, they also banned together in protest of Leon Davis's detainment and lauded his efforts to "bring a measure of dignity and self-respect to these terribly victimized workers." Ultimately, the union threatened to initiate additional strikes throughout the state, which caused New York Governor Nelson Rockefeller to intervene with assurances to support legislation that allowed union recognition.[1]

SCLC and Local 1199 began to foster their mutually supportive relationship in the late 1950s. The national union, for example, hosted a "Negro History Week" and donated the funds to SCLC. As a demonstration of solidarity with the civil rights movement, Local 1199 members participated in New York sit-ins and the 1961 Freedom Rides. Dr. Martin Luther King Jr., among SCLC's founders and the organization's original leader, spent time at the Local 1199 headquarters and regularly served as a speaker for union rallies. In July 1962, during an interracial meeting of New York's community leaders, a telegram sent from Dr. King offered his public support of Local 1199 by asserting, "I am fully confident that your historic organizing crusade will be successful in eliminating poverty wages and winning decent standards in Local 1199 contracts, and I bid you Godspeed as you move upwards and onwards."[2]

In 1969, as Local 1199 realized that it was going to need assistance with garnering local support for Charleston's striking hospital workers, SCLC emerged as the natural choice. The timing of Local 1199's call on the civil rights organization in the spring of 1969 could not have been better. Reverend Ralph David Abernathy, SCLC's new leader and Dr. King's successor, was searching for ways to carry on the work that King started. King had begun to expand the organization's focus and revamp its efforts within the African American community in the early 1960s. In public appearances, private meetings, and personal conversations, he frequently pointed to the overlap between the labor and civil rights movements' legacies and aims. In a speech to the 1961 Fourth Constitutional Convention of the AFL-CIO, he poignantly explained his interpretation of the connection between the two movements. Beginning with a discussion of the history of labor organizing, including how the laws for which early unionizers fought established the right to organize, King illustrated a common thread within the movements:

> Negroes in the United States read the history of labor and find it mirrors their own experience. We are confronted by powerful forces telling us to rely on the goodwill and understanding of those who profit by exploiting us. They deplore our discontent, they resent our will to organize, so what we may guarantee that humanity will prevail and equality will be exacted. They are shocked that action organizations, sit-ins, civil disobedience, and protests are becoming our every day tools, just as strikes, demonstrations and union organizations became yours to insure that bargaining power genuinely existed on both sides of the table. If we do not advance, the crushing burden of centuries of neglect and economic deprivation will destroy our will, our spirits and our hopes. In this way labor's historic tradition of moving forward to create vital people as consumers and citizens has become our own tradition, and for the same reasons.[3]

King's longtime adviser, A. Philip Randolph, was the ideal choice as the leader for this movement. The March on Washington for Jobs and Freedom embodied the link between the labor and civil rights movements in the early 1960s. As the founder of the Brotherhood of Sleeping Car Porters and one of the founders and first president of the Negro American Labor Council, he understood the critical nature of the African American economic status and the desperate need for good jobs and fair wages as a central component of the civil rights movement. Randolph worked quickly to garner support and spread the word about the march. In a letter dated July 19, 1963, the labor leader described that the goal of the campaign was to "demonstrate in an orderly way their deep desire for federal action to meet the most burning needs for full employment and for equal rights for all American citizens."[4]

Years after the March on Washington, King envisioned another confrontation when those individuals directly affected by economic injustices, unemployment, inequality in the workplace and poverty would take their issues to the front door of the nation's capital, forcing the American government to face the ills of its citizens and develop a solution:

> We ought to come in mule carts, in old trucks, any kind of transportation people can get their hands on. People ought to come to Washington, sit down if necessary in the middle of the street and say, "We are here, we are poor; we don't have any money; you have made us this way; you keep us down this way; and we've come to stay until do something out it.[5]

King began to formulate the core aims of a broader endeavor that would be called the Poor People's Campaign just prior to his death. While some members of SCLC did not support the idea of the Poor People's Campaign, King and Abernathy realized that it would take the organization in a new direction. As plans for the campaign began to take shape, the Memphis garbage workers' strike erupted in February 1968, providing SCLC with a timely opportunity to engage in the practical application of its vision aimed at eradicating economic injustice. Members split over concerns around deviating from traditional movement aims, especially in the face of an emerging Black Power Movement, and whether going to Memphis was the right call for the organization.[6]

Unionized workers of Local 1733 of the American Federation of State, County, and Municipal Employees (AFSCME) called a strike due to racist inequality, unfair wages, and poor working conditions. Workers, who had been organizing since 1959, overcame the fear of losing their jobs and challenged the system that they believed undercut their dignity and humanity. King and SCLC arrived in Memphis in March 1968 to offer their support to the striking workers. King's vision for SCLC and the movement was clear: establish an inextricable link between the struggles "for jobs and freedom" and reframe the movement to take a more holistic approach to the challenges that African Americans faced.[7]

After King's death, the question of who would and could lead the organization immediately emerged. Conflict among SCLC members materialized around the issue, but according to Reverend John Reynolds, an SCLC staff member, Abernathy was King's choice for successor. Abernathy took the reins to lead SCLC and continued with his predecessor's work. He argued that at that point the civil rights movement had already reached its pinnacle and

SCLC's influence was beginning to wane. He quickly moved to finalizing plans for the Poor People's Campaign, which was set to kick off in May 1968. Abernathy and SCLC staff moved forward with King's vision of a model city on the National Mall where "poor folks would have homes of their own," placing poverty on display for all Americans to witness. They acquired permission to build "Resurrection City" on the Mall, the grassy stretch of land between the Lincoln Memorial and the Capitol. While Resurrection City symbolized SCLC's aims to revive the organization and the movement as a whole, it also offered Abernathy the opportunity to prove himself as a leader.[8]

By the time the lease for Resurrection City expired, even with a week's extension, SCLC had made minimal headway with achieving the goals it originally set. The peaceful demonstrations and attempts to meet with government officials bore little fruit. Unwilling to concede defeat, Abernathy developed the idea of a grand rally to close out the campaign, which SCLC leaders called Solidarity Day. They scheduled the rally for June 19. An estimated fifty to two hundred thousand people attended. The rally garnered a decent amount of political support, but it was not enough to turn the tide or make a sizable impact on SCLC's efforts to attain its goals. Realizing that Resurrection City had reached its end, Abernathy and SCLC decided to drive their point home with a final nonviolent demonstration, and in true SCLC tradition members planned to be arrested. As expected, they were arrested and detained outside of the city. Shortly after they were removed from the premises, local police descended on Resurrection City, cleared out the remaining residents and arranged for their transportation away from the city. Before Abernathy and his followers were released from jail, Resurrection City had been dismantled. In the aftermath, the leader feared that the participants would not be able to understand the impact of this movement and ultimately deem it unsuccessful. He concluded that, even though the campaign did not achieve its original goals, the mere presence of America's poor in the nation's capital for approximately a month brought much needed attention to their circumstances, needs, and demands.[9]

When the Charleston hospital workers' strike erupted the year after Resurrection City ended, SCLC was mired in uncertainty. There were ongoing concerns about the relevance of a traditional approach to civil rights activism, particularly in the face of a growing Black Power movement. Internally, the organization was dealing with turmoil and dissent over the issue of Abernathy's leadership. SCLC needed a win after the disappointing outcome in DC, and leaders believed that issues relating to economic injustice and inequality were so salient that the organization would be able to secure a clear victory in Charleston in a way that it had not in DC. However, SCLC leaders also knew that taking on Charleston was an enormous gamble. Facing another ambiguous outcome, the organization might not survive. If, however, they could walk away with the city of Charleston counted among their victories, it could be a major step in reinvigorating the relevance of the nonviolent, direct-action approach to organizing and the organization.[10]

SCLC needed to address several obstacles and questions before it officially agreed to take on Charleston. How could it deliver a decisive blow in South Carolina, a staunchly anti-union and right-to-work state? The organization quickly ascertained that it would need the full support of Charleston's Black community for its part in the campaign to be effective. Abernathy agreed to join the campaign on the condition that he and SCLC had permission from the Black community to be there. Both Local 1199 and SCLC sent in representatives, David White and Carl Farris, respectively, to serve as community relations liaisons to garner support for the organization's presence. White and Farris encountered a great deal of suspicion and fear. Some citizens expressed explicit resistance to SCLC on the grounds that, "wherever they go, they cause turmoil." Many leaders within the community hoped for a diplomatic resolution to the situation and had little interest in bringing in outsiders to deal with the dispute. They requested a meeting with members of the Concerned Citizens of Charleston, a local organization led by Black and white ministers that included several other local Black leaders. White and Farris, complete strangers working together as if they had known each other for years, spent hours stalling by dragging out the conversation long enough for those who were staunchly opposed to leave. They then persuaded those who remained to agree to invite SCLC to assist with resolving the strike. Leaders of the Concerned Citizens of Charleston offered the official invitation.[11]

On the evening of Monday, March 31, Abernathy addressed a crowd of more than 1,500 people from all over the state gathered at the Fourth Baptist Church and pledged his support for striking workers. The SCLC leader, and eventually the entire staff, returned to Charleston three weeks later ready to devote himself and his organization to the cause of the striking workers. While happy to have Abernathy and SCLC's support, workers did not passively wait for their return. Just days after the SCLC leader left Charleston, they and their supporters executed an approximately five-hundred-person memorial march in honor of Dr. King with hopes of drawing more attention to their campaign and symbolically reiterating the ongoing connection between the civil rights and labor movements. The march took two hours and spanned three and a half miles through the city, beginning at the union hall and passing five hospitals, including the two where workers maintained picket lines. Workers moved peacefully through the city singing "We Shall

Overcome" and other movement songs before dispersing around 6 p.m. Later that week, they spread across the city seeking moral and financial support at approximately eighty churches. They passed out leaflets explaining to the church community that they were seeking "resurrection" and that it had "justice and dignity attached to it." The following day, representatives of the striking workers traveled to Columbia to petition local unions and other organizations for support. Workers appealed to the community from the position of hard-working individuals who "represent years of service to the city," arguing that they had made major contributions to the Charleston community and deserved to earn a living wage and to be treated with respect. They also began soliciting donations from local merchants and threatened boycotts against those that did not contribute. A group of women from the union visited several stores on King Street, Charleston's main thoroughfare, requesting assistance. When they met with refusal, they threatened to add the store to a growing "blacklist." Workers took a multidimensional approach to garnering support, building their finances and exposing the surrounding community to the issues at the center of their campaign.[12]

Workers also requested a meeting with South Carolina Governor Robert E. McNair during this period. A week into the strike, McNair announced that he planned to appoint a three-person committee that would be charged with studying the various aspects of the strike, "correcting any existing problems and establishing equitable personnel practices consistent with those of other state institutions and agencies." The individuals appointed to the committee would be guided by and report directly to McNair and ultimately report their findings to him and the Budget and Control Board. He appointed Earl Ellis, director of the personnel division of the state's Budget and Control Board, as the chair of the committee. In the meantime, workers wanted more immediate answers.[13]

On April 8, McNair met with a group of five workers and two attorneys, F. Henderson Moore and George Payton. The meeting took place days after he met with six members of the Concerned Clergy Committee, who aimed to mediate a resolution to the strike, and a little more than twenty-four hours after approximately forty workers picketed the State House and requested the meeting with the governor. Mary Moultrie, her second vice president Jack Bradford, and three other workers met with the governor. The state maintained its position on its inability to negotiate with a union while workers remained unwilling to end their protest. According to McNair, "the only thing that will satisfy Miss Moultrie and those who follow her would be recognition of and bargaining and contracting with them as union representatives." He asserted that, based on the laws of the state, that would be impossible.

He suggested that "the others who are interested in returning to the hospital present themselves and request re-employment. Should this not prove satisfactory, then I would suggest that you get in touch with Mr. Edwin Schachte, chair of the board of trustees, which has the authority over the policy for the College Hospital." In the end Moultrie, representing the workers, deemed the meeting a "waste of time." She argued, "We got nothing from him. I don't know whether he rejected our requests or not. We got no concessions from him. It is the same story we've been getting. I don't know where this will end but we won't give up. We'll keep trying."[14]

Workers began to deliberately be arrested, a tactic often employed by civil rights activists as a form of protest, in order to bring more visibility to their cause—in some instances acting out of pure anger and frustration. In the previous weeks, workers were being arrested for violating the injunction, but they had not employed being jailed as a resistance strategy. Judge Singletary, in response to the open defiance, issued a third injunction on April 10, just a few of days after workers and their representatives met with McNair, restricting the picket line to ten workers, requiring members of the union not on the line to maintain a distance of five hundred yards, and prohibiting "intimidation, threats and harassment" of those who continued to work. During the morning shift change that same day, strikers attempted to prevent two workers from entering the hospital, causing law enforcement to address the situation. Amid the confrontation, one of the striking workers allegedly threw some pepper that hit one of the officers in the eyes. Subsequently, more strikers gathered to prevent workers from entering the hospital. Within minutes, officers arrested a total of five individuals. The following day, thirty-one striking workers were arrested for defying the injunction.[15]

Workers were "determined to stay in jail without bail until their rights are established and steps to end poverty are taken." These instances together demonstrate two things: First, they served as a reminder that framing this as a movement about union recognition and rehiring the twelve workers Medical College administrators terminated severely underestimated the feelings of discontent and the "by any means necessary" attitude at the core of the movement. Second, they highlight the multiple layers of the approach to organizing, activism, and resistance within this movement. Workers fighting for the same cause demonstrated varied responses and tactics to reach the common goal, but at the center of each approach rested a spirit of fearlessness and determination that were increasingly difficult for local authorities to contain.[16] Mary Moultrie made this clear during a speech that she rendered at a public event. She spoke directly to the South

Carolina governor in her speech, but her message emphasizes the power and dedication of striking workers:

> Mister governor, this strike has been going on for over ten weeks now. I know that surprises you. You thought we'd just die out after a day or two of marching. You thought we'd just give up and scratch our heads and shuffle back to those hospitals. You thought we'd say "sorry, boss" and put those handkerchiefs back on our heads. Sorry about that, governor, but we just had to disappoint you. The fact is, governor, we're stronger than ever. We've been going ten weeks, and we'll go another ten if you want it that way. We've kept on walking and we've kept on talking. And we're going to keep right on until you come to your senses. Mister governor, we've got something here that you'll never be able to beat. Not you, not your cops, not your National Guard. Because mister governor, we've got a winning combination. We've got our union, mister governor, Local 1199B. And we've got the SCLC and its great president, Reverend Ralph David Abernathy. Mister governor, you might as well face up to it. Neither of us is going to sit down and die—neither of us, at no time. You know why we're not going to die, mister governor? Because we're strong and we're getting stronger every day. We're getting support from all across this nation, and all you're getting is one big headache. And a headache can make you weak, mister governor. And that's bad because, mister governor, you're getting weaker and we're getting stronger. And you know, mister governor, that only the strong survive.[17]

When Abernathy and SCLC staff finally returned to Charleston three weeks after his first visit, they arrived with plans to structure their approach based on previous campaigns in Birmingham and Selma, where large-scale demonstrations and boycotts created enough disturbance to compel local and state government to negotiate. To that end, organizers aimed to achieve three main goals: mobilize the entire community, including the youth; draw national attention to the movement; and compel federal intervention on the workers' behalf, if necessary. Like Local 1199 and Local 1199B, SCLC understood the importance of community support and knew that it would have to mobilize the community in support of striking workers. SCLC also agreed with Local 1199 that, considering the resistance from the state, it would take federal intervention to override anti-union state law in order to resolve the situation. It would also take increased and consistent national attention to get the White House involved. With these things in mind, the organization set up its headquarters in a local Black hotel and hit the ground running. Abernathy placed Andrew Young, executive vice president of SCLC, in charge of the day-to-day operations as he made plans to be jailed as a symbol of resistance to the injustices that striking workers faced and as a show of solidarity with them in their cause. A community rally at Morris Brown African Methodist Episcopal Church on April 22 kicked off SCLC's arrival in Charleston while simultaneously marking the beginning of the end of the strike.[18]

SCLC's Southern evangelical roots allowed it to utilize local churches to gain access to the community. The organization's full-throttle community mobilization campaign began with organizers contacting local ministers to get permission to use their churches for meetings and rallies. Organizers also reached out to ministers in the surrounding areas such as Johns Island, Edisto, and Columbia to widen the support base. David White, Local 1199 organizer, concluded that in the South, particularly among Black people, "without the church you can't do a thing." With that being the case, every move that SCLC made "was through the church." The organization hosted meetings at a different church each night. Representatives from SCLC and Local 1199B, especially Abernathy and Moultrie, usually spoke at each meeting. Often representatives from local and national government, national and international unions, and community organizations would be added to the roster of speakers. Once SCLC solidified the support of local churches, organizers immediately sprang into action orchestrating massive marches through the city as one of its main tools to draw national attention to the workers' cause. The organization's notoriety and use of traditional community mobilization tactics instantaneously stimulated local and national interest. Its involvement had two immediate effects: a substantial increase in the number of people physically on the ground and daily coverage in the national news. SCLC gave the local civil rights–based labor dispute national visibility.[19]

On the morning of April 22, 1969, Mary Moultrie, linked arm-in-arm with Reverend Ralph David Abernathy, led the first mass march organized by SCLC in Charleston. They were followed by approximately eight hundred people singing "Ain't nobody turning 'round, keep on walking down to freedom land." Abernathy brought his Bible and a toothbrush to the march with hopes of implementing the civil rights movement tradition of arrest as a demonstration of protest. Striking hospital workers, their families, and numerous supporters made their way down Calhoun Street and stopped at Charleston County Hospital, where they sat on the pavement. Surrounded by bowed heads, Father William Joyce, member of the Concerned Clergy Committee, offered a prayer, "Negroes who have been caught up in centuries of serfdom and slavery might be free. Peace is our goal. Not an empty vapid peace, but a peace with justice on our side. The truth, when it is known, will make us all free." The group traveled on, and as they marched through the Medical College complex past the hospital, nonstriking workers watched the procession from the windows. The marchers encouraged onlookers to join. The march ended at Morris Brown African Methodist Episcopal Church with Abernathy addressing the crowd, assuring them that he would return, announcing several upcoming community rallies, and promising to get "Mrs. Martin Luther King" to visit Charleston. He also announced that in addition to a mass meeting, which would be a nightly occurrence, there would also be a youth rally the following night. Regarding the youth, Abernathy warned, "I don't want parents to get disturbed if their children go to jail instead of school. There are some things you can't learn in school."[20]

SCLC's first major demonstration was among its most significant. It introduced the city to the style and scale of mobilization that SCLC intended to orchestrate. The march was almost double the size of the one that hospital workers had organized in memory of Dr. Martin Luther King Jr. on April 4. The dramatic increase in hospital workers' supporters and growing tensions prompted Governor McNair to call in the National Guard, members of which were in place by the end of that week. When approximately 2,500 individuals marched on the Medical College on the following Saturday, several hundred National Guardsmen, armed with "rifles and fitted bayonets," lined the streets. A group of more than a hundred protesters broke off from the march and formed a picket line around Medical College Hospital. This violated the injunction order and resulted in the entire group, including Abernathy, being arrested. SCLC aimed to use high profile arrests, such as having its leader jailed, and the increasing number of hospital workers and their supporters inside the local jail to draw national attention to the movement.[21]

Early in the strike, workers, backed by local leaders and the union, garnered some local support, but the campaign received sporadic national media attention. Prior to Abernathy's visit to Charleston in late March 1969, the *Charleston News and Courier* provided daily coverage of the strike while reports from national news outlets and the Black press were infrequent. Moe Foner, Local 1199 director of public relations, recalled the general feeling among union organizers, "We're going to die here. We cannot make it here the way we're going. This has to become a big thing." After Abernathy's first visit, while still not daily, reports on the strike began to steadily increase in mainstream and Black-owned newspapers. On the day of the first major march, *The Washington Post* reported that Abernathy told a crowd of 3,500 at a rally the night before that he planned to "sock it to Charleston." The following day, *The New York Times* ran an article including a picture of Moultrie and Abernathy with the caption, "Prepared for the Worst: The Rev. Ralph David Abernathy, head of the SCLC, carrying toothbrush and paste as he leads striking workers of Local 1199B, National Hospital and Nursing Home Employees Union, through Charleston, SC." After law enforcement arrested Abernathy on April 25, 1969, the campaign became daily national news.[22]

Despite Abernathy's willingness to go to jail as a protest strategy, he attempted to distance the movement from the ongoing violence that had become a persistent occurrence, arguing that it "discredited" nonviolent direct action. He claimed that SCLC would use its resources to identify and expose those causing disorder because "we don't believe in violence." Ironically, according to William Saunders, leader of the semisecret militant Hospital Workers Defense Team, after Abernathy arrived and began making plans to go to jail, the Defense Team already had people in place on the inside to ensure Abernathy's safety. Saunders recalled that young members of the team would approach him in the mornings asking, "Mr. Bill, you want me to go to jail today, sir?" Many of them had experience with the penal system and had few reservations about going to jail, especially for what they believed to be a worthy cause. These individuals would find reasons to be locked up and, according to Saunders, would go in and take over the inside of the local jail by doing jobs such as working in the kitchen or becoming trustees. Like the striking workers, neither Abernathy nor any of his people seemed to have been aware of the protection or of who provided it.[23]

Mary Moultrie also challenged the notion that hospital workers were responsible for the violence spreading throughout the city. She asserted that they were constantly blamed for the chaos, generally and in regard to specific incidents, but according to her, "a lot of it is not true." She recalled numerous moments of violence and unrest that took place in the evenings after the curfew began but argued, "When we really got down to it, they were not strikers. There are going to be people somewhere that are going to capitalize off somebody's efforts, and these were onlookers or whatever you would call them. They certainly weren't supporting us in that manner." Naomi White and Jessie Jefferson agreed with Moultrie's assertion. White remembered workers being held responsible for the growing violence but argued, "all of that was attributed to us, which we had no part in it." Jefferson concurred, saying "that was a time for other people to take advantage of what was going on (to do what they wanted to do). But it wasn't the strikers." Contrary to those assertions, workers were indeed involved in violent activity. In fact, White led hospital workers in a group known as Hell's Angels, which organized to address the scab issue, that was known to have committed acts of violence against scabs.[24]

Abernathy acknowledged that the violence associated with the movement was a growing issue. He admitted, "there were times when we weren't quite in control." He cited local Black youth as the root cause. The leader contended that though SCLC workshopped its followers in Charleston the same way that they had in other campaigns, external variables made that tactic less effective. He pointed to growing anti-Vietnam War sentiments and lingering emotions connected to Dr. King's assassination as the sources of unrest, which resulted in demonstrations and riots that sprang up across the nation. He reasoned that Charleston youth were being exposed to the riotous behavior through the media and would then bring that approach to SCLC's "peaceful and nonviolent demonstrations."[25]

Hospital workers and their supporters shouldered accusations of inciting the growing disorder in the city, while they suffered brutalization that largely went unnoticed. According to Moultrie, the treatment that hospital workers endured included being dragged and violently thrown into police vans, having their arms twisted, and even getting punched. Naomi White recalled moments when "they roughed us up." She explained, "One worker, she was beaten and after they got her in the paddy wagon, they closed the door and beat her. And we couldn't get in to help." Jessie Jefferson, a nursing assistant at Medical College who had just returned to the area when the organizing began, shared the story of Thelma Buncum, a fellow striker, being attacked while in jail:

> The policemen got mad at us, because we keep coming on the picket lines. In fact, we even had one that went into the cell and attacked one of the nurses. We had pictures blown up. He went in and did her face and everything and beat her. When we went in the jail, they said that when we were out there, they said that was Black power. When we came into the jail that was white power. They took over. That's what they said.[26]

The violence against workers was not always behind closed doors. Beverly Kennedy, a nurse's aide from Medical College, recalled state troopers brutalizing a woman she referred to as "Miss Richards" in broad daylight on King Street, the city's main shopping area. Hosea Williams, a member of SCLC's executive staff, shared a memory of the strike when he sustained and witnessed violence at the hands of local police. He and Abernathy led a march together, and toward the end several officers began to demand that they immediately end the march. When marchers seemed to be ignoring their command, Williams recollected, "Those police unleashed on us. They beat that little Black girl. The blood, that beat up, and she wasn't doing anything.

They really roughed us up too. Yeah they kicked our butts. They did a good job of kicking my butt and they carried us on down and finally us into jail." Workers who fought back or intimidated scabs were often criticized for their behavior. But White reasoned that they were merely reacting to how they were being treated:

> Well, I mean you know somebody rough you up and hit you, you not just going to stand there and take it, you know, you will retaliate. In some instances if they had intended to do things that wouldn't even be publicized like little underhanded things. 'We can beat this one up or shove them around. Nobody is really around to report it.' And then when you get done there it's my word against yours, the officer.

She framed their actions as a natural response to and a reiteration of their unwillingness to tolerate disrespect.[27]

In addition to working through the churches, orchestrating a national publicity campaign, and grappling with the persistence of violence in the movement, SCLC also made youth a key aspect of its community mobilizing efforts. Carl Farris, the Charleston project director for SCLC, took charge of organizing the student-led arm of the movement. While a youth arm of the campaign emerged prior to the arrival of SCLC, during this phase of the strike the number of involved youths quickly grew as a formally organized faction of the movement. Approximately four hundred students, some as young as eight years old, gathered for the initial youth rally on April 23. Farris warned students that if they chose to support hospital workers they needed to prepare to be arrested. Despite the words of caution, students cheered and pledged their support. By the end of April, school attendance reports indicated the level of student involvement. More than 4,300 students were reported absent from city and county schools, compared to the normal average of 1,100 absences. SCLC used the churches during the day to organize the youth, providing them with movement training and lessons in African American history.[28]

The day after Abernathy's first arrest, a group of nearly a hundred protesters, the majority of whom were students, attempted to march through Charleston's main business district. Led by Farris and Jerome Smalls, a Burke High School student, the group was instructed to march in pairs in an orderly manner from the Central Baptist Church. Within a short distance from the church, the group ran into Charleston City Police Chief John F. Conroy, local law enforcement officers, and National Guardsmen preventing them from proceeding. After a four-hour standoff, Conroy demanded that the marchers disband. The group followed Farris's earlier instruction: "If we are stopped by the police, just wait there until they let us go by." They refused to move, and the entire group was arrested. The next day, Father Leo Croghan and Father William Joyce, both local Catholic priests, led a group of 140 students down King Street. They were accused of violating a city ordinance that required them to have a march permit. When they refused to disperse, they were also arrested. The youth were motivated by a multi-layered sense of purpose. One said, "We want justice for our hospital workers, our parents, as well as ourselves." Their participation added complexity to the movement. As young people had done throughout the civil rights era, Charleston youth expanded definitions of leadership and activism. Their presence on the picket lines and at marches, coupled with increasing numbers of arrests, framed the struggle as a battle fought by and for entire families.[29]

Some members of Charleston's local leadership took issue with the youth arm of the movement. Father Henry Grant, an African American Episcopal priest of Charleston's St. Stephen's Episcopal Church and chair of the city's Community Relations Committee, criticized SCLC for organizing the youth. He argued that the civil rights organization encouraged students to tell their parents that they were "traitors" if they did not support the hospital workers. He called attention to the hypocrisy of how SCLC leaders, particularly Abernathy and Andrew Young, handled Charleston youth when he said, "You tell them that this is more important than them going to school every day and to stay out of school. And I know damn well, Andy Young, you have your children in a private Episcopal school in Atlanta, and Reverend Abernathy, you do, too, and none of you have taken your children out of school." He argued that, while these leaders rested assured that their children received an education, a private education in fact, they entered other communities and advised "Black kids" who could not afford to miss any days of school not to go. Father Grant's assessment sheds light on the sacrifices that communities made in the name of change and uplift. It also reveals a clear line of distinction between movement leaders and those folks on the ground whose lives were directly impacted by their participation.[30]

When Coretta Scott King arrived in Charleston on April 29, she spent the afternoon visiting the county jail where Abernathy remained along with more than two hundred hospital workers and their supporters. Later that evening she spoke at a rally held at Emanuel AME church to prepare for the march she planned to lead the following day. Mrs. King, who had been named the chair of Local 1199's national organizing committee, stood in front of the crowd wearing a blue and white Local 1199 hat and assured them that she was fulfilling "her husband's dream" and that if he were "alive today, he would be right here with you" because he often referred to Local

1199 as "his favorite union." Martin Luther King Sr. also attended the rally, his presence further solidifying the connection between his son and the Charleston movement.[31]

The following day, less than a month after the one-year anniversary of her husband's assassination, Mrs. King led a peaceful march through the city of Charleston. The *Chicago Tribune* compared her to Dr. King, reporting that she "walked today where her late husband had walked hundreds of times in cities across the South—at the front of more than 1,500 Negroes in a protest march." At this point, approximately 845 National Guardsmen, highway patrolmen, and South Carolina Law Enforcement Division agents were on duty. They stood by as marchers gathered at Morris Brown AME Church and headed to Medical College. Approximately 150 marchers started a picket line at the hospital while the rest of the crowd moved ahead. Even though the size of the picket line clearly violated the injunction order, Conroy excused the crowd on the grounds that his officers were preoccupied with guarding Mrs. King. At the end of the march, she gave a short speech in which she compared the Charleston movement to Selma and Memphis, asserting that each of these moments had become, "a national test of purpose with tremendously important implications for decent-minded Americans everywhere." She vowed her support, claiming that she would be a part of "this historic struggle no matter what."[32]

When SCLC arrived in Charleston, the hospital workers' campaign was in full swing. Workers had forged a movement that expanded traditional notions of African American women's activism by shedding light on its distinctive nature. While their protest and resistance had not reached the end of its effectiveness, workers certainly needed additional support and guidance in their efforts to have their grievances acknowledged and resolved. SCLC's arrival critically impacted the local movement's landscape with experience, connection, and the full weight of tried-and-true civil rights movement strategy. The organization's presence propelled Charleston into becoming a location for a nationally recognized civil rights–based labor movement location. In the meantime, the majority of workers at the center of the campaign were steadily being rendered voiceless and faceless in media and, eventually, in the historical narrative.

Chapter 5

RESPECTABLE AND DISORDERLY

As the hospital workers' civil rights–based labor campaign gained traction in late 1960s Charleston, competing voices and aims surrounded and certainly shaped the movement. However, despite the challenges to their autonomy and leadership in the moment, workers focused their energy on the day-to-day struggles they hoped would result in a living wage, improved working conditions, and union representation. Their activism and resistance at the front line of the strike emerged in many forms but often failed to gain widespread public attention. The moments that made the news or garnered public discussion were often regarded negatively. Despite the lack of attention paid in that moment to the contributions of working-class Black women on the front line, the experiences of those women shaped key aspects of the movement and shed light on the distinct nature of Black women's activism at the intersection of the civil rights and labor struggles. The narrative of the hospital workers' campaign adds to the ever-expanding discourse on African American women's experiences and their activism by highlighting several critical components: distinct aspects of women-driven movements, influence of gender norms, and militancy. The working-class Black women who took on a major portion of Charleston's health-care system in the late 1960s were a beautiful mix of grace and grit. Their approach to activism in this movement was simultaneously fueled by the tenets of nonviolence and labor militancy. Kali Nicole Gross, in *Hannah Mary Tabbs and the Disembodied Torso*, confronts the tendency to render African American women as one dimensional and to favor a narrative that focuses mainly on "suffering, resistance, and, ultimately, redemption." Gross urges a reconsideration of Black women's experiences and insists on the importance of giving Black women the space to be "fully visible, fully legible, fully human, and thus vulnerable, damaged, and flawed." Charleston's hospital workers forged a movement that demonstrated the fullness of what Black women activists confronted, asserted, and accomplished in addition to the scope of their organizing influence.[1]

Striking hospital workers regarded their ability to support their families and feed their children as the driving force for their activism. The bulk of organized workers became activists for the moment and out of necessity, with earning a wage that allowed them to support their family as a clear priority. Beverly Kennedy, an employee of Medical College, asserted, "Everyone on earth wants their children to have, and be able to live like humans." Many workers were single parents and the only source of financial support for their families. Though some married workers could rely on their spouse's income, many of the striking women provided a critical portion of the household income. Local 1199 provided striking Charleston workers with fifteen dollars a week. Prior to the strike, the lowest paid workers earned approximately three times that amount and yet they made the sacrifice in an effort to bring about change. If workers found themselves in a serious financial bind such as needing help with rent or a utility bill, the union would assist. For those workers who needed further help, several sought assistance from the Charleston County Welfare Department to apply for food stamps and other government assistance. According to Margaret Rose, in her discussion of Filipino women in the 1965 Delano Grape strike, having the responsibility of supporting one's family created a complicated situation for female unionists. For women workers "activism was complex as they juggled competing interests of family, work and trade unionism." Those competing interests made women's activism in labor movements distinctive. The nature of their experiences and responsibilities outside the job and away from the picket line shaped their activism at every turn.[2]

The daily presence of children and young people in the union hall and on the picket line underscored mothering as one of the intricacies of women-centered activism within this movement. Mothers faced the challenge of balancing their families and their activism. Some women on the picket line were single mothers with as many as ten children. Workers relied heavily on food prepared daily in the "strike kitchen" staffed by striking workers, even though it was usually just beans and rice, and utilized it as a resource for feeding their families. Many workers brought their children with them to the union hall every day to eat. Even for the married women, the amount of time they spent away from home became a source of tension. Husbands began to resent having to take over traditionally female responsibilities such as cooking, cleaning and grocery shopping. Since childcare was generally a woman's responsibility, workers conducted activities and games in the union hall to keep children occupied, allowing mothers to participate in the day-to-day union and strike activities. Many mothers took their children with them to the picket line. A scene from *I Am Somebody*, a documentary about the Charleston strike, showed a group of women marching and singing as they were being loaded into a bus after being arrested. One of the women was shown moving along with the group while carrying an infant until an officer stopped her from getting on the bus with the baby.³

For some workers, the intersection of mothering and activism presented itself in the form of personal loss. Rosetta Simmons, then vice president of Local 1199B, recalled a moment of her experience that confirms the fact that their activism was colored by strikers' distinct roles as women. When workers at Charleston County Hospital walked out in late March of 1969—several days after the MCH strike began—Simmons, who was single at the time, was pregnant. Days later, she went into premature labor and delivered a baby girl, who lived only four days. Devastated by the loss of her daughter and needing time to recuperate from the ordeal, Simmons stayed away from the protest for only a short time. Motivated first by her faith in God and then by her desire to be a part of the movement she believed would bring about change for workers and their families, she pulled herself together and returned to the picket line. "I said it's God's will and I can't question the work of the Lord," she said. "I said my job is to get back out there, and I did. I just wanted to be a part of what we started." Simmons's experience with the pregnancy, premature birth, and subsequent loss of a child in the midst of her role as a local leader within the union and among the other women on strike, emphasizes the fact that the responsibilities of womanhood and work together defined women's activism in this movement. In that moment, for Simmons, being a recently bereaved mother complicated her role as an activist and organizer. It did not, however, undermine or negate it. Simmons discussed the loss of her daughter with as much passion as she displayed when she spoke about her beliefs and ideals as they related to the movement. The mere fact that she quickly returned to the picket line after childbirth and the death of her daughter speaks volumes about her commitment and the importance of the movement.⁴

The involvement of women fostered another distinct aspect of the campaign: the emergence of a youth arm of the movement. It became customary to see women on the picket line with young children in strollers or being supported by older children who volunteered to assist in the day-to-day aspects of the strike. Naomi White recalled that all her children, from the oldest to the youngest, participated in some capacity throughout the strike. Both her oldest son and daughter, the son returning to Charleston occasionally from

Wilberforce University, stood on the picket line. Even though White's mother would sometimes forbid them to participate out of fear for their safety, the younger children also supported their mother's commitment. The number of children on and around the picket line motivated workers to organize youth marches during the strike. Over time, Charleston youth unrelated to the strikers began to pay closer attention to the movement in progress and offered their support.[5]

Charleston youth, whether they connected to women on the front line directly or not, began to form a broader student-led arm of the campaign. Students chose fellow students James Jones, Jerome Smalls, and Linda Harvey as their leaders and began to operate in the tradition of civil rights organizing in support of striking workers. To train and prepare for their roles and responsibilities, students led daily workshops to develop strategies, discuss expectations, and motivate each other. They also staged school walkouts, organized marches and demonstrations, and participated in local boycotts. Hundreds even went to jail. Students found themselves motivated to act for a few different reasons. First, they viewed the movement as an important cause. Second, many had family members, specifically parents, on the picket lines and therefore they had a personal interest in the workers' success. Finally, they saw this moment as an opportunity to create change for their own future. For them, the strike symbolized their own freedom and what lay ahead in their lives. Ultimately, students were adamant about their support of striking workers and made their commitment clear: "There is nothing or no one who can stop us. There is no law that says we had to stay in school, and we did not stay. We belong with the workers and will stay with them. We closed the schools but learned much more outside the classroom, in the street."[6]

The student arm of the movement became strong enough to cause concern among state leaders due to its reach and ability to connect with other student-led protest organizations and efforts across South Carolina. The youth arm of the Civil Rights Movement demonstrated the effectiveness of grassroots efforts to confront and eradicate racism and discrimination through disruptive campaigns such as the 1961 Freedom Rides and the 1964 Freedom Summer. State leaders were wise to be uneasy. In late March, just days after the strike began, Henry Nichols, one of Local 1199's national organizing committee directors, sent Clifford B. Smith, an Internal Revenue Service agent affiliated with Local 1199B, to South Carolina State College, one of two historically Black colleges in Orangeburg, South Carolina. The HBCU had been struck with tragedy just over a year prior, in early February 1968, when three unarmed Black students were killed by police during a protest. Nichols tasked Smith with picking up students to bring back to Charleston.

Those students provided support to striking workers by "picketing, making signs, . . . and running little errands for the union. . . ." As the unrest in Charleston continued to swell, an armed, student-led protest emerged at Voorhees College in Denmark, South Carolina, less than a hundred miles away, that South Carolina Governor Robert McNair feared would influence or heighten an already unstable situation. In a report from Chief Joseph Strom of South Carolina Law Enforcement division (SLED) on the afternoon of April 28, 1969, the governor received news that students from "the militant crowd" had taken over the library and administration buildings of the predominately Black, Episcopal-affiliated institution. On the same day, students at Memphis State University, Queens College in New York City, and St. Louis University engaged in acts of protest as well. These demonstrations emerged as a part of an ongoing movement of mostly Black college student protests across the country.[7]

Voorhees students, thirty Black men and women armed with guns and knives, barricaded themselves inside after escorting faculty, staff, and other students out. They made it clear that they were armed for their own protection: "These students have secured guns for self-defense purposes only and they have refused to leave the building. We aren't going to allow another Orangeburg." The Voorhees students issued a list of demands addressing the development of a Black Studies program, appointing Black department chairs, health care, living conditions, raises for nonacademic college employees, and immunity for those students who participated. They covered the large windows of the building with newspapers, Malcolm X posters and handwritten signs with slogans such as, "no Viet Cong ever called me a [n----r]" and "the liberated Malcolm X University." In support of the students inside the building, approximately a hundred students reportedly descended on the cafeteria and demanded that everyone leave. Two members of the group removed George W. Wilbur, the cafeteria manager, at gunpoint while the rest gathered up all of the food from the refrigerators and serving lines. Based on Wilbur's approximation, in addition to the cooked food, they delivered enough nonperishables and dairy products to the administration building to sustain the protesters for a week. Another group of students assembled outside the home of Dr. John F. Potts, the college president, chanting, "Ungawa, black power."[8]

The students had seized the buildings at around noon. Governor McNair received confirmation at two o'clock that there was an armed protest. Potts requested assistance from the state in the matter. McNair declared a state of emergency on the campus approximately an hour later, and by 4:30 p.m., National Guardsmen and SLED agents had surrounded the campus.

Members of the college's administration and faculty negotiated with the students on the inside prior to the troops' arrival, and thirty students subsequently vacated the buildings unarmed. Potts, with authority over only institution-based situations, granted the students amnesty as a part of their settlement. However, shortly after the students emerged from the buildings, and despite the administrator's objections, Chief Strom arrested the entire group, saying that "they violated the laws of this State and I have to help uphold those laws." The students were transported to Bamberg County Jail and held on the charges of "unlawful assembly and riot." In the aftermath, the college president closed the campus until May 12, 1969, at which time most of the students returned to classes.[9]

Governor McNair faced the reality that "South Carolina stood at a very important crossroad." Fearing that the already tense situation in Charleston could be exacerbated by a national student protest movement and the Voorhees situation, he had to figure out how to avoid having another movement emerge alongside the hospital workers' campaign. The steady surge in the number of demonstrators and supporters for the hospital workers' campaign caused trepidation among local and state leaders regarding safety and revenue. In addition, local businesses and the city as a whole were starting to feel the financial impact of the growing turmoil. The fact that the city's troubles had become a part of the national conversation was also disturbing.[10]

In response, the governor drew a line in the sand regarding potential student uprisings and the hospital workers' campaign. In a press conference on the morning of May 1, his main theme was "no surrender." He warned South Carolina students, particularly those in Charleston, that if they attempted to do what the Voorhees students had done, he would not hesitate to call in National Guardsmen and SLED agents. The offenders would be charged and jailed. He reiterated his unwillingness to concede—"not to the SCLC or Charleston's unionized hospital workers; not to anyone, student or otherwise, who seizes a public or private building in South Carolina." He insisted that only the state's legislature could revise the state's policy on collective bargaining. However, he vowed that the legislature would not be able to make changes to the policy "without a fight into which he will throw every ounce of his influence and prestige."[11]

Later that day, McNair declared a state of emergency in Charleston and imposed a daily curfew in the city from nine o'clock in the evening until five o'clock in the morning. Until that point, the National Guard's presence had reportedly been "sobering and prevented violence and destruction." However, the governor cited a fear of the growing possibility of "fire, vandalism, break-ins and other harm which may come to persons or property." The curfew mandated that citizens stay home and that businesses close during the designated times. Only those who needed to conduct emergency or essential business, with approval from Strom or his designee, were allowed to move around within the city during the restricted hours. The proclamation included additional restrictions regarding the possession of weapons and the number of people allowed to gather.[12]

Despite these efforts to control and de-escalate the situation, Charleston became a powder keg, and according to McNair, the circumstances grew "more serious as each hour and day has passed." Reports of "roaming groups of Negro youth" who allegedly shattered windows in at least five local stores emerged hours after Mrs. King's march ended. Later on the day of the curfew announcement, several instances of violence and vandalism took place: A state highway patrol car and a local fire truck were struck by bullets, three local buildings were set on fire, and there were several instances of rocking throwing. Other examples of mayhem, including "firebombs, scattered sniping and roads littered with broken glass," spread across the city and into outlying parts of the county. At 10 p.m. on May 2, county police officers apprehended a suspect after a group of "Negro" youth built a "concrete block barricade" allegedly to impede and terrorize motorists. At 11 p.m. firefighters were called to another part of the city to deal with a case of arson. As they attempted to control the fire, residents assaulted them with rocks. A local supermarket sustained fire damage after being set afire with the use of kerosene as an accelerant.[13]

The confrontation accomplished by the youth was a part of a broader tradition of protest and organizing that coupled nonviolent direct action, an ideal often viewed as the only tactical approach employed in the civil rights movement, with armed resistance. The Charleston hospital workers' campaign emerged at the intersection of the civil rights and labor struggles that employed both labor militancy and armed resistance. On one hand, the hospital workers campaign developed within what Karen Brodkin Sacks referred to as an era of "labor militancy in hospitals." This era of labor resistance began in Northern hospitals in the late 1950s and continued in hospitals across the nation until the mid-seventies. In her study of unionized hospital workers at Duke Medical Center in Durham, North Carolina, Sacks argued that African American and/or Hispanic women stood at the center of this wave of resistance, by establishing a direct link between the issues at the center of the labor and civil rights movements. As a result, labor organizations came face-to-face with issues of race and the impact of racial inequality on workers, and the civil rights movement began to grapple with the realities of economic injustice and the actualization of Black freedom. On the other hand, according to Akinyele Omowale Umoja, "armed resistance," has always been a critical aspect of the Black Freedom Movement despite the movement's reliance on nonviolence as a central guidepost. The author defines armed resistance as "individual and collective use of force for protection, protest, or other goals of insurgent political actions and in defenses of human rights." The author further explains that "armed resistance" includes "armed self-defense, retaliatory violence, spontaneous rebellion, guerrilla warfare, armed vigilance/enforcement, and armed struggle." Hospital workers forged a movement in which they employed militant tactics and ideologies that were certainly common in both civil rights and labor movements. The key distinction was that they were women carrying out these acts of militancy and armed resistance. The hospital workers' campaign expands the parameters of African American women's activism to include a multitude of ways in which they resisted, protested, and triumphed, regardless of whether those things were becoming of a lady.[14]

Charleston's hospital workers battled with feelings of frustration and resentment in their efforts to secure higher wages, union representation, and respect for human dignity, and that occasionally erupted into physical violence. On the first day of the strike, Naomi White, a five-foot three inch, forty-something year old married mother of six, assaulted another Black woman who worked in housekeeping as she attempted to breach the picket line. According to White, the woman only made about ninety cents per hour and had hired someone to bring her to work and get her through the picket line. White vividly recalled the incident, "I told her I didn't object to her going in but she wasn't going to break my line. And this guy, he says, 'Oh yes she is because that's what I'm being paid for.' I said, well that is your business. You can get her in any way you can but you ain't going through here. He said, 'Oh yes she is.'" In the midst of this exchange, the woman from housekeeping offered a few derogatory remarks aimed at White. White bristled at the woman's disrespect and disregard for what striking Black hospital workers were attempting to achieve. She recalled during a 1990s interview for the *Charleston Post and Courier*, "There is no use for us going out there with the sun baking us and these scabs crossing the line. I grabbed her. I started beating her, and the cop grabbed me. Then all hell broke loose." White snatched the woman by the jewelry she wore around her neck, and "that's when the free-for-all started." Members of local law enforcement, already on the scene, attempted to gain control of the situation. One officer endeavored to restrain White, asserting, "Sweetheart, you're going to jail." Undoubtedly, the officer was caught off guard when she retaliated by shoving the officer against his car declaring, "The chief shouldn't send a boy to do a man's job." White was arrested and charged with "disorderly conduct, creating a disturbance on the street, and assaulting with her hands a police officer." Isaiah Bennett, along with two local attorneys, posted her $201 bail within hours of her arrest. Unscathed and undaunted, she returned to the picket line the following day.[15]

Naomi White's experience demonstrated the complex emotions and concerns that fueled the striking workers' actions and reactions in this moment. It also confirmed the simultaneous existence of armed resistance and nonviolence as mainstays of the modern civil rights movement. When the organizing began, White, due to her schedule, was often unable to attend the regular meetings. However, she approached the movement with a deep sense of purpose and a great deal of intensity. When the moment arrived to stage a walkout, White was off on a long weekend. While she was unable to literally walk out of Medical College with other strikers, when she was due to return to work she simply refused to go. Regardless of her minimal participation in the yearlong organizing prior to the strike, she showed up on the picket line on day one of the strike, bold in her opposition to the treatment that Black hospital workers had been experiencing and eager to confront the power structure that perpetuated it. White became a part of a broader collective of Black women workers who aggressively and physically confronted the obstacles that challenged their ability to provide for their families. Her reaction to the nonstriking worker's attempt to break the picket line in late 1960s Charleston, South Carolina bore a striking similarity to the actions of three women on strike from Mount Sinai Hospital in late-1950s New York. Three striking hospital workers were arrested for disorderly conduct and felonious assault after a local patrolman was assaulted while attempting to escort a nonstriking worker into the facility. In a 2008 interview, White, then in her early eighties and with a soft and trembling voice, still conveyed the intensity of her resistance to the disrespect and discrimination that Black women workers suffered in Medical College. She made her unwillingness to stand by and allow herself or her coworkers to be mistreated abundantly clear. She shared a memory of a situation with a white coworker that occurred not long before the strike where she unleashed a bit of her fury at being disrespected:

> We had this night nurse, which they could never keep a nurse on 11:00 to 7:00. And I went to put some instruments in the autoclave because them babies was coming like rain, and she came in the work room and said something. I can't remember what she said, but whatever it was I answered her. And she tells me to shut up, don't talk back to her. And if it wasn't for a couple of the nurses coming out the nursery I

was going to autoclave her ass, because I had done opened the door and said, "Who do you think you're talking to?" I said, "I want you to know I'm a grown woman." I think I was forty-seven years old. I said, "I got grown children. I don't allow them to speak to me any kind of way." I said, "And I ain't taking that off of you." I said, "Now one more word out of you and your ass is going. They'll just find you revolving in the autoclave."[16]

Even as she chuckled at herself at the end of the story, the strength of her convictions came through loud and clear.

White's contribution to the organizing efforts away from the picket line reveals the intentionality that undergirded militant action among striking workers. White had virtually zero tolerance for what strikers referred to as "scabs": individuals who refused to strike and continued to work while their coworkers were on the picket line. She adamantly resisted the idea of someone breaking the picket line because it conveyed disrespect and disregard for the myriad sacrifices that those on the front line made every day. The word "scab" has deep roots in labor movement history. In Charleston's labor history, scab activity and the ways in which striking workers responded demonstrated another link between the tobacco workers strike of 1945 and the hospital workers strike of 1969. Lillie Doster, a tobacco workers union member and veteran of Charleston's tobacco workers strike who supported workers during the hospital strike, shared a story of a much more violent response to scabs during the tobacco strike. As the strike dragged on, many of the striking workers grew weary and began to return to work. Many succumbed to the fears associated with being out of work and the impact of having no income. Rather than going in through the front of the factory, these workers were loaded into a truck that would drop them off at a rear entrance of the building. According to Doster, a group of striking workers made it their business to inflict harm on those individuals who opted to return to work. She recalled one instance in particular:

And it was a group of girls, all of them are dead now. But they had hoe handles and sticks and axes with nails in them. It was seven of them. . . . So the girls brought in all those things. I said, "What are you going to do with that?" "We're going to beat the you-know-what out of them when they get out of the truck and as soon as the truck pulls off we're going [to] go out there and we're going to put a beating on them." They were on strike. They were going to beat the people who went back to in the plant. . . . We used to call them "scabs" when you'd go back to work.¹⁷

Naomi White became as adamant in her opposition to scabs' presence in the hospital workers' strike as striking tobacco workers had been two decades prior. In response, she organized a group of workers who called themselves "Hell's Angels" to monitor scab activity and resolve any related issues. Generally, striking workers picketed during the same times that they would have normally been working at the hospital. Part of the reason for this was so that those workers on the picket line could pinpoint those workers from their unit and shift who were still working. According to White, early in the strike, things remained relatively peaceful. She asserted that the situation became tenser when those who stayed began to taunt those who walked out. She recalled the growing animosity: "And things seemed like they were going so smoothly, I said, you know, as long as we be nice and just picket, and that hot sun burning you, and they're just making fun. Something's got to be done." White recalled taking matters into her own hands and leading the Hell's Angels, which consisted of a handful of women and one man, in seeking out those individuals whom they identified as scabs and punishing them: "We ripped them scabs up if we caught them. That's what we did. That was our mission—We'd ride around [at night] and we'd get out at certain places where we know they was coming, you know. Some of them, they would change their route and we find out where they change, where they're going to come, and we'd be right there to greet them."[18] As White shared her recollections of those moments, her calm demeanor and matter-of-fact retelling of the group's approach to dealing with scab activity revealed a sense of certainty about their undertaking. She expressed no remorse and seemed to have no qualms about the manner in which they dealt with the individuals that disrespected them, disregarded their movement, and undercut their ability to stand up for themselves and fight for their rights.[19]

Workers had to deal with other efforts to undermine their movement as well. Rosetta Simmons recalled an issue with workers whom they believed served as spies for the hospital. These individuals would attend union meetings but continue to report to work. Simmons and a group of striking workers would ride around, with her as the driver, to catch those folks who were attending meetings and going to work. Their goal was to identify the individuals and expose them at the meetings, not to harm anyone. According to her, the striking workers were able to bring an end to the spying. The organized workers employed espionage as a strategy as well. They selected hospital workers who were affiliated with their group to remain at work in order to keep a steady stream of information flowing from the hospital back to their meetings. Simmons and White's recollections of the movement unveil moments of violent confrontation and tactical strategizing that have been left out of the broader historical narrative but that were critical aspects of their individual and collective activism.[20]

According to William Saunders, these direct confrontations merely scratched the surface as it pertained to militant activity within the movement. He and Otis Robinson, a local Muslim leader, organized a semi-secret organization that he loosely referred to as the "hospital workers' defense team" whose purpose was to protect the striking hospital workers and in some cases members of SCLC: "I had this little group of bad fellas and a couple of women and we used to take care of business if we had to." Saunders contended that the group operated so far under the radar that even the individuals for whom they provided protection usually remained unaware of their presence and purpose. Seven leaders knew the identity of the members, but the members generally did not know each other. Saunders believed that keeping the details about the group to a minimum even internally made it more difficult for members to disclose information if questioned by authorities. The group was extremely cautious in their operations, even down to the logistics. For example, they usually met in locations such as juke joints near the jukebox to head off any surveillance or monitoring. Their approach was that the striking workers handled their business during the day and members of the organization covered the night.[21]

The "hospital workers' defense team" provided protection in a number of different capacities within the movement. Eva Alston, a member of the defense team, served as Mary Moultrie's bodyguard. Moultrie remained unaware of Alston's role but Rosetta Simmons recalled her reputation and a personal encounter with her during her stay in the hospital after the birth and death of her newborn baby. Simmons, who was hospitalized at Medical College, recalled Alston coming to her hospital room with two armed individuals worried that she was in a hostile environment and wanting to verify her well-being. She recalled, "I leaped out of bed when I heard her voice. I said, 'Oh my God!' She said, 'I just wanted to know that you. . . .' I said, 'I'm alright, I'm okay. Okay. Just, you know, take it easy.' Because she was about to take them down. I mean she was equipped to take them down." According to Saunders, Alston, who was a woman of few words, had a powerful presence and cared a great deal about the striking workers, Moultrie and Simmons in particular. White and Simmons's recollections reveal that some striking workers were as committed to and as fully engaged in armed resistance as Saunders and Robinson's and their secret organization members. Women at the front line of the movement engaged in clandestine organizing, vigilante justice, and physical confrontation asserting their power, autonomy, and leadership. According to Simmons, the workers had no other choice, "Look at all the ladies who were out. I get so frustrated. Some of your Black men are saying that independent African American women are something but we have to be. You won't stand up to the plate so we have to do it ourselves." That sense of woman-centered purpose and drive operated at the core of the entire movement.[22]

As a campaign that emerged as both a civil rights and labor movement, the Charleston hospital workers' strike drew on many of the traditional values of each movement and the time in which it occurred. In the late 1960s, strong distinctions between men and women's roles in American society prevailed. Many of those distinguishing features carried over into the civil rights movement, particularly within the traditional civil rights organizations like SCLC, where women generally served behind the scenes as the backbone of the movement while the men positioned themselves out front and in positions of leadership. Female leaders of the movement were described in gender-specific language. Septima Clark, for example, was referred to as the "Mother of the Movement" and Ella Baker, as the "lady" whose contributions to and influence on the movement had been deemed among the most valuable. Traditional gender norms thus restricted women's work within the movement by imposing boundaries on what they could do or be and casting a negative light on their contributions in public discourse.[23]

Examining a comparison drawn between Naomi White and Coretta Scott King by the *Charleston News and Courier,* the major local newspaper during the strike, offers some insight into the role that gender and class play in defining a "woman's place" in this historical moment. It also reveals a broader resistance to the break from tradition being carried out by striking workers. After the law enforcement officer arrested White for initiating a physical altercation with a scab, the newspaper reported that, "Mrs. White" had been "disorderly" and "assaulted with her hands a police officer." The local newspaper quoted portions of Medical College's complaint against striking workers to further explain workers' behavior, which included "threats, cursing, obscenities, acts of intimidation and acts of violence." Approximately two weeks later, the same newspaper published an article about "Mrs. Martin Luther King, Jr." and how she had taken up her husband's mantle in continuing to push for "peace and brotherhood." The author described her as a "resolute, attractive 41-year-old widow" praising her for being a pioneer in a number of firsts for women. More importantly, the author highlighted the fact that even with her extensive travel and busy schedule, "She also has been caring for their four children." Further, the article highlighted her contributions to her deceased husband's life and the "strong will that lies beneath the placid calm and dignity" of her character. The local media created an important distinction between Naomi White's "disorderly" behavior unbecoming of a woman and Coretta Scott King's seeming adherence to the traditional norms of a woman's role.[24]

Despite the effort to polarize the images of White and King, the two Southern Black women actually had quite a bit in common. Both women came from working-class families that, with increased wealth, access, and opportunity, were able to experience positive shifts in their socioeconomic status. King came from rural Alabama, where she grew up on the family's farm picking cotton as a young person. Her father attained relative wealth among farmers by acquiring approximately one hundred acres of farmland. She obtained her grade school education from a local church-based private school. White grew up within the city of Charleston. Her mother worked as seamstress and her father as a janitor for the College of Charleston for fifty years. While White attended public school, due to her Catholic faith, all of her children attended parochial school. At the time of the strike, White was forty-four, and King was forty-one years old. Both women married and had multiple children; King had four children, while White had six. The author used the term "placid" to describe King's brand of determination. White's actions on the picket line on the first day demonstrated her tenacity and resolve. While White's approach lacked subtlety, she and King shared a staunch commitment to their convictions and the movement.[25]

When the newspaper reporter referred to Naomi White as "disorderly," it connected her to generations of "disorderly" women, such as those involved in the walkout of over five hundred women in 1929 from American Glanzstoff in Elizabethton, Tennesee. Trixie Perry, whose story reveals a longer history of the gendered nature of labor organizing, has a strike story that is akin to White's in the pair's willingness to challenge the expectations of a gendered society. Perry, twenty-eight at the time of the strike, allegedly had been married and divorced several times and had children for a number of different men. For the women on strike in 1929 and forty years later in 1969, the mere fact that they, as members of what was considered the fairer sex, had the boldness to challenge male-dominated power structures undermined the gender norms that dictated that women be seen and not heard. "Disorderly" women like Perry and White confronted the system with loud voices and brute force, defying the rules of traditional femininity. When onlookers celebrated women like King, Clark, and Baker for being "placid," a "Mother," and a "lady" and chastised Perry and White for being "disorderly," they obscured the common threads of their activism and disregarded the reasons for their activism. All of these women, in spite of their differences, shared similar experiences with discrimination, exclusion, and being overlooked due to their gender. For that reason, each of these women, regardless of their individual ideologies and methods, had the same basic goals: equality and access.[26]

Hospital workers, as an all African American and mostly female group, struggled to earn validation for their cause and the efforts to resolve the issues at its core. The *Charleston News and Courier*, beginning on the first day of the strike, consistently reported that the conflict emerged because workers had "two demands: the right to union recognition and the rehiring of twelve discharged workers." This assessment of what motivated workers to strike oversimplified the impetus of the movement. The women who stood at its center took up the mantle because they wanted to be treated with respect, resented the racial discrimination they faced on a regular basis, and needed to earn a decent wage. The myriad expressions on the front line of their dissatisfaction and resistance highlights the fact that their decision to strike had a breadth and depth that could not be summed up in "two demands."[27]

At the center of the hospital workers' campaign were women who approached the conflict with respectability and disorder. The efforts to balance their activism with the demands of family—often resulting in the two aspects of their experiences overlapping and intersecting—reveal an aspect of women's activism that clearly distinguishes it from moments of protest carried out by men during that era. Shifts in workers' visibility created holes in the narratives that surrounded their activism; however, it also created space and opportunity for clandestine militant activity. Militant protest among striking workers demonstrated the range of tactics that they employed in their daily efforts to achieve social and economic justice. It also emphasizes the dynamic nature of their engagement. Hospital workers adhered to societal norms and expectations in regard to family and mothering while they challenged the local health-care system through any means necessary.

Chapter 6

"MCNAIR FIDDLES WHILE ROME BURNS"

As hospital workers persisted in their boots-on-the-ground efforts to confront social and economic injustice, the campaign morphed into a national movement. SCLC's arrival, the "soul power," grounded the campaign in traditional civil rights tactics, and it ushered in the full strength of national civil rights organizing. Local 1199's involvement, the "union power," and the chartering of Local 1199B in the city, gave hospital workers access to wealth of labor organizing resource. Together Local 1199 and SCLC positioned striking hospital workers at the precipice of generations of labor and civil rights organizing and activism. The might of the movement garnered attention and concern from local, state, and national leaders causing the resolution of the strike to become a matter of national importance. Political power plays marred the road to resolution casting a shadow over the grassroots activism that laid the foundation for the movement.

As hospital workers and their supporters prepared for and then executed the April 30 march supported by Mrs. Coretta Scott King, on the other side of town critical meetings took place regarding the progress and potential outcome of the campaign. These meetings were conducted on behalf of workers but not necessarily with their knowledge. On April 28, the State Attorney General Daniel R. McLeod and State Director of Personnel F. E. Ellis traveled to Charleston at the behest of SCLC to meet with Andrew Young, Carl Farris, and Abernathy's administrative assistant. They arrived expecting to be bombarded with a list of demands from the organization on behalf of the workers. However, according to Young, the only purpose of the meeting was to establish a line of communication with state officials about the situation in Charleston. He also expressed SCLC's confidence that it would be able to achieve the same results in Charleston as it had in previous campaigns. Ellis concluded that, while he did not agree with Young's prediction of the outcome, he did get the sense that SCLC believed that its position was "right and justified." This meeting became the first of many in which the civil rights organization spoke and negotiated on behalf of striking workers without their presence or knowledge. SCLC provided Medical College administrators an important workaround in the midst of the labor dispute. They could meet with leaders of the civil rights organization, which arguably represented striking workers without violating state laws that prohibited negotiations with labor organizations.[1]

The following day, state officials met with seven people representing the workers and the union, including Eugene Eisner, Local 1199's attorney, Young, Isaiah Bennett, and Moultrie. The "white organizer from New York," most likely Henry Nicholas or Elliot Godoff, led the meeting with input from Eisner. He clarified the union's position, declaring that "all demands, all negotiations, and all future conversation was predicated on all employees being reinstated, including the twelve who had been discharged, and all charges pending against the strikers being dropped." On behalf of workers, the union representative provided the state officials with a list of nine demands. The demands addressed reinstatement, a wage increase and minimum, a willingness to "forego [sic] the recognition of the union" for the development of an employee committee, a grievance procedure, a system for dues, medical insurance, the observance of Martin Luther King Jr. Day, payment of lost wages incurred during the strike, and an improvement of the annual leave system. At the end of the meeting, McLeod assured that group that while he did not have the authority to make decisions regarding their demands, he would present them to the appropriate people and get back to the union with the outcome.[2]

That same day, McNair met with the Charleston County Legislative Delegation to discuss the current situation in the city. Several of the members expressed their concerns. Representative Leonard Crawcheck referred to the presence of National Guardsmen and the increased number of law enforcement officers in the city as "repugnant." The governor responded that the safety of South Carolina citizens should be ensured using all of the state's power. He asserted that the state's position on its responsibility to its citizens "would not be weakened on account of Charleston" and that the National Guard would remain in the city until "peace and tranquility" had been restored. He warned the delegation that, if the situation in Charleston continued to worsen, he would impose a curfew on the city. Senator Robert B. Scarborough expressed concern that the people of Charleston did not know enough about where the state stood regarding the turmoil. McNair suggested that the state would continue to handle the situation behind closed doors stating, "there would be no public debate through the news media." Scarborough partially conceded, responding that he would support McNair's position in the matter but not that of Medical College. He argued that the administration had "made some serious blunders and many mistakes and that he personally could not endorse legislative resolutions endorsing the hospital's action." As the meeting wrapped up, McLeod interrupted to present McNair with the workers' demands. The governor shared the information with the delegation but made no comment. At the end of the meeting, the consensus was that the delegation had sided with the state. The march orchestrated by striking workers, the protest accomplished by the march, and the meetings being held on behalf of workers, some without workers, foreshadowed the intricacies of the campaign's progress in the wake of SCLC's arrival.[3]

On the heels of the march led by Mrs. King in late April, Charleston Mayor J. Palmer Gaillard appointed a citizen-based committee. The committee's main goal was to reopen the lines of communication between hospital workers and Medical College Hospital. The mayor emphasized his hope that the "matter will be resolved at the conference table and taken off the streets." He gave the committee the initial task of meeting with representatives for the workers and the hospital. Workers quickly agreed to meet with the committee. Isaiah Bennett affirmed that the union was "willing to cooperate fully with the mayor and the people on the committee." Elliott Godoff backed Bennett's response, saying, "We have nothing better to do than negotiate a settlement. We are available at any time of day or night." The hospital, on the other hand, was less congenial. J. Edwin Schachte, chair of the Medical College board, responded to the request by stating that while he had the "fondest hopes that this thing is going to lead to some kind of concrete avenue of improving the relationship that exists at this time," but he would not commit the board to a meeting until the committee submitted a formal request that the board would then decide upon. He claimed that the board would offer as much cooperation as possible but ultimately wanted to see the situation handled at a local level. Andrew Young responded that SCLC would support any effort to resolve the strike, but the organization would stay in Charleston "until the workers tell us to get out that they no longer need our help," affirming that the situation had passed the point of being just a local issue.[4]

Governor McNair did not oppose the mayor's decision to appoint the committee, but he had clear expectations regarding its boundaries. He took the opportunity to reiterate the state's position in the matter, emphasizing that, "no committee appointed by anyone can compromise the policy of

South Carolina in reference to collective bargaining or union recognition." In addition, they could not make any suggestions regarding wages beyond the boundaries of the state employee classification system. He also cautioned against anyone publicly advocating that the state make adjustments to current public policies. McNair blamed the hospital workers' movement for the turmoil, referring to their demands as "unreasonable" and "ridiculous":

> The state of South Carolina did not choose Charleston as the site where the state policy should be tested. Someone else chose Charleston. Unfortunately, our state policy is being tested in Charleston and I would say that it was unfortunate if it were in any other city or town in South Carolina. However, we will not sacrifice the state of South Carolina for the sake of Charleston in this situation. If we allow our policy to be bargained away and change our position in Charleston, that will be the foot in the door that will spread to every other state and public institution.[5]

He offered a plea for support in resolving the situation so that "peace and tranquility" could be restored. He concluded the summary with the hope that "everyone concerned will recognize our state policy and will be willing to express themselves honestly and sincerely, or don't express themselves at all."[6]

While the union and SCLC offered their support to the citizens' committee, members of the executive committee of the Political Action Committee (PAC) joined the effort by petitioning the legislature and the governor to develop a "meaningful solution to the hospital strike." The petition was in response to a public statement by South Carolina Senator Rembert C. Dennis, a Medical College trustee, in which he commended the governor and the hospital for how well they had handled the strike to that point. Further, he recommended that the general assembly pass a resolution that lauded the governor and hospital administration for their efforts in managing the strike. Herbert U. Fielding, chair of the PAC, challenged Dennis's statement, taking issue with the fact that it did not mention the hundreds of workers at the center of the conflict, disregarding the significance of their movement and grievances. Additionally, the chair expressed concern about the fact that the statement excluded any discussion of justice for all those involved.[7]

Part of the petition was addressed to Dennis, reprimanding him for the "utter disregard and disrespect for the rights and future welfare of the hundreds of workers" and his indifference to the safety and outlook of the entire community. The other portion of the petition appealed to local legislators and the governor, contending that their power and influence should be used to bring a reasonable end to the strike. The committee insisted that rather than upholding a staunch position against collective bargaining, resolving the "crisis" and "maintaining justice" should be the focus. The petition included a request that the general assembly adopt a resolution that was "pertinent, healthy, morally sound and expedient," as opposed to one that glorified inaction. The committee requested the removal of the National Guardsmen and any other "foreign police forces." It encouraged a more inclusive interpretation of the situation, arguing that "all citizens of the community" were interested in the "the social, educational, economic and political development of all our people" and that the striking hospital workers had to be considered in that effort. The petition closed with a humble but powerful plea, "We recognize and respect you as our political leaders, but remind you that such leadership demands faithful, forceful, dynamic and imaginative action in times of crisis. We would only further petition you to understand that law and order without justice is neither realistic nor lasting."[8]

McNair called a meeting on April 29, 1969, and briefed the attendees on the situation in Voorhees and Charleston. In response, House Speaker Solomon Blatt suggested the introduction of a resolution "with both houses concurring, reaffirming the State's position concerning negotiation and collective bargaining for state employees." All of the meeting attendees agreed, and an ad hoc committee gathered later that afternoon to draft the resolution.[9]

Later that day the General Assembly found itself at an impasse. Questions arose regarding the state's general position on collective bargaining and specifically on how it and the hospital were handling the ongoing labor dispute. The House Military, Municipal and Public Affairs Committee introduced the resolution that would uphold the governor's previous refusal to negotiate with the union representing striking workers on the grounds that there was "no constitutional or statutory authority permitting the state, its subdivisions, agencies, or institutions to bargain collectively with their employees."[10]

Representative Robert W. Turner of Charleston, who had attended the meeting with the governor earlier in the day, served as the chair of the committee that introduced the resolution and also as an ex officio member of the Medical College Board of Trustees. As the Senate prepared to vote on the resolution, Senator Scarborough, speaking on behalf of the Charleston senatorial delegation, emphasized that his support of the resolution did not mean that he was unconcerned about the situation. He added that it stood "firmly for fair, non-discriminatory treatment for all state employees, including those at Medical College" and that they would work with "any group of employees" to address their grievances fairly. He added that the resolution did not "represent an inflexible position by the state." After it was approved, Representative Joseph P. Riley Jr. rebuked the haste with which the measure was passed, noting that "the situation is serious and so important that nothing should have gone through this House today without serious consideration and study." Despite his disappointment, he clarified hopefully that "the resolution that was passed today says simply the state can't negotiate without specific legislation being passed to permit it." Representative Thomas F. Hartnett of Charleston, who had not been given the opportunity to view or analyze the resolution prior to its passing, questioned "the timeliness and effectiveness of it helping the strike situation."[11]

The Charleston County Council also issued a resolution unanimously supporting McNair's position. Unlike the general assembly's resolution, which was brief and focused on the state policy, the council's decree had an indignant tone. The council argued that the community had "suffered traumatic and unwarranted strife and unrest" at the hands of hospital workers and their supporters. It declared that their presence and actions were "abhorred by the loyal and thinking citizens of our community, who, shoulder to shoulder, have built and maintained its legacy over the years as a proud, fair, peaceful, and understanding community." The council's resolution praised the governor and his team for "their exemplary performance of duty" in providing the "support and protection" and commended the Charleston County Hospital workers who remained on the job as well as the "law abiding white and Negro" citizens who they believed had been a part of the peace keeping efforts.[12]

Mary Moultrie offered a rebuttal in which she challenged the state, and McNair in particular, on its stance on the strike and unwillingness to negotiate. She emphasized that the "hospital workers' organization is here to stay." She argued that workers were prepared to continue the strike well into the summer months because the governor offered solutions that were "impossible for the workers to accept." She placed responsibility for the growing unrest within the city squarely on the governor's shoulders, asserting that "the city is in crisis but McNair fiddles while Rome burns." She argued that, while he continued to disregard the issues at the core of the movement and to reject unionization, the problems remained unresolved. She acknowledged the fact that the governor had plans to convene a committee of selected hospital workers as a means of settling the labor dispute, but she avowed that striking workers would "never accept any form of negotiations whatsoever without the [union] elected committee of workers despite the governor's attempts to handpick those workers." She made it clear that hospital workers, while open to negotiations, were adamant about having a say in how the resolution would be reached.[13]

Ralph Abernathy, who had been released from jail after eight days, realized that the governor needed a stronger influence to change his mind about the dispute. He petitioned President Richard Nixon on May 2, 1969, for assistance in resolving the hospital workers' campaign. Jack Greenberg, then director of the NAACP Legal Defense and Educational Fund, reached out to the President on behalf of Abernathy and SCLC stating, "We must have the intervention of the office of the President of the United States immediately so that this problem can be brought to a speedy solution and peace and tranquility restored to this old historic community." Even though he was scheduled to visit Columbia, South Carolina, the following day, Nixon responded that he did not see the need for him or a representative to visit Charleston because "our information is that efforts of a citizens' committee are progressing very well."[14]

Ironically, on April 30, the governor's office received a phone call from James Turner, an attorney with the Civil Rights Division of the US Department of Justice, questioning the state's position regarding the hospital workers' campaign. Bert Goolsby, a representative from the state attorney general's office, reported that their office had also received a call from Turner asking the same questions. According to Turner, the Justice Department's inquiry was for informational purposes only. However, just days later, on May 5, a team from the Community Relations Division of the US Justice Department and a representative from the US Commission on Civil Rights (USCCR) arrived in Charleston. Jacob Schlitt, director of the USCCR's Mid-Atlantic field office, characterized their visit as a "preliminary fact-finding" endeavor. While in the city, Schlitt met with Black and white community leaders and representatives from Medical College in an effort to identify the issues at the core of the situation and ascertain whether a resolution could be reached.[15]

Meanwhile, state and local leaders continued to search for answers. Charleston County's Democratic senators offered an alternative that they believed would not violate state policy. In a press conference on May 2, they suggested that Local 1199 "back off" as a bargaining agent and that hospital workers consider SCLC as representatives for their negotiations, essentially relying more heavily on the racial aspects of their grievances rather than those that were labor based. They reiterated that state employees had the right to join a union. They also clarified that, even though the state could not legally "recognize the union as a collective bargaining agent," the state could "acknowledge a union's existence." Although the state was barred from negotiating "wages, grievances, or working conditions" with a public sector union, a labor organization could function in the same capacity as any other professional association, including by ensuring that workers' grievances were "recognized administratively either by the hospital officials or the General Assembly." The senators' motivation for offering another resolution option was to remove the union from the bargaining table, which the state had clearly identified as the main obstacle to resolving the conflict.[16]

A few days later, the Citizens' Committee suggested a meeting of all concerned parties aimed at opening up the lines of communication. In response, Attorney General McLeod and Fred H. Moore, the striking workers' attorney, set up a meeting that would involve five hospital workers, including Mary Moultrie, chosen by the committee along with members of Medical College's Board of Trustees. When the meeting convened and members of the Board realized that Elliot Godoff, director of Local 1199's national organizing, and the Local 1199 attorney were in attendance, they refused to proceed with the meeting, arguing that they initially agreed only to meet with the selected workers without union representation. McLeod suggested that the union officials could wait in another space nearby. The workers and Moore were unwilling to meet without the union officials present. According to the statement later released by the hospital, union officials and the hospital workers left the meeting, rebuffing the idea of moving forward without the union. Godoff offered another explanation for why they walked out. He explained that in addition to the five selected workers, an advisory committee chosen by the workers to provide "immediate consultation" was also a part of the meeting arrangement. He also claimed that the space where McLeod suggested that he and the Local 1199 attorney wait was the restroom. He argued that, "under such insulting circumstances a meeting couldn't possibly be productive." The union official expressed a willingness to meet and open the lines of communication but only if handled appropriately.[17]

Charleston County Council Chairman J. Mitchell Graham, speaking on behalf of the Charleston County Hospital, affirmed his refusal to meet with unionized workers or union representatives, despite their ongoing efforts to see him. During a meeting behind closed doors guarded by county and state law enforcement officers, the chair discussed the fact that he had selected a committee of council members and county officials that would meet with hospital workers currently on the payroll in order to discuss their grievances. However, he stated that striking workers would not be allowed to take part in the meetings. They would have to reapply for one of the vacant positions; and, if hired, they would then be able to participate. Approximately twenty-four employees, most of whom were Black, attended the two-hour session. According to Graham, many of the attendees wanted to discuss grievances such as holidays, shift differentials, additional operating room staff and seniority. He claimed that none of the employees mentioned any issues with racial discrimination. He referred to the meeting attendees as "loyal, hard-working employees who have not abandoned their positions." He assured workers that that "the minimum county pay scaled will be raised from $1.30 to $1.50 per hour starting July 1" and that the pay would increase by another fifteen cents per hour in July of the following year. In addition to an increase in wages, Graham avowed that the Council would address the other grievances as well.[18]

Despite the curfew and National Guardsmen occupying the city, on Mother's Day evening thousands gathered inside Charleston County Hall while thousands more waited outside preparing to stage the largest march in the city to date. Abernathy addressed the crowd, proclaiming, "the eyes of the world today are seeing a great, a growing, a mighty movement against economic injustice in Charleston, South Carolina. Poor hospital workers here in Charleston have risen up against exploitation and oppression by the ruthless political, military and economic machine of South Carolina." Although the march did not bring in the twenty-five thousand people that SCLC originally projected, it prompted an estimated five to ten thousand people to descend on the city.[19]

The makeup of the crowd confirmed that the campaign had made the leap from a national news story to a national issue. Masses of people, including busloads representing local SCLC chapters from Pennsylvania, Mississippi, North Carolina, and Washington, DC, offered support. A group of United States Congressmen, including Representatives William Fitz Ryan, Edward I. Koch, and Allard K. Lowenstein, all from New York, along with Representatives John Conyers Jr. and Charles C. Diggs, both from Michigan, joined workers for the march. Conyers, serving as the group's spokesperson, called for unity in the struggle to eradicate economic injustice; "this message must be learned: the black and white people together are going to overthrow the racism and economic deprivation that brings us together in Charleston today."[20]

Because it began at 7 p.m., three hours behind schedule, the threat of the 9 p.m. curfew loomed over the march. Nonetheless, hospital workers and their supporters left the auditorium and proceeded to Medical College of South Carolina and later to Charleston County Hospital. Under the watchful eyes of approximately eight hundred National Guardsmen and four hundred law enforcement officers, protesters marched through the streets of Charleston, moving to the beat of soul music and freedom songs rendered by a brass band. The march ended without incident just before the curfew and buses transported thousands out of the city. The Mother's Day March proved to be a watershed moment in the movement. The growing violence and unrest leading up to the march, coupled with the massive display of support for workers caused more concern among local and state leaders. As a result, the state of South Carolina and the city of Charleston, both having been supportive of the hospitals' refusal to negotiate, began to seek definitive ways to resolve the strike.[21]

Communication between unionized workers and the hospitals stalled while McNair grew increasingly frustrated with the mounting outside interference. He rebuked SCLC and the union arguing that their presence in the city did "not add anything to the situation" and reiterated that none of their tactics would force his hand in regard to state policy. The governor snubbed the congressmen who participated in the Mother's Day demonstration arguing that "they have every right to be here as Americans," but they needed to "sweep under their own steps before coming to observe civil disorders somewhere else."[22]

Prior to their arrival in Charleston, those five congressmen and fourteen others had reached out to Nixon regarding the strike. They requested that he send a representative to the city to demonstrate to hospital workers that they had his support. He replied:

> I question whether the presence of a presidential representative would aid in a fair resolution of the controversy under the circumstances. I think each of us has an obligation in situations of this kind to do what we can to urge contending parties to resolve their differences in a calm atmosphere of mutual good faith. Let us join in urging the parties to quiet the situation and continue to seek a peaceful and mutually satisfactory solution to their problems.[23]

Despite the reserved tone of Nixon's response, the inquiries via telephone and subsequent visit by representatives from the Justice Department and USCCR in early May indicated a growing concern within the White House about the dispute. After corresponding with the group of congressmen, the president tasked US Attorney General John N. Mitchell with assigning individuals to be observers in the city and to provide him with regular reports on the developments.[24]

Less than a week later, a bipartisan group of seventeen senators, each representing a different state, sent a letter to the president petitioning him to send a mediator to Charleston. They cited the hospital workers' campaign as an important demonstration of "non-violence" as a "strategy for social change" particularly during an era when so many believed that Black Power and armed self-defense had more relevance. The letter highlighted the fact that the situation in Charleston bore a striking resemblance to the garbage workers' strike in Memphis the year prior. Both disputes emerged in response to low wages, poor working conditions and a lack of respect for Black workers.[25]

The key aspects of each movement were almost identical. They were sparked by a group of Black workers who called on a national union and SCLC for assistance. In response to the strike, the local court issued an injunction in both cities. Due to growing support and an increase in the violence around the movement, the city implemented a curfew. A demand for respect lay at the center of both campaigns. The garbage workers issued "I Am a Man" as their unifying refrain, which was a declaration of their refusal to be emasculated. The hospital workers' battle cry, "I Am Somebody" emerged as a rebuttal to a history of disregard for their humanity. Early in the movement hospital workers began asserting, "I might be Black, but I am somebody" to challenge the notion that their race and socioeconomic status automatically deemed them inferior and their grievances meaningless. Both movements, rooted in a history of African Americans connecting issues of labor and civil rights that dated back to the 1940s, grappled with the question of how to be truly free without the economic means to do so. Considering the similarities between the campaigns, the senators reminded Nixon that after Dr. King's assassination and the subsequent riots across the nation, President Lyndon B. Johnson sent in Undersecretary James Reynolds, from the US Department of Labor, to mediate the situation in Memphis. They warned the president that the hospital workers campaign could have the same "broad national implications."[26]

McNair's response to the senators' request reeked of frustration and illuminated his growing resentment toward the hospital workers and the movement. He condemned their request for a mediator and countered with accusations that the senators were proponents of the "open and willful violation" of the state's laws and policies. He questioned how they could be concerned about hospital workers considering that they had no respect for the law or those in need of health care. He proposed that it would be "much more helpful if they would issue a call for public respect for the law and for placing the care of the ill above selfish personal interests." McNair challenged the notion that the hospital workers movement was a test of nonviolence by arguing that, "the theory of nonviolence in this case has not always been consistent with the actual incidents of violence." Despite the push for resolution, the governor continued to stand firm in his refusal to negotiate.[27]

Considerable financial and organizational support for the movement emerged as the antithesis to the governor's staunch opposition to it. Local and national civil rights contributors banded together to offer their support to hospital workers. Leaders of all of the major civil rights organizations, along with five Black elected national and state officials, issued a joint statement that placed the campaign in a broader context, arguing that "it is part of the larger fight in our nation against discrimination and exploitation—against all forms of degradation that result from poverty and human misery." It was the first time since Dr. King's death that the national civil rights organizations had spoken collectively on an issue. The statement also included another comparison between Memphis and Charleston, asserting that McNair's refusal to acknowledge or bargain with the union was the same kind of resistance that led to tragedy in Memphis in 1968. This collective of supporters petitioned South Carolina's governor and the administrators of both hospitals to "grant the workers this elementary right" of union recognition "as a minimal gesture of justice and humanity."[28]

Two days after the civil rights organizations issued the joint statement, Reverend Matthew D. McCollom and Paul W. Matthias, president and executive director, respectively, of the South Carolina Council on Human Relations (SCCHR) offered support on its behalf. The SCCHR, an interracial organization founded in 1957, aimed to "foster better living and social conditions for African-Americans" and promote "racial harmony" within the state, throughout the 1960s and '70s. The leaders of the 1,500-member statewide organization issued a statement arguing that the issue was much deeper than money, even though the issue of low wages was among the core grievances. It was a "demand for dignity for laboring men and women who have too long been denied it in a system of paternalistic dependency." They pointed to unionization as a means to that end and chastised state officials who opposed it: "to deny this right is to seek to perpetuate the kind of plantation politics that makes decisions for people rather than with them." They insisted that state leaders had "both the responsibility and response ability" to address the workers' grievances "expeditiously and openly." They were concerned that a resolution would become more difficult to reach as those on each side of the dispute became increasingly unyielding in their stance and added, "Charleston need not become another Memphis."[29]

The nation's largest and most powerful labor organizations also stepped in to back the campaign. Harry Van Arsdale Jr., president of the New York City Central Labor Council AFL-CIO, shed light on what the hospital workers campaign meant to the labor movement, characterizing it as "no ordinary strike." He explained that a win in Charleston would be a win for the entire movement during a time when union membership had been steadily declining. It would highlight unionism as the "broad road out of poverty, out of segregation, and into the mainstream of American life." In addition to the wider implications of the win, he argued that victory against such an unyielding adversary was important to demonstrate the power of labor organizing as a vehicle for economic and social change. George Meany, president of AFL-CIO, and Walter Reuther, president of United Auto Workers (UAW), set the tone for labor organizations across the nation by putting aside their institutional differences to unify in support of hospital workers. Each organization sent representatives to Charleston to assist on the ground and donated a combined amount of more than thirty thousand dollars. William F. Kircher, national organizing director of the AFL-CIO, pledged that his organization would develop "a nationwide program of support" for the campaign, which would mean more than sixty thousand locals banning together for the cause. Members of Local 1199, including both the hospital and drug divisions, sent nearly forty thousand dollars to hospital workers. Other New York locals, such as the Bedding, Curtain and Drapery Union and the United Department Store Workers, collected approximately eight thousand dollars. National unions contributed more than fifty thousand dollars. Smaller donations from individuals and organizations such as Jacqueline Kennedy, a Mount Desert Island civil rights group, representatives from Harvard University, and the Astoria Branch of the NAACP totaled almost thirteen thousand dollars. By the end of the strike financial contributions amounted to more than $125,000.[30]

Even though McNair maintained substantial support for his stance on the strike, his constituents grew increasingly frustrated by the ongoing fallout of the strike. Local businesses, particularly small businesses, experienced considerable financial setbacks as a result of the curfew. In its first week, local businesses reported minor reductions in business and revenue but realized that the situation could rapidly deteriorate. The Sheraton-Fort Sumter Hotel had to cancel five evening events, the hotel restaurant closed an hour early in the evening, and convention attendance was down by 25 percent. F. William Broome, executive vice president of the Charleston Trident Chamber of Commerce, highlighted the fact that the tourist season was in full swing and that a number of potential visitors were changing their minds due to the unrest and curfew. He expressed concern regarding how the city's "$30 million a year tourist industry" would be affected. The city was already seeing lost revenue in theaters, restaurants, and other businesses that catered to the masses of tourists who visited the city each year.[31]

SCLC added to the pressure by calling on African American citizens to boycott local businesses. Andrew Young said we will "stay out of downtown and keep our money in our pockets." Supporters were supposed to purchase only food and medicine. The boycott targeted stores on King Street, the city's main shopping district. Local food markets and grocery stores reported only slight declines in revenue compared to other businesses, which could have been an indication of the boycott's effectiveness within the city and in outlying areas of the county.[32]

By day nine of the curfew, local businesses saw a drastic decline. The downtown Holiday Inn, forced to cancel all evening functions, reported that its revenue had been reduced by 50 percent since early May. Jason C. Travis, owner of three establishments throughout the city, claimed to be losing nearly six hundred dollars each month and had to lay off seven employees. Businesses outside the curfew area were also suffering losses. Johnny Howe, owner of the local bowling alley, stated that on a night that the lanes usually did well, post-curfew he was taking in four or five dollars. He asserted, "I'm losing my shirt. I'm not doing enough to pay the light bill." In addition to lost revenue due to the strike, many businesses also dealt with the expense of having to make repairs after window-breakings and other acts of vandalism.[33]

Thirteen owners of businesses that required twenty-four-hour operation reached out to McNair in hopes of finding a suitable solution. While they expressed their collective opposition to the "likes of Mr. Abernathy and his sordid clan going around stirring up trouble," they requested permission to remain open after the curfew hours. They argued that based on their locations, which were anywhere from two to five miles away from the curfew boundaries, they should be allowed to conduct business as usual. Otherwise, most of them would have to close their doors due to continued loss of revenue. Travis attached a personal plea to the governor, claiming that he could not "afford to remain open another two weeks if the curfew continues." He informed McNair that if the situation persisted, he would have to "close his businesses, sell my home and move to another location."[34]

In response to stalled talks between state and local officials, the hospitals, and hospital workers, the South Carolina Task Force for Community Uplift added to the push to reach a resolution. The task force, formally established in 1967 as a statewide organization, was "designed for community uplift and to preserve and expand racial harmony" within the state. The South Carolina branch of the NAACP had proposed the development of the organization, and Governor McNair endorsed it. On May 16, 1969, the task force issued a petition to the General Assembly requesting an open forum to discuss the strike, a study of state policies regarding unions, and the development of a policy that would resolve the strike. The group offered three main justifications for the petition. First, it expressed concerns regarding the safety and well-being of the Charleston community and the potential for more conflict due to the tense atmosphere surrounding the campaign. Second, it highlighted the impact of the dispute on the functioning of Medical College and Charleston County and the bearing that had on health care. Finally, the organization quoted the cost—"$10,000 per day"—of keeping the National Guard on duty and questioned the implications of that for local taxpayers.[35]

The task force petitioned the general assembly to take a more active role in resolving the strike. It requested that the legislative body hold an open meeting to give citizens a detailed account of the workers' grievances, information as to whether and to what extent the grievances had been dealt with prior to the strike, and more transparency about what exactly has happened during the course of the dispute and the policies surrounding it. The organization called on the legislative body to initiate a "thorough study" of current state policy regarding unionization and to establish legislation to "protect the general citizenry against the loss of vital public services due to strikes, while at the same time providing adequate legal machinery to protect the constitutional rights of workers." The task force closed by urging the general assembly to address the requests "as expeditiously as possible" in order to develop a policy that would lead to an immediate resolution that would be "fair to all parties and in a way that will promote the progress of South Carolina in matters relating to its employed citizens." [36]

In May 1969, HEW initiated a second investigation of Medical College, officially bringing the federal government into the dispute. Like the masses of African American workers who used Titles VI and VII of the Civil Rights Act of 1964 to combat work-related injustices and discrimination, the twelve hospital workers whose termination sparked the strike had submitted a discrimination complaint to HEW against Medical College in early March 1969. In response to the allegation, Hugh Brimm, the chief of the Contract Compliance Branch of the Office for Civil Rights, conducted a preliminary investigation by interviewing each of the twelve discharged workers and McCord in early April 1969. On May 19, 1969, the Federal Contract Compliance Division of HEW launched a "full-scale investigation" of Medical College as a result of findings from the study. Owen Kiely, chief of the Compliance Division, arrived in Charleston to conduct the inquiry. Based on Title VI mandates, which banned racial discrimination by federally funded institutions, Medical College, if found to be in violation as a federally funded hospital, risked the suspension of its federal contracts, including those that made it eligible to accept Medicare and Medicaid.[37]

The mounting pressure to resolve the strike put McNair in a precarious situation. All parties involved, himself included, remained unwilling to yield their positions; yet the Medical College and the city as a whole could be jeopardized if the strike continued unresolved. The governor, indirectly acknowledging how ineffectively McCord had handled the situation to date, instructed

William Huff, vice president of development, to unobtrusively take the lead on behalf of the hospital. McNair reached out to William Saunders to work with Huff in setting a meeting between Medical College and the hospital workers. Based on his absence from media coverage, Saunders seemed to have taken a back seat in the campaign. In reality, though, he had continued to work outside the spotlight as one of the leaders of the semi-secret "hospital workers' defense team" and as an unofficial adviser to the hospital workers. McNair saw him as an ideal go-between as he had connections with the workers but no obvious association with the union. Saunders agreed to work with Huff at the governor's behest to organize another meeting. The five hospital workers who had attended the halted May 8 meeting, plus Saunders and Fred Moore acting as their advisers, participated in the meeting on behalf of striking workers. Huff, the state personnel officer, two hospital personnel officers, and three members of the hospital's board of trustees were also in attendance. McCord, Local 1199, and SCLC were excluded from the gathering, but Saunders informed Local 1199 and SCLC that it was planned.[38]

The group met on May 26, 1969, at the Santee-Cooper hydro-electric plant in Moncks Corner, a community nearly thirty miles north of Charleston. According to Saunders, as everyone arrived, the trustees got chairs so that the female hospital workers could sit. That small gesture helped to alleviate some of the tension and set a relatively congenial tone for the meeting. The agenda focused on issues pertaining to wages, grievance procedures, an employee credit union, and the rehiring of the twelve fired workers. F. E. Ellis started the meeting by responding to the question of wage increases. He explained that a new state employee classification system had been proposed and was due to begin on July 1, 1969, with the minimum wage raised to $1.60 per hour. The hospital representatives did not have a solid plan for the grievance procedure. They offered several options but made it clear to workers that they would not be able to use union-elected workers to represent them in the grievance process. The workers inquired about the possibility of an employee credit union and payroll deductions for union dues. The hospital representatives—based on the fact that other state institutions had such a system in place—agreed to acknowledge a credit union and allow the payroll deduction.[39]

The group saved the hot-button issue of rehiring the twelve workers until the end of the meeting. The hospital representatives readily agreed to rehire anyone who was not terminated by the administration or who had not been charged with major violations of the law. They argued that rehiring would have to be handled on a case-by-case basis because the circumstances of the separation would determine how or whether persons could be rehired. They suggested that a representative of the workers consult Charles Fennessy,

Medical College personnel officer, to sort out the details of rehiring. The meeting closed with an agreement to keep the specifics confidential and to wait for the HEW report to decide the next steps.[40]

HEW sided with hospital workers and issued a forceful reminder to Medical College of the consequences of noncompliance. Brimm, verbally and in a letter dated June 5, presented McCord with the results of the HEW investigation. He stated that the "Medical College of South Carolina together with its hospital facilities is in non-compliance with the requirements of Executive Order 11246." He advised the administrator that, in order for the hospital to maintain its status as a federal contractor receiving approximately $12 million in government funding, it would be required to implement an affirmative action plan that adequately addressed the ideals of equal employment opportunity set forth by the order. Brimm recommended that reinstating the twelve workers with retroactive pay and without penalty be "a first step in the demonstration of an affirmative equal employment opportunity program." Even though Brimm could only urge the rehire, linking it to the directive regarding affirmative action and the threat to the hospital's federal funding implied that it was nonnegotiable.[41]

Heeding the HEW warning, on June 9, McCord announced the hospital's decision to reinstate the twelve workers. In the days after the announcement, Medical College finalized the details of the settlement with the hospital workers and McNair approved it. The governor addressed Medical College employees, primarily to calm the resistance he knew had been brewing even before the announcement to rehire. He applauded the workers who stayed on the job for their dedication and commitment. He assured them that neither the state nor the hospital had surrendered to union demands and that the returning workers had already begun to abandon the idea of union recognition. The governor referred to the twelve workers as "the symbol of the strike" and said that "there is a chance right now that taking the twelve back could open the door to breaking the strike and solving our problems." McNair urged workers to consider that, "in a situation such as this, and considering the alternatives, I believe some sacrifices are necessary on everybody's part to bring peace to the community of the state of South Carolina and particularly to your own home city and this institution."[42]

In an unexpected twist on June 12, moments before the settlement documents were due to be signed, Saunders received a call informing him that there was an issue with the settlement. Less than an hour later, a messenger delivered a note to Saunders that read, "Please be advised that the offer to employ the twelve discharged workers made on June 9, 1969, is now withdrawn as of Thursday, June 12." In a letter to McNair, McCord vaguely explained that "an ultimatum was presented to me in regard to the twelve being hired." In a press conference on June 19, he clarified what caused the abrupt about-face. He stated that in addition to the meeting where the governor addressed the hospital's faculty and staff, he had held an additional meeting with hospital employees regarding his plan to rehire the discharged workers. He claimed that, based on the response of his employees to the news of the workers return, if he had not rescinded the offer he would have been "forced to close the hospital." Some hospital employees, particularly nurses, had indeed threatened to quit if the striking workers were allowed to return. But a political intervention by US Congressmen from South Carolina was actually the impetus for ceasing the settlement.[43]

After HEW issued its report, three US Congressmen reached out to Robert F. Finch, Secretary of HEW, initiating communication that promptly caused the proposed settlement to unravel. Republican Senator Strom Thurmond, a steadfast segregationist and former governor of South Carolina, met with Finch on the same day that McCord withdrew the offer. The senator persuaded him to refrain from cutting off Medical College's federal funds pending a more thorough investigation of the allegations. Democratic Representative Mendel Rivers, also a segregationist and white supremacist, had a separate meeting with Finch with the same aim of halting any obstructions to the hospital's funding. Democratic Senator Ernest F. Hollings, characterized as a "Southern moderate politician," also intervened on the hospital's behalf. He requested information regarding the basis of the report that deemed the hospital noncompliant. Hollings had taken a special interest in issues of poverty among African Americans in South Carolina. Local leaders had guided the senator through the state's poorest areas and introduced him to its most impoverished residents. In February 1969, amid the hospital workers' pre-strike organizing, he spoke before the Senate Select Committee on Nutrition and Human Needs and shared the details of the destitution that he witnessed throughout the state, imploring it to assist in eradicating the deficiencies. Yet the senator ignored the hospital workers' opposition to "poverty wages" as a driving force in their campaign. Ultimately, Finch assured Thurmond that he would not tamper with the hospital's federal funding. The "unexpected poison" injected by the "Dixie" Congressmen worked, and within hours of the threat being removed the proposed settlement between Medical College and the hospital workers had been retracted.[44]

On the heels of the rescinded settlement offer, SCLC intensified its efforts. Organization leaders openly defied the ban on night marches in the name of civil disobedience and organized a group of approximately four hundred supporters to march on the evening of June 20. Abernathy set the tone, avowing, "We've played around with Charleston long enough." As law enforcement officers ordered the crowd to disperse under threats of arrest, Abernathy, joined by Hosea Williams, refused and instead knelt in prayer. Violence erupted as officers physically carried them both to the awaiting paddy wagon. Marchers reportedly threw bricks and bottles, causing minor injuries to several officers, which led to Abernathy and several others being charged with inciting a riot and held under fifty-thousand-dollar bonds. As Abernathy appeared before the magistrate the following day, approximately forty strike supporters attempted to organize a demonstration downtown. When law enforcement officers ordered them to disperse, they lay down in the street, blocking midday traffic. Again, officers were forced to physically remove demonstrators, and a scuffle ensued. In response to rising tension, McNair reinstated the 9 p.m. to 5 a.m. curfew.[45]

Local law enforcement officers found it increasingly difficult to control the once relatively easily managed masses of demonstrators, and FBI agents were sent to Charleston. Workers and their supporters continued to show up to the picket line and various demonstrations daily in the sweltering Charleston heat while they and their families dealt with the personal and financial repercussions of being on strike. Abernathy argued that all of that was exacerbated by the fact that, despite SCLC's commitment to nonviolence, a faction of supporters was intent on violent action. Recognizing that the movement had reached the boiling point, FBI agents reached out to Saunders with concerns about the possibility of riots. He declared, "We would never have a riot in Charleston, we would have a war." He warned that if the situation arose, African Americans in the city would not "throw bottles at tanks like folk did all over the country" because they "all had guns." The FBI had a deeper fear that the hospital strike would expand into a moment of national unrest.[46]

By mid-June, Charleston and the campaign had reached a tipping point, garnering national attention as hospital workers gained increasing support. Local businesses and the tourist industry suffered as a result of boycotts and the presence of striking workers and their supporters throughout the city and surrounding areas. Hospital administrators, along with local and state leaders, grappled with the pressures of federal interests and expectations. The movement had reached a crossroads, and the next move would determine its outcome and Charleston's immediate future.

Chapter 7

RESOLUTION AND DISILLUSION

Despite the major transformation of the movement in the second phase, hospital workers remained constant in their core demands: a decent wage, an effective grievance process—which included union representation—and respect. The collaborative efforts of Local 1199 and SCLC gave the movement credibility and situated the hospital workers' campaign firmly in the tradition of struggles to simultaneously eradicate racial and economic injustices. Their presence gave the Charleston movement a spot on the national stage, but it too often overshadowed the women at the center. Those in the various iterations of leadership put such an emphasis on settling the strike that as it reached an end, the grievances that sparked the movement tended to be eclipsed.

In the wake of the failed resolution, Local 1199 and SCLC made decisive moves on the workers' behalf but without their participation, which led to the resolution of the dispute. First, in order to suppress the growing violence, they decided to refrain from direct confrontations with law enforcement. For example, SCLC attempted an alternative to civil disobedience by organizing groups of African Americans to attend local all-white churches as a demonstration of peaceful protest on Sunday, June 22, 1969. During a candid conversation that included Stoney Cooks, SCLC executive director, and Local 1199 leaders, Andrew Young realized that the union was reaching the end of its rope. Union leaders expressed concerns about how much longer they would be able to maintain in the struggle. Their energy and funds were nearing depletion. He shared with them that he had read an article indicating that McCord's parents were missionaries in South Africa and that he had grown up there. Based on that information he deduced, "a guy like that can't be all bad" and suggested that they go talk to him. He called the hospital and requested a "chat" with McCord, who agreed. Young did not share with union leaders the fact that there had been several conversations going on behind the scenes that made the meeting possible. He had a friend in New York, Jay Islan, an editor at *Harper's Magazine*, who was originally from South Carolina. Islan had connections in the governor's office and was acquainted with Charleston's mayor. Islan verified Young's credibility and advised Mayor Gaillard that he would be the ideal person to help settle the strike. According to Young, that affirmation, his rapport with Chief Conroy, and the fact that he had "always dealt straight with everybody" encouraged McCord to consent to the meeting. Young and Cooks met with the administrator that day. Young recalled spending the first two hours just allowing McCord to vent. In the end, Young assured him that they were "interested in finding a way to go on from here together." He explained that they wanted to figure out the most expedient and efficient way to "get these workers back to work and settle the strike" and that they wanted to work with him on a resolution.[1]

There was one more hurdle to address at Medical College—the ongoing threat of nurses quitting if the original twelve hospital workers were reinstated. Moe Foner and Young worked together to remove the final obstacle. Barbara Schutt, editor of *The American Journal of Nursing* with whom Foner had become personally acquainted prior to the strike, introduced him to the leader of the South Carolina Nurses Association. Once the lines of communication were opened, he spoke with her regularly throughout the campaign to get updates on the situation inside the hospital. When the word that "white nurses" would walk out reemerged, Foner reached out to his association contact, who confirmed his fears. Young, who had met with McCord several times at this point, reached out to the administrator for support in resolving the matter. Young "was slipped in the back door" of the hospital to meet with the nurses. According to Foner, when he spoke to his association contact again to inquire about how Young was received and the outcome of the meeting she asked, "Do you have any more people like him?" Apparently, by the end of the meeting, the nurses agreed not to walk out and even joined the civil rights organizer in singing, "We Shall Overcome."[2]

While Young met with McCord and worked to sway the nurses, Foner reached out to the White House. Shortly after the strike began, he had contacted Daniel Moynihan, then serving as a domestic policy adviser to President Nixon, to inform him of the situation in Charleston. Moynihan requested that he be kept in the loop regarding developments in the dispute. After the incident with the retracted settlement offer, Foner recognized that "things were getting very hot;" and one evening as he and Godoff were strategizing it occurred to him that he needed to call Moynihan. When the union organizer finally got Moynihan on the phone, he explained, "I'm not going to be responsible, but I just thought you ought to know we've had another night march here tonight. This city is going to blow up. You just have to trust me on this. You know what's happened on how they ended the settlement. This thing is not going to go on like this. This city is going to go. And you're going to have it on your hands." Moynihan advised Foner that the White House would send George Schultz, US Secretary of Labor, and other observers to Charleston to assess the situation. Foner met with Schultz and brought him up to speed on all that had transpired in the campaign to date. According to Foner, after the visit, the White House sent word that "they're going to reinstate the settlement."[3]

At the eleventh hour, hospital worker supporters, most of whom were unaware of these backroom negotiations, also turned up the heat in an effort to force Medical College to resolve the strike. On June 26, 1969, William Kircher, director of the AFL-CIO announced that if the hospital did not settle the strike, Local 1422-A of the Longshoreman's Association would initiate a strike, shutting down Charleston's port. The longshoremen handled approximately 5.5 million tons of freight worth nearly $500 million in a year. Staging a strike at one of the largest ports on the Atlantic seaboard would "paralyze the city and have serious impact on most of the state." He argued that a port shutdown was not their first choice but that they had reached the decision after exhausting every other possibility. The following day, Reverend Walter Fauntroy, a Washington SCLC representative, led a demonstration at the HEW headquarters for the second time. The first protest took place on June 20, lasted for ninety minutes with less than twenty demonstrators while HEW employees and others merely watched. The June 27 demonstration was larger and longer, with thirty protesters, including HEW employees, picketing for two hours. They insisted that HEW step in on behalf of the workers to end the strike.[4]

By the end of June, it was clear that McCord was the only obstacle to resolving the strike. Schultz ordered Robert Finch of HEW to issue an ultimatum, not a recommendation, which stated that if the administrator did not settle the dispute, the hospital's federal funding would be cut, which he did. McCord conceded, ending the walkout at Medical College after one hundred days on June 27, 1969. He announced in a press conference that, "all those working on March 15 [including the twelve] will return to their jobs on Tuesday." Workers were guaranteed a minimum wage of $1.60 per hour, effective July 1, 1969, in accordance with the new state job classification and compensation plan. The settlement included a six-step grievance procedure that would allow workers to bring in another employee to assist "at any and all stages" of the process. However, it placed limits on the number of times any one individual could serve in that capacity. Local 1199 accepted this concession as a substitute for union recognition. The resolution also included plans for a credit union that would facilitate payroll deductions for union dues.[5]

When news of the settlement reached hospital workers and their supporters, the union hall filled with celebration, hugs, kisses, and freedom songs. In separate public statements, McNair expressed relief and hopes that the "peace and calm" would be restored in the city. The mayor shared feelings of delight regarding the settlement. Abernathy had been temporarily released from jail in order to speak at a "victory rally." Hospital workers had seemingly won the battle, but they had not yet won the war.[6]

Once Medical College and its hospital workers reached a settlement, Local 1199 and SCLC turned their attention to Charleston County Hospital. Just two days after the first strike resolution, the Charleston County Council, the county hospital's governing body, announced that it would not rehire all of the sixty-nine striking workers. When Andrew Young met with members of the council, J. Mitchell Graham, the council chair, offered a compromise that would give thirty-five workers jobs at the hospital and another twenty-five top priority for other county positions. Graham argued that the hospital could not afford to rehire all of the workers because permanent replacements had been hired in their absence. He claimed that a complete rehire would leave the institution with only two options: terminate those employees who "stood by the sick and the dying through the strike" or spend $250,000 to overstaff the hospital. The council did not consider either as a viable solution. After workers rejected the first proposal, the council offered to reinstate half of the workers at Charleston County and place the remainder of the workers in positions at the Veterans and Naval Hospital, which workers also refused. The council submitted a "final offer" to take back thirty-seven of the workers and place the rest on a "standby employment list." It demanded that the workers accept the settlement or the hospital would begin filling the available positions with permanent employees the following Monday. Again, workers refused and referred to the ultimatum as a "declaration of war." Since most of the workers' original grievances were addressed in the resolution of the larger state hospital, the issue of rehiring striking workers was the only obstacle to ending the strike.[7]

Local 1199 and SCLC vowed to remain in Charleston and support the striking workers until they reached a settlement. Abernathy, who had been in jail since his June 21 arrest for "inciting a riot," remained there until July 3 in protest of the ongoing dispute and as a demonstration of his commitment to the campaign. Leon Davis, Local 1199 president, suggested that the movement would be better served if Abernathy were out of jail. After conferring with his top aides, he agreed to leave, posting the significantly reduced five-thousand-dollar bond. Davis returned to New York to galvanize support for the remaining striking workers. The Local 1199 Hospital Division Delegates Assembly pledged to continue their financial support of Local 1199-B after voting to "double the strike benefits for the county hospital workers."[8]

Medical College Hospital workers continued to stand with Charleston County Hospital workers in solidarity, even as one group returned to their jobs and the other returned to the picket line. Initially, Medical College workers asserted that, even though they had been reinstated, they would not return until the second part of the strike had been resolved. However, county employees urged them to return to work to avoid any further adversity. On July 2, approximately eighty of the one hundred workers scheduled to return to Medical College on that day stopped by the County Hospital picket line and demonstrated briefly as a show of support on their way to work. McNair amended the curfew, decreasing it from "dusk to dawn" to midnight to five in the morning. Sporadic instances of violence persisted throughout the city, but the situation was not nearly as tense or as worrisome for local and state leaders as it had been.[9]

County Hospital workers eventually extended an olive branch by relaxing their original "all or none" approach to their demands for rehiring. They expressed a willingness to accept a reinstatement plan that did not include the immediate rehire of all workers as long as the hospital set a firm deadline by which all workers would be back on the job. On July 18, 1969, three weeks after the Medical College strike was settled, Charleston County Hospital and its striking employees reached an agreement. The two parties decided that forty-two out of the sixty-five workers who wanted to return to the hospital would be reinstated immediately. In regard to the remaining workers, the council committed to "make every effort" to rehire them within three months. Even as the settlement was being finalized, there were still some issues regarding the grievance procedure; but both parties agreed to move forward with the assurance that they would work out the details. In the news conference announcing the settlement, the council chair simplified the resolution as a relief for the city, saying, "I am happy that the strike and turmoil in the streets of Charleston have ended." Rosetta Simmons's assessment of the strike and what it meant for workers spoke to the essence of what initially motivated them to respond to the call to action: "We are returning to work with a relation of mutual respect and dignity. We gained recognition as human beings. We gained that recognition as human beings."[10]

CHAPTER 7

Once the strike was settled in July 1969, the majority of Local 1199 staff returned to New York, and SCLC prepared to host its twelfth annual convention in Charleston a month later in mid-August. As the union and the civil rights organization set their sights on their next endeavors, hospital workers were left to confront the aftermath of a movement that had brought the city to its knees. Immediately after the strike ended, workers grappled with what felt like an abrupt end to the campaign. According to Mary Moultrie, many of the workers were confused and caught off guard by the settlement. She was the person the workers chose as their leader, yet she and her officers had been excluded from the final negotiations. As a matter of fact, Moultrie was in New York when the settlement occurred. Workers did not regard Local 1199 or SCLC as their leaders. They took direction from Local 1199-B officers and identified the national organizations as a support system. So when news of the strike settlement hit, the union hall workers had mixed feelings of both triumph and disappointment. Moultrie admitted that she probably felt more strongly about the terms of the settlement than other workers did and criticized how it was handled:

> In spite of the fact that most of our demands had been met, I felt the terms were agreed upon too quickly. I felt that those representing us should have brought the package back to the strikers and have us vote on whether we agreed with it or not, or at least explain why we had to accept that agreement. I felt at that time that I had been cheated out of something. I really felt that I should have been a part of that bargaining session, because that was the most important meeting of all meetings.[11]

Moultrie believed that workers would have been willing to hold out for as long as necessary in order to gain union recognition but "just accepted it" because they felt like they had no other choice but to return to work once they had lost their support system. She contended that, "if the bargaining had been done between the workers and management, we would have gotten a contract or would have held out longer." She eventually accepted that the union and SCLC "had exhausted all of their resources suitable to our cause, and anything else would have become more complicated and more expensive." She also recognized that had workers been in a position to refuse the settlement, they could have been left with nothing. In her assessment of the situation, Moultrie also examined the role of local leaders: "While we were fighting just to get our jobs back and to get better working conditions and more money, they were community people doing their own thing. But at the time we couldn't see it. Now we know." She asserted that she had lost respect for those that she had traditionally held in high regard as leaders of the Black community. At the end, Moultrie found herself "more hurt and disappointed than angry" about what looked and felt like desertion as both national and local leaders left workers to pick up the pieces.[12]

As workers grappled with mixed emotions after the strike, hospital workers quickly recognized that the settlement agreement was not "worth the paper it was written on." Rehiring discharged workers, the main obstacle of both settlements, continued to be an issue. Some workers realized that they would not be able to get their jobs back. Others decided not to go back in an effort to avoid the uncomfortable return to work, unsure of the consequences of their involvement. Workers from Medical College returned to their jobs relatively quickly, while more than two dozen of the County Hospital workers never regained their positions.[13]

Rosetta Simmons, Local 1199B vice president, was an LPN at Charleston County Hospital prior to the strike, but afterward she was labeled an agitator. As a result, hospital administrators tried to avoid reinstating her. According to her, if it had not been for her former manager, a white RN who lived on Wadmalaw Island, she would never have been rehired. The RN reached out to Simmons to inform her that the hospital was in the process of reinstating LPNs in the operating room, which was where she worked prior to the strike, but she had not been notified. She contacted the manager who originally hired her to inquire about the hospital hiring LPNs even though they claimed they did not have a position open to rehire her. The manager lied, saying that they had not hired any LPNs. The RN had given her all of the new hires' information, including the hire dates and the locations of each position, which Simmons provided to the manager. He directed her to the hospital's administrator who told her that she would not be able to return to her former position and that she would be placed somewhere else. She returned to work on November 10, 1969, well beyond the agreed upon three-month limit.[14]

The newly implemented grievance procedure looked good in print, but it too turned out to be ineffective in practice. Initially, the process worked well. Workers were given the option to be accompanied by another employee, even if it was a unionized worker. Moultrie recalled several occasions when she provided support to coworkers. However, the grievance procedure included a restriction on the number of times that one individual would be allowed to serve in that capacity. Eventually, administrators used the loophole to bar Moultrie from participating in grievance proceedings. She questioned the grievance process's usefulness, arguing that it was pointless to have a system in place for workers that management controlled. She recalled, "we finally got the channels that you go through, but once you got to your last step, it was as if you had never started out. Most of the time, the decision was never reversed." According to her, in a short time, the process of addressing worker grievances bore a strong resemblance to how it had been handled prior to the strike.[15]

In accordance with the settlement agreement, a credit union was established, but it fell short of what workers envisioned. Based on the agreement, workers would be able to set up payroll deductions to pay their union dues, but that never came to fruition. Hospital administrators, taking their normal anti-union stance, refused to allow the credit union to handle dues, citing a lack of staff and funding. Alternatively, workers were instructed to withdraw money and pay union dues on their own. This approach worked well at first, but over time workers became markedly less committed to the process, which had a devastating impact on the local union.[16]

Hospital workers returned to the job labeled as agitators and stained by their decision to confront the hospitals, the city, and state. Personal reflections about the aftermath from a handful of workers provide a window into the post-strike hospital environment. Their experiences shed light on the range of reactions to their reinstatement and the forms of retaliation they confronted. One of the main concerns for hospital administrators and those who stayed on the job was the potential for ongoing hostility between unionized workers and "scabs." Naomi White characterized her return to work as "fine" but insisted that some hospital employees were fearful after their reinstatement. She recalled, "They were afraid of us, because they didn't put us on the floors we came off. They said the scabs didn't feel too comfortable." She found their solution laughable because workers could request to be moved back to their original location within a month. And even if they did not go as far as to request to be moved, there were few boundaries in place to stop confrontations. She asserted that, for example, "if somebody up on the ninth floor I want to cut their behind, I'm going on the elevator and do what I got to do and come back." She also pointed to the fact that in spite of the fear associated with rehired workers, they experienced moments that revealed the value of their labor. Supervisors who became frustrated with the incompetence of the new hires would ask rehired workers to return to their old positions. According to White, many workers refused, saying that "since they did what they did to distribute us like they did, we stayed wherever they put us and let them see wherever they puts us we were capable."[17]

Workers confronted the realities of rebuilding an on-the-job rapport under problematic circumstances. Carrie Mitchell recalled how deliberate supervisors had been in placing reinstated workers. She worked as a nursing assistant in pediatrics prior to the strike and had been assigned to handling medications upon her return. Supervisors were also mindful of the number of former strikers they put in one department. She remembered mixed emotions among those workers who stayed. She contended that the workers who had been hired as replacements "didn't know what to expect" when the strikers came back. Like White, she recalled feelings of fear and skepticism abounding. She asserted that, despite the discomfort and uncertainty, those who had been reinstated handled themselves well, "They ain't never treated us so good at all, but personally, I think people was ready to go back to work and had to do what they had to do. I think that the people that was on strike were mature about—you know, had responsibilities and so they knew what they had to do." Despite the unease, some of the work-based friendships that had been affected during the strike survived and workers were able to resume those relationships.[18]

Coworkers and supervisors surreptitiously antagonized former strikers. Rosetta Simmons faced concerted efforts to force her resignation. Her supervisor would schedule her for three different shifts in one week, which was against hospital policy. One day she would work seven to three, the next day three to eleven and her next shift eleven to seven. Initially, she took matters into her own hands and would only work the first two shifts and call in sick for the third, but her supervisor continued to assign the same shifts. Eventually, she decided to just work the shift, and over time the supervisor stopped scheduling her in that manner. In addition to scheduling issues, she recalled her superiors attempting to "blackball" her by heavily scrutinizing her work, trying to find a mistake and a reason to fire her. Simmons recalled that she responded by being extremely thorough with her work, controlling her normally brazen attitude, and making sure she prayed to stay on the job.[19]

Mary Moultrie had become the face of Local 1199B and the strike. Hers was often the image that represented workers in national and local publications. She traveled all over the country delivering speeches and making appearances on behalf of striking workers. She recalled people referring to her as "Mary Moultrie, you know, she led the hospital workers." Her visibility during the movement made her a target in the aftermath. She characterized her return to work as "hell." When, in an interview nearly forty years later, she was questioned about how things were for her at work after the strike, the lingering pain was obvious. After a moment she replied, "It was hard and I hadn't really gotten to the point that I could actually talk about it. There's been a lot of workplace mobbing, if you are familiar with that. I went through a lot. It's not easy. I can't talk about that at this point. But I have overcome. I stuck it out as long as I could." While she could not articulate the details of her experience, the emotion-filled reaction was a clear indication that she had been traumatized. William Saunders, a close friend of Moultrie's, expressed feelings of regret over how she had been treated. He argued that she experienced more backlash than anyone who had been involved in the strike. So much so that she had blocked most of it out. She only worked at Medical College for six years after the strike. She left and began working for the city in recreation. She thought that leaving the hospital meant leaving her troubles behind, but she faced some of the same retaliatory acts in the new position.[20]

Despite the challenges that workers faced on the job in the aftermath, they returned to work emboldened by a greater sense of dignity, power, and purpose. According to Moultrie, the movement was transformative. "Those of us who had been seen as nobody were soon respected as somebody," she said. Claire Brown asserted that workers learned that their voices mattered, and when they joined together as one voice it was incredibly powerful. For most workers, the strike symbolized their unwillingness to accept a "life of poverty, exploitation, or discrimination."[21]

By the end of 1969, Local 1199B had begun to decline. There were approximately 250 workers on the Local 1199B roster compared to the four to five hundred that initially struck from the two hospitals. Less than twenty of them paid their monthly dues consistently from August through December. The majority of the workers, including some officers, only paid August dues and only a few of them paid in September. The fact that the newly established credit union did not allow payroll deductions for union dues made it difficult for hospital workers to keep up with their contributions. However, the deeper reason for the decline was that for many workers the union had been a means to an end; and once they achieved the strike settlement, it had no purpose. According to Moultrie, in the months that followed, it became clear that many of the former strikers no longer wanted to be associated with the union or even be seen talking to her. The same workers who had been on the picket line singing "We Shall Overcome," would see Mary Moultrie in the hospital halls and duck into the nearest open door or turn to walk in the other direction.[22]

The local union attempted to transition from the strike to a grassroots organizing campaign with unsteady leadership. Those who remained committed to Local 1199B came to realize that they were ill-prepared for the task of transitioning from unionizers organized under duress to union builders. Leon Davis, after a visit to Charleston, wrote to Moultrie in December 1969 with detailed instructions on how to structure the local and conduct the day-to-day union business, indicating that he also had some concerns about Local 1199B and possibly her leadership. Davis refused to provide additional support or make any other changes until the local proved its viability. Moultrie affirmed Davis's concerns when she expressed feelings of abandonment and a lack of confidence in her ability to run the local union and maintain full-time employment at the hospital. According to her, Local 1199 left the local chapter without resources or guidance. In interviews decades after the strike, she argued that, in addition to the lack of support, the leaders of Local 1199B lacked the training and skill necessary to organize other Charleston hospitals and build the union. By February 1970, her assessment rang true, as the local chapter had not successfully organized any new hospital workers. The national began to explicitly express their loss of faith in the local's ability to "function and not merely live on its past and act as a drain on 1199." Local 1199 leaders pressured the local for results that justified the money being invested. Isaiah Bennett, still on loan from Local 15A, continued to serve in the capacity of organizer for the local, but he also failed to meet their expectations. In the meantime, the national union sent Doris Turner, Local 1199 vice president, to assess the situation. She was told to ascertain whether Local 1199B leadership followed the instructions on how to manage the union, to examine Bennett's contributions and determine whether he needed to be terminated, and "investigate" Moultrie's and Rosetta Simmons's leadership and decide whether they needed to be replaced.[23]

The decline of Local 1199B became a personal cross for Moultrie to bear. During the strike she had been characterized as the "real leader" and as a "Barbara Jordan" kind of speaker, yet by mid-1970, national leaders and members of the local had begun to raise concerns about her leadership. Union leaders professed that she had been exactly what the movement needed in the moment due to her charisma and ability to connect with the rank and file. However, after the campaign, their opinion of her quickly deteriorated with criticisms that she needed more discipline and that becoming a national figure overnight had become too much for her. Horace Small, Local 1199 organizer, characterized her as "prestige and power mad." Members of Local 1199B expressed frustration with the decline of the local and pointed to the ineffectiveness of Moultrie's leadership as the central issue. Bennett, on the other hand, spoke on Moultrie's behalf highlighting the fact that she was given an enormous task for which she was not properly prepared. He revealed that, even though the union sent Moultrie to New York during the strike to take classes and acquire some training, she couldn't "learn that overnight. You learn organizing by doing it." Moultrie found herself caught in a web of accusations that culminated with responsibility for the local's regression being placed squarely on her shoulders. Local 1199B members eventually voted her out as president, and she withdrew from hospital organizing completely. Despite the shift in leadership, the local continued to decline and dissolved in the mid-1970s.[24]

Despite the challenges hospital workers faced in the aftermath, their campaign set the stage for another group of Charleston's service employees. On August 15, 1969, more than two hundred Black sanitation workers pulled a "surprise move" and walked off the job. Organized by the National Council of Distributive Workers of America, workers issued demands for high wages, increased benefits, and union recognition. Mayor Palmer Gaillard immediately responded with a threat to hire replacements if workers did not return to work. Mary Moultrie offered the sanitation workers the full support of Local 1199B declaring that, "A wrong against one is a wrong against us all." Workers attempted to strengthen their position, as hospital workers had done, calling on SCLC for support. The strike emerged while the civil rights organization was hosting its twelfth annual convention in Charleston. A delegation of sanitation workers petitioned the organization for support during one of the event meetings. While their proposition garnered cheers and applause from the crowd, SCLC did not fully commit to backing them as they had the hospital workers. The organization led several demonstrations in the city to draw attention to the workers' cause but only obligated themselves to the campaign on an as needed basis.[25]

The strikers endured for eleven weeks before they reached a settlement with the city of Charleston. Early in the strike, the mayor agreed to reduce the work week from six days to five but refused to negotiate with the union and offered an explanation of his inability to make adjustments to pay rates during the fiscal year. After several closed meetings between him and the striking workers, they reached an agreement in early November 1969. Workers received a nominal pay raise, a grievance procedure, and reinstatement. The main obstacle in the negotiating proceedings had been the issue of union recognition, which the sanitation workers had to ultimately relinquish. Many considered the resolution only a partial win. In conjunction with the hospital workers campaign, however, their stance had broader implications. It marked the beginning of a shift in Charleston's race relations, on and off the job. For example, in the years following these labor disputes hospital workers experienced more congenial working relationships across the racial divide, and increased numbers of African Americans were being elected in local politics. Most important, these movements exposed members of the local Black working class to the possibility of recourse, challenging the belief that they had "to sit and take a situation."[26]

Despite the decline of the Charleston chapter, Local 1199 leaders used the momentum from the strike to situate the union as the preeminent national hospital workers union. They began by transforming their national campaign to organize hospital workers into a permanent union structure. To that end, the union petitioned the RWDSU to establish a division for the sole "purpose of representing and organizing hospital and nursing home employees throughout the United States." In early October 1969, the executive board of RWDSU voted to establish the National Hospital and Nursing Home Employee Union, a Division of the RWDSU, AFL-CIO, which incorporated Local 1199 and all its affiliates.[27]

The Charleston campaign marked the beginning of the union's national organizing efforts and became the symbol of its new direction. Local 1199 characterized the hospital workers movement as the epitome of the "principles of nonviolence massively organized and militantly conducted in the best traditions of nonviolence." Moe Foner initiated the idea of developing a visual representation of the union's contributions in Charleston. In October 1969, Local 1199 commissioned the production of a documentary about the hospital workers' campaign. The final product was a thirty-minute film comprised of interviews with local leaders and hospital workers, news clips highlighting key aspects of the campaign, and narration by Claire Brown, an obstetric technician who had been on strike from Medical College. The documentary became a valuable element of the national organizing strategy as they used the Charleston campaign for credibility.[28]

Local 1199 capitalized on the hospital workers strike for nearly a decade, using the threat of "pulling another Charleston" as its calling card. A decisive victory in Baltimore bolstered by "the grim reminder of recent events in Charleston, S.C., in the background," set the tone for the union's vision of its organizing future. In late summer 1969, the union answered the call to organize hospital workers across the city. There were several hospitals involved in the dispute but Local 1199 chose to focus its energy on Johns Hopkins Hospital, a "symbol of Baltimore's elite white power structure," anticipating that a victory there would lead to resolutions at the other institutions. In August 1969, Hopkins hospital workers voted Local 1199 in just a month after their employer, plus Lutheran and North Charleston General hospitals, agreed to recognize collective bargaining agreements. Before the close of the following year, the union had added approximately six thousand Baltimore hospital workers to the roster and established agreements at six hospitals. During the 1970s, the union suffered missteps and failed organizing attempts, while dealing with broader questions about the fate of labor unions in an uncertain economy. Despite the challenges, Local 1199 had still been successful in hanging its hat on the Charleston campaign. By 1979, the union had more than one hundred thousand members representing thousands of employers across the nation.[29]

SCLC failed to reap the same kind of benefits from the Charleston movement. A dramatic victory could have revitalized it and the nonviolence ideology. Instead, the campaign's lukewarm resolution caused more membership depletion. In the years after Charleston, its leaders struggled to organize campaigns that garnered significant national attention or achieved clear victories. That failure coupled with internal conflicts made the future of SCLC uncertain. Andrew Young, a pillar in the organization, resigned just months after the hospital workers' campaign to pursue a career in politics. By 1973, the organization's staff had dwindled from 125 to seventeen. Getting involved in the Charleston movement had been a gamble for the organization, and in the end, it failed to get the expected return.[30]

Hundreds of Black women, whose voices have been generally unheard and the majority of whom remain nameless, stood at the core of the Charleston hospital workers' campaign of 1969. Many had experience in civic engagement through their churches and in their communities but saw themselves as removed from the 1960s national movements against racial and economic injustice. It could be argued that most of the hospital workers did not fully understand what they were about to embark upon or how their involvement would impact the city. Even though only a small number of the hospital workers came from or were familiar with a "protest community," they became a community of organizers and activists in the moment. Motivated by frustration and resistance, whether it was conscious or unconscious, they confronted their employers, the city of Charleston, and the state of South Carolina with a powerful challenge to the notion that as working-class Black women they were inherently inferior and unequal.

Hospital workers could not have built the national movement they did without the support of local and national labor and civil rights leaders. Yet, at times, the presence of these leaders overshadowed the critical nature of workers' contributions, undermined their ability to advocate for themselves, and obscured their enormous personal sacrifices. Despite the challenges, hospital workers concentrated on what the outcome of the campaign would mean for their families rather than how the movement evolved. For them, it was always a grassroots endeavor; and their focus throughout was to assert their right to be treated with respect and to be fairly rewarded for their labor.

CONCLUSION

Charleston and the state of South Carolina, and even many of the workers, wanted to get as far away from the strike and its memory as possible. Immediately after the strike, local and state leaders saw the strike as a blemish on the port city. During the campaign words like "ridiculous," "unreasonable," and "agitator" were used to describe hospital workers, their supporters and their cause. In the decades following the strike, however, a shift in local memory transformed hospital workers from villains to heroines. By the early 1990s, a mainstream celebratory narrative began to emerge. Local newspapers praised the movement as a "an important episode in Black history and in Charleston's history." Reporters applauded former strikers who "stood up for what was right." Efforts to redirect local perceptions of the hospital workers strike, however, led to the oversimplification of their protest, a slow-growing regard for its contribution to the broader civil rights and labor movements, and often negated its impact on the workers' personal lives.[1]

In 2007, the Charleston County Library hosted a reunion of the strikers, Local 1199 and SCLC in an effort to recognize the strike's contribution to the city's history. Henry Nicholas, who had become Local 1199 president, interpreted the shift in attitude toward the strike as an opening for the union. He approached Mary Moultrie about revitalizing Local 1199B, arguing that it was an ideal time for another attempt to organize hospital workers. She agreed, claiming that she had been "waiting for this opportunity for a long time." She called on Rosetta Simmons and Naomi White to help her rebuild the union. Moultrie and Nicholas seemed to have gotten swept up in the euphoria of the redirected narrative or simply rewrote the history in their minds. Nicholas dismissed his earlier critiques of Moultrie's leadership as ineffective and undisciplined. He ignored the fact that Moultrie had not been involved in labor organizing in over thirty years. In later interviews, she generally attributed the demise of the local union to the lack of dues, a shift in interest, and a lack of training. However, she did not mention being voted out. A family trip to New York City, in 1973, revealed the breakdown in her relationship with Local 1199. While in the city she visited the headquarters of the national union. After seeing a life-size image of herself during the strike at the end of a hallway, the feelings of disappointment and disrespect flooded her mind, and she left the building without speaking to her former colleagues. She lost contact with all of them over the years. When Nicholas approached her about Local 1199-B, she seemed to divorce herself from the realities of her personal narrative and accept the commemorative version.[2]

The Preservation Society of Charleston unveiled a historic marker of the strike on the campus of Medical University of South Carolina (MUSC), formerly Medical College, on October 1, 2013. It was the last of five markers designated to recognize key civil rights events and sites. The marker read:

> Hospital Strike of 1969: Civil rights marches on Ashley Avenue and elsewhere occurred during the strike at two hospitals from March 20 to July 18, 1969. Workers, mostly Black women, cited unequal treatment and pay when they organized and walked out of the Medical College Hospital (MCH) on Doughty Street and Charleston County Hospital (CCH) on Calhoun Street. Some picketers were arrested, the state of S.C. refused to sanction a union, and talks stalled.[3]

The wording failed to encompass the true character of the strike or pay homage to the workers. As a result, the Preservation Society experienced some backlash, particularly from William Saunders. However, from a broader perspective, identifying the strike as a moment in Charleston's civil rights history and erecting the marker at MUSC symbolized the movement as a critical demonstration of the intersectional struggles against racial and economic injustices during that era. It was also an indication of former striking hospital workers now being lauded as heroines and not villains.[4]

The most recent rendering of the Poor People's Campaign, now the Poor People's Campaign: A National Call for Moral Revival (PPC), launched in May 2018 with forty days of "protest and civil disobedience" led by Reverend Doctor William Barber II and cochair Reverend Dr. Liz Theoharis. According to Dr. Barber, the current campaign is a "reenactment and reinauguration" of what Dr. King envisioned over fifty years ago. During the PPC's inaugural march on Capitol Hill, Dr. Barber conjured the spirit of the March on Washington and Resurrection City in a speech outlining the revised vision of the movement. The leaders of PPC argue that it has been resurrected with Dr. King's vision at the foundation but that they have also taken steps to ensure that its current aims are inclusive and address twenty-first century issues such as: voting rights, tribal recognition and sovereignty, living wages, unionization, equity in education, and poverty. Working-class South Carolinians have established a branch of the PPC in order to address the needs of the state's poor and disenfranchised. Charleston, South Carolina has emerged as one of the major hubs for the movement in the state. South Carolinians involved in the PPC have deliberately and consciously connected themselves to the local protest tradition.[5]

March 2019 marked the fiftieth anniversary of the hospital workers' strike. MUSC hosted a four-day event in May of that year commemorating the importance and success of the movement. The South Carolina Poor People's Campaign advertised its event in honor of the strike in a Facebook post on March 5, 2019, with an image of Dr. Barber, Dr. Theoharis, and Louise Brown, one of the hospital workers involved in the 1969 hospital workers' campaign and now a key contributor to the SC PPC. The event advertisement read: "We can't just honor the 1969 strikers with words. We must honor them with action, by picking up the baton and continuing their organizing work and building a statewide Poor People's Campaign." Interestingly, the statement responds to the challenge that Rosetta Simmons issued to future activists during an interview with me in 2009 where she said, "We paved the way. There is a corridor here. Why can't you get in line and do something for yourself?"[6]

The movement that culminated with the spring 1969 strike has taken on different meanings for the various parties involved which ultimately shaped the movement and its outcome. Looking back at this moment in labor and civil rights history, workers' demand for equality and economic justice coupled with their insistence on being treated with respect and human dignity were the central motivations of organized hospital workers. Workers viewed these as their inalienable rights and believed that achieving them would provide a means to ensure a better life for themselves and their families. Hundreds of working-class African American women forged the 1969 hospital workers' campaign in opposition to years of discrimination, disrespect, and disregard. While both local and national leaders viewed this as an opportunity to further their perspective agendas, for hospital workers it was a response to a need and a rejection of the persistent efforts to undermine their livelihood and dignity.

NOTES

Introduction

1. Jacquelyn D. Hall, "The Long Civil Rights Movement and the Political Uses of the Past," *The Journal of American History* 91, no. 4 (March 2005): 1233–1263; Mary Moultrie, interview by author, June 23, 2008, digital voice recording, Charleston, SC; United States Department of Labor, accessed October 12, 2023, https://www.dol.gov/agencies/whd/minimum-wage/history/chart; U.S. Bureau of the Census, "24 Million Americans: Poverty in the United States, 1969," in *Current Population Reports*, series P-60, no. 76, accessed April 11, 2017, https://www2.census.gov/prod2/popscan/p60-076.pdf.

2. Robert Korstad, *Civil Rights Unionism: Tobacco Workers and the Struggle for Democracy in the Mid-Twentieth-Century South* (Chapel Hill: University of North Carolina Press, 2003), 120–23; Robert Korstad and Nelson Lichtenstein, "Opportunities Found and Lost: Labor, Radicals, and the Early Civil Rights Movement," *The Journal of American History* 75, no. 3 (December 1988): 786–811; Karen B. Sacks, *Caring by the Hour: Women, Work, and Organizing at Duke Medical Center* (Urbana: University of Illinois Press, 1988), 13–14, 65–67.

3. Adam Parker, "A lunch unserved: How the 1960 Kress sit-in changed Charleston," *The Post and Courier*, August 3, 2010; Judge Clarence Singletary, interview by Leon Fink, voice recording, February 27, 1980; Millicent Brown, Clerc Cooper, and John Hale, *Somebody Had to Do It: First Children in School Desegregation*, Lowcountry Digital History Initiative, College of Charleston, accessed July 24, 2016, http://ldhi.library.cofc.edu/exhibits/show/somebody_had_to_do_it; Hall, "The Long Civil Rights Movement," 1233–1263. In 1959, J. Arthur Brown, then-president of the Charleston chapter of the NAACP, filed a lawsuit to have to his high school age daughter, Minerva, attend an all-white school. While the case was pending, in the fall of 1960, several other Black students, including his younger daughter Millicent, applied to transfer to all-white schools. The local school board denied their applications. Before Minerva's case was settled, she graduated from high school, and her younger sister Millicent became the first listed plaintiff out of eleven on the case of *Millicent Brown et al v. Charleston County School Board, District 20*. Judge Robert Martin of the United States District Court of South Carolina ordered the school district to accept the students' application and admit them to the all-white schools to which they applied.

Chapter 1: Charleston's Local Protest Tradition

1. Aldon D. Morris, *The Origins of the Civil Rights Movement: Black Communities Organizing for Change* (New York: The Free Press), x.

2. Felice F. Knight, "Portrait of a Community Activist: William 'Bill' Saunders and the Black Freedom Struggle in Charleston, SC, 1951–2004" (MA thesis, The College of Charleston, 2006), 11–12; Morris, *The Origins of the Civil Rights Movement*, x; William Saunders, interview by Kerry Taylor and author, June 17, 2008, digital voice recording, Charleston, SC; Editorial, "That's Esau, as in Literacy," *The Charleston Post and Courier*, April 27, 2012; Peter F. Lau, *Democracy Rising: South Carolina and the Fight for Black Equality since 1865* (Lexington: University of Kentucky Press, 2006), 219–20; The Progressive Club, "Our History," accessed November 9, 2022, https://progressiveclub.org/our-history/.

3. Katherine M. Charron, *Freedom's Teacher: The Life of Septima Clark* (Chapel Hill: University of North Carolina Press, 2009), 223–25; Knight, "Portrait of a Community Activist," 11–12; Mary Moultrie, June 23, 2008; Editorial, "That's Esau, as in Literacy," *The Charleston Post and Courier*, April 27, 2012; The Progressive Club, "Our History"; Stephen O'Neill, "The Struggle for Black Equality Comes to Charleston: The Hospital Strike of 1969," *South Carolina Historical Association*, 1986, 82–91, from the "Hospital Strike" folder, Avery Research Center for African American History and Culture, Charleston, SC; Lau, *Democracy Rising*, 137, 219–20; Esau Jenkins Biographical Note from the Esau Jenkins Papers, Avery Research Center for African American History and Culture, Charleston, SC.

4. Charron, *Freedom's Teacher*, 223–25; Knight, "Portrait of a Community Activist," 11–12; Mary Moultrie, interview by author, June 23, 2008; Editorial, "That's Esau, as in Literacy," *The Charleston Post and Courier*, April 27, 2012; The Progressive Club, "Our History"; Lowcountry Digital History Initiative, "The Progressive Club, Johns Island," accessed November 9, 2022, https://ldhi.library.cofc.edu/exhibits/show/septima_clark/virtual-tour/the-progressive-club; "This civil rights-era bus was in a backyard on Johns Island. Now it's on display in D.C.," *The Post and Courier*, September 17, 2019, https://www.postandcourier.com/news/this-civil-rights-era-bus-was-in-a-backyard-on-johns-island-now-its-on/article_48695ae2-d005-11e9-bb6d-932ad4c6f156.html; O'Neill, "The Struggle for Black Equality Comes to Charleston," 82–91; Lau, *Democracy Rising*, 137, 219–20; Esau Jenkins Biographical Note from the Esau Jenkins Papers.

5. *Sisters in the Struggle: African American Women in the Civil Rights-Black Power Movement*, edited by Bettye Collier-Thomas and V.P. Franklin, *Women in the Civil Rights Movement: Trailblazers & Torchbearers, 1941–1965*, edited by Vicki L. Crawford, Jacqueline Anne Rouse, and Barbara Woods, and *How Long? How Long?: African American Women in the Struggle for Civil Rights* by Belinda Robnett are seminal works on Black women in the civil rights movement that explore the distinct nature of Black women's activism and provide key terms for defining it; Linda A. Lennon and Ruth M. Miller, *The Angel Oak* (Charleston: Tradd Street Press, 1989), 24–26; Charron, *Freedom's Teacher*, 2, 226; John Meffert, Sherman E. Pyatt, and the Avery Research Center, *Charleston, South Carolina* (Charleston: Arcadia Publishing, 2000), 56.

6. Charron, *Freedom's Teacher*, 2, 5, 217, 226–30; Belinda Robnett, *How Long? How Long?: African-American Women in the Struggle for Civil Rights* (New York: Oxford

University Press, 1997), 36–37; Jacqueline A. Rouse, "'We Seek to Know . . . in Order to Speak the Truth': Nurturing the Seeds of Discontent—Septima P. Clark and Participatory Leadership" in *Sisters in the Struggle: African American Women in the Civil Rights-Black Power Movement*, ed. Bettye Collier-Thomas and V. P. Franklin (New York: New York University Press, 2001), 96.

7. Mary Moultrie, interview by author, June 23, 2008; Mary Moultrie, interview by author, June 26, 2009, digital voice recording, Charleston, SC; Mary Moultrie, interview by Leon Fink, February 28, 1980, voice recording, Charleston, SC, National Union of Hospital and Health Care Employees (Local 1199) Records, 1938–1972, Catherwood Library Kheel Center, Cornell University, Ithaca, NY; Mary Moultrie, interview by Jean-Claude Bouffard, July 28, 1982, cassette recording, location unknown, National Union of Hospital and Health Care Employees (Local 1199) Records, 1938–1972, Catherwood Library Kheel Center, Cornell University, Ithaca, NY.

8. Mary Moultrie, interview by author, June 23, 2008; Mary Moultrie, interview by author, June 26, 2009; Mary Moultrie, interview by Leon Fink, February 28, 1980; Mary Moultrie, interview by Jean-Claude Bouffard, July 28, 1982.

9. Mary Moultrie, interview by author, June 26, 2009; Mary Moultrie, interview by Jean-Claude Bouffard, July 28, 1982; David White, interview by Leon Fink, June 5, 1979, audio recording, location unknown, National Union of Hospital and Health Care Employees (Local 1199) Records, 1938–1972, Catherwood Library Kheel Center, Cornell University, Ithaca, NY.

10. Mary Moultrie, interview by author, June 23, 2008; William Saunders, interview by author, June 23, 2008, digital voice recording, Charleston, SC.

11. Mary Moultrie, interview by author, June 26, 2009; Mary Moultrie, interview by Leon Fink, February 28, 1980; Mary Moultrie, interview by Jean-Claude Bouffard, July 28, 1982; John E. Wise, interview by Leon Fink, February 28, 1980, voice recording, Charleston, SC, National Union of Hospital and Health Care Employees (Local 1199) Records, 1938–1972, Catherwood Library Kheel Center, Cornell University, Ithaca, NY; United States Department of Labor, accessed October 12, 2023, https://www.dol.gov/agencies/whd/minimum-wage/history/chart. John E. Wise's assertion is partially corroborated by a hand-written document that includes a list of workers, their positions and their hourly wage. The document also includes another list of positions that striking workers held at the time with the associated hourly wage. The hourly wages listed ranged from $1.33 to $2.12 per hour.

12. Mary Moultrie, interview by Leon Fink, February 28, 1980; Mary Moultrie, interview by Jean-Claude Bouffard, July 28, 1982; Mary Moultrie, interview by author, June 23, 2008; O'Neill, "The Struggle for Black Equality Comes to Charleston," 82–91; Naomi White, interview by author, June 25, 2008, digital voice recording, Charleston, SC.

13. Leon Fink and Brian Greenberg, *Upheaval in the Quiet Zone: 1199SEIU and the Politics of Healthcare Unionism*, 2nd ed. (Urbana: University of Illinois Press, 2009), 33–34; William Saunders, interview by Kerry Taylor and author, June 17, 2008; William Saunders, interview by author, June 23, 2008; William Saunders, interview by Leon Fink, March 1, 1980, audio recording, Charleston, SC; Mary Moultrie, interview by author, June 26, 2009; Andrew Young, interview by Leon Fink, January 31, 1980, audio recording, Chapel

Hill, NC, National Union of Hospital and Health Care Employees (Local 1199) Records, 1938–1972, Catherwood Library Kheel Center, Cornell University, Ithaca, NY.

14. Knight, "Portrait of a Community Activist," 11–12; William Saunders, interview by Kerry Taylor and author, June 17, 2008; William Saunders, interview by Kerry Taylor, June 9, 2011, video recording, Charleston, SC; Oceanic Linguistics Special Publications, "Gullah," in *A Bibliography of Pidgin and Creole Languages* (Honolulu: University of Hawaii Press, 1975), 468; Herb Frazier, "Saving Gullah Culture," *The Charleston Post and Courier*, May 25, 2004, sec. A1; National Park Service, "The Gullah Geechee," Gullah Geechee Cultural Heritage Corridor Commission, accessed September 8, 2023, https://gullahgeecheecorridor.org/thegullahgeechee/.

15. Knight, "Portrait of a Community Activist," 11–12; William Saunders, interview by Kerry Taylor and author, June 17, 2008.

16. Knight, "Portrait of a Community Activist," 11–12; O'Neill, "The Struggle for Black Equality Comes to Charleston"; William Saunders, interview by Kerry Taylor and author, June 17, 2008; William Saunders, interview by Kerry Taylor, June 9, 2011; Esau Jenkins Biographical Note from the Esau Jenkins Papers.

17. William Saunders, interview by Kerry Taylor and author, June 17, 2008; William Saunders, interview by Kerry Taylor, June 9, 2011.

18. William Saunders, interview by Kerry Taylor and author, June 17, 2008; William Saunders, interview by Kerry Taylor, June 9, 2011; Knight, "Portrait of a Community Activist," 11–12.

19. William Saunders, interview by author, June 23, 2008, digital voice recording, Charleston, SC; William Saunders, interview by Leon Fink, March 1, 1980; Knight, "Portrait of a Community Activist," 28–29; William Saunders, interview by author, July 7, 2010, digital voice recording, Charleston, SC.

20. Mary Moultrie, interview by Jean-Claude Bouffard, July 28, 1982; Isaiah Bennett, interview by Leon Fink, February 29, 1980, National Union of Hospital and Health Care Employees (Local 1199) Records, 1938–1972, Catherwood Library Kheel Center, Cornell University, Ithaca, NY; Isaiah Bennett Biographical Note from the Isaiah Bennett Papers, Avery Research Center for African American History and Culture, Charleston, SC. It is difficult to determine from the archival material the exact year he joined the union, but based on interviews and conversations with members of the Charleston community, Bennett was a staunch union man. It is therefore safe to assume that he joined the union as soon as he began working at the American Tobacco Company's Cigar Factory.

21. Isaiah Bennett, interview by Leon Fink, February 29, 1980; Lillie Doster, interview by author, June 25, 2008, digital voice recording, Charleston, SC; Karl Korstad, "Tobacco Road, Union Style," *New Masses*, May 7, 1946, 13–15; Dwana Waugh, "Charleston's Cigar Factory Strike, 1945–1946," Lowcountry Digital History Initiative, College of Charleston, Charleston, SC, accessed October 2, 2015, http://ldhi.library.cofc.edu/exhibits/show/cigar_factory .

22. Isaiah Bennett, interview by Leon Fink, February 29, 1980; Lillie Doster, interview by author, June 25, 2008; K. Korstad, "Tobacco Road, Union Style," 13–15; Waugh, "Charleston's Cigar Factory Strike, 1945–1946."

23. Isaiah Bennett, interview by Leon Fink, February 29, 1980; Lillie Doster, interview by author, June 25, 2008; K. Korstad, "Tobacco Road, Union Style," 13–15; Waugh, "Charleston's Cigar Factory Strike, 1945–1946."

24. Isaiah Bennett, interview by Leon Fink, February 29, 1980; Lillie Doster, interview by author, June 25, 2008; K. Korstad, "Tobacco Road, Union Style," 13–15; Waugh, "Charleston's Cigar Factory Strike, 1945–1946."

25. Isaiah Bennett, interview by Leon Fink, February 29, 1980; Lillie Doster, interview by author, June 25, 2008; K. Korstad, "Tobacco Road, Union Style," 13–15; Waugh, "Charleston's Cigar Factory Strike, 1945–1946."

26. Isaiah Bennett, interview by Leon Fink, February 29, 1980; Lillie Doster, interview by author, June 25, 2008; K. Korstad, "Tobacco Road, Union Style," 13–15; Waugh, "Charleston's Cigar Factory Strike, 1945–1946."

Chapter 2: Hospital Workers and Health-Care Activism

1. The name "Medical Society of South Carolina" was a partial misnomer, as the society was located in Charleston and was not a statewide organization. Joseph I. Waring, "History of Medical University of South Carolina," *Southern Medical Journal* 67, no. 8 (1974): 888; Joseph I. Waring, *A History of Medicine in South Carolina* (Columbia: The South Carolina Medical Association, 1964), 119; The City of Charleston, "Centennial Celebration of the Incorporation of the City of Charleston," August 13, 1883, in the University of North Carolina-Chapel Hill Digital Library, accessed April 10, 2017, https://babel-hathitrust-org.libproxy.lib.unc.edu/cgi/pt?id=loc.ark:/13960/t54f2jh7c;view=1up;seq=175; Joseph I. Waring, "Charleston Medicine 1800–1860," *Journal of the History of Medicine and Allied Sciences* 31, no. 3 (1976): 320–22, 340.

2. Simon Lewis, "Slavery, Memory, and the History of the 'Atlantic Now': Charleston, South Carolina and Global Racial/Economic Hierarchy," *Journal of Postcolonial Writing* 45, no. 2 (2009): 125–26; Blain Roberts and Ethan Kytle, "Looking the Thing in the Face: Slavery, Race, and the Commemorative Landscape of Charleston, South Carolina, 1865–2010," *The Journal of Southern History* 78, no. 3 (August 2012): 640; Waring, "History of Medical University of South Carolina," 888; Waring, "Charleston Medicine 1800–1860," 329, 340; Philip G. Grose, *South Carolina at the Brink: Robert McNair and the Politics of Civil Rights* (Columbia: University of South Carolina Press, 2006), 242. Medical College of South Carolina opened as an educational institution in 1824. The hospital was not established at the same time that the school opened.

3. Medical Society of South Carolina, *Rules and Regulations for the Government of the Trustees and Officers of Roper Hospital* (Charleston: Evans & Cogswell, 1861), 6–7, in Rare Books Collection, Perkins Library, Duke University, Durham, NC; Waring, "Charleston Medicine 1800–1860," 340–41; The City of Charleston, "Centennial Celebration of the Incorporation of the City of Charleston," August 13, 1883, in the University of North Carolina-Chapel Hill Digital Library, accessed April 10, 2017, https://babel-hathitrust-org.libproxy.lib.unc.edu/cgi/pt?id=loc.ark:/13960/t54f2jh7c;view=1up;seq=175.

4. *Missouri ex rel. Gaines vs. Canada*, 305 U.S. 337 (1938) in *The Greenwood Dictionary of Education*, John W. Collins III and Nancy P. O'Brien, eds (Santa Barbara: ABC-CLIO, 2011), 294; Karen K. Thomas, *Deluxe Jim Crow: Civil Rights and American Health Policy, 1935–1954* (Athens: University of Georgia Press, 2011), 165–66; Karen K. Thomas, "Dr. Jim Crow: The University of North Carolina, The Regional Medical School for Negroes, and the Desegregation of South Medical Education, 1945–1960," *The Journal of African American History* 88, no. 3 (Summer 2003): 229–33; E. H. Beardsley, "Good-Bye to Jim Crow: The Desegregation of Southern Hospitals, 1945–70," *Bulletin of the History of Medicine* 60, no. 3 (Fall 1986): 368; Hall, "The Long Civil Rights Movement," 1243–1247, 1252–1253; Rosetta Simmons, interview by author, June 25, 2008, digital voice recording, Charleston, SC. The sources do not make it clear when Medical College Hospital began accepting African American patients.

5. U.S. Congress, *Hospital Survey and Construction Act with Amendments*, Public Law 725, 79th Cong., 2d sess. (August 13, 1946), 3–4.; US Commission on Civil Rights, *Equal Opportunity in Hospitals and Health Facilities: Civil Rights Policies Under the Hill-Burton Program*, Commission on Civil Rights Special Publication, no. 2 (March 1965), 3–5, accessed December 15, 2022, https://www.nlm.nih.gov/exhibition/forallthepeople/img/1706.pdf. The Hospital Survey and Construction Act of 1946 (also known as the Hill-Burton Act) was developed with the premise that it would provide federal funding for hospital construction to improve health care for everyone by increasing the number of facilities and renovating those in need of upgrade. The legislation mandated that all persons, regardless of race, creed, color, or ability to pay, within the vicinity of these hospitals be served. However it supported the Jim crow ideology, "but an exception shall be made in cases where separate hospital facilities are provided for separate population groups, if the plan [state plan] makes equitable provision on basis of need for facilities and service of like quality for each group"; Thomas, "Dr. Jim Crow," 229–33; John Dittmer, *The Good Doctors: The Medical Committee for Human Rights and the Struggle for Social Justice in Health Care* (New York: Bloomsbury Press, 2009), 133–34; "'Separate but Equal' Hill-Burton Clause Held Unconstitutional," *Afro-American*, November 9, 1963; "High Court Leaves Ban on Separate-But-Equal Clause in Hill-Burton Act," *Wall Street Journal*, March 3, 1964; David B. Smith, "Stealth Capture: The Civil Rights Movement and the Implementation of Medicare," *Poverty and Race* 25, no. 2 (April–June 2016): 1–2; Catherine Conner, "'The University That Ate Birmingham': The Healthcare Industry, Urban Development, and Neoliberalism," *Journal of Urban History* 42, no. 2 (January 29, 2016): 288. Abraham Ribicoff, US Department of Health, Education, and Welfare Secretary under President John F. Kennedy, had recommended to Congress that the "separate-but-equal" clause be removed from the Hill-Burton Act in 1962. See "HEW for Changing Hill-Burton Act," *Afro-American*, June 23, 1962, for the complete article.

6. Dittmer, *The Good Doctors*, x, 18–19; Beardsley, "Good-Bye to Jim Crow," 367.

7. US Congress, *Hospital Survey and Construction Act with Amendments*, 3–4; US Commission on Civil Rights, *Equal Opportunity in Hospitals and Health Facilities*, 3–5; Ezelle Sanford III, "Civil Rights and Healthcare: Remembering Simkins v. Cone (1963)," *Black Perspectives*, February 4, 2017, accessed December 22, 2022, https://www.aaihs.org/civil-rights-and-healthcare-remembering-simkins-v-cone-1963/#:~:text=Cone%20

Health%20commemorated%20the%20legacy,of%20the%20Guilford%20County%20 Courthouse; Karen Kruse Thomas, "Simkins v. Cone," *Encyclopedia of North Carolina*, ed. William S. Powell (Chapel Hill: University of North Carolina Press, 2006, accessed January 16, 2023, https://www.ncpedia.org/simkins-v-cone; Karen K. Thomas, "Dr. Jim Crow: The University of North Carolina, The Regional Medical School for Negroes, and the Desegregation of South Medical Education, 1945–1960," *The Journal of African American History* 88, no. 3 (Summer 2003): 229–33; Dittmer, *The Good Doctors*, 133–34; "'Separate but Equal' Hill-Burton Clause Held Unconstitutional"; "High Court Leaves Ban on Separate-But-Equal Clause in Hill-Burton Act"; Smith, "Stealth Capture," 1–2; Conner, "'The University That Ate Birmingham,'" 288. The Public Health Service, founded in 1912, is moved to the Department of Health, Education, and Welfare in 1953.

8. US Commission on Civil Rights, *Equal Opportunity in Hospitals and Health Facilities*, 3–5; Smith, "Stealth Capture," 1–2, 12; Waring, "History of Medical University of South Carolina," 893–94; Grose, *South Carolina at the Brink*, 242–43; "41 Complaints Filed Against: 29 More Dixie Hospitals," *Afro-American*, March 13, 1965; "NAACP Complaints Aims to Cut Funds to Biased Hospitals," *New York Amsterdam News*, March 13, 1965; "HEW Urged to End Bias in Southern Hospitals," *New York Amsterdam News*, March 26, 1966. Complaints had also been filed against St. Francis Xavier Hospital, another Charleston institution.

9. Hugh A. Brimm to Dr. William McCord, September 19, 1968, Governor Robert McNair Papers, South Carolina Political Collection, University of South Carolina, Columbia, SC; Hugh A. Brimm to Dr. William McCord, June 5, 1969, Governor Robert McNair Papers, South Carolina Political Collection, University of South Carolina, Columbia, SC.

10. Hugh A. Brimm to Dr. William McCord, September 19, 1968.

11. Fink and Greenberg, *Upheaval in the Quiet Zone*, 131–33; Jack Bass, "Hospital Strike," 8. The source of this article is unknown but according to the context its approximate publication date is May 1969; Dr. William McCord to Attorney General Daniel R. McLeod, November 26, 1965, William M. McCord Papers, Waring Historical Library, Medical University of South Carolina, Charleston; John E. Wise, interview by Leon Fink, February 28, 1980, audio recording, Charleston, SC, National Union of Hospital and Health Care Employees (Local 1199) Records, 1938–1972, Catherwood Library Kheel Center, Cornell University, Ithaca, NY; Hugh A. Brimm to Dr. William McCord, September 19, 1968.

12. According to the US Department of Labor website (https://www.dol.gov/agencies /whd/minimum-wage/state#sc), South Carolina does not have a minimum wage law. Based on the oral interviews, the grievances around low wages were based on "nonprofessional" wages as compared to the wages white nurses and doctors were paid. It seems that even the Black women who had formal training were paid substantially less than their white counterparts. Handwritten lists of workers that included their hourly wage at the time of the strike from Medical College Hospital, Roper Hospital, and Charleston County Hospital from the National Union of Hospital and Health Care Employees (Local 1199) Records, 1938–1972, Catherwood Library Kheel Center, Cornell University, Ithaca; Fink and Greenberg, *Upheaval in the Quiet Zone*, 131; Hugh A. Brimm to Dr. William McCord, September 19, 1968; United States Department of Labor, accessed October 12, 2023, https://

www.dol.gov/agencies/whd/minimum-wage/history/chart; United States Department of Labor, "History of Changes to the Minimum Wage Law," accessed February 16, 2025, https://www.dol.gov/agencies/whd/minimum-wage/history#:~:text=The%201961%20amendments%20greatly%20expanded,an%20hour%20in%20September%201963.

13. Laurie B. Green, *Battling the Plantation Mentality: Memphis and the Black Freedom Struggle* (Chapel Hill: University of North Carolina Press, 2007), 1–2, 259.

14. Rosetta Simmons, interview by author, June 25, 2008; Rosetta Simmons, interview by author, August 26, 2009, digital voice recording, Charleston, SC; Dr. William McCord to Attorney General Daniel R. McLeod, November 26, 1965; Mary Moultrie, interview by Leon Fink, February 28, 1980.

15. Moe Foner and Dan North, *Not for Bread Alone: A Memoir* (Ithaca, NY: Cornell University Press, 2002), 36–38; John Hennen, *A Union for Appalachian Healthcare Workers: The Radical Roots and Hard Fights of Local 1199* (Morgantown: West Virginia University Press, 2021), 17–18; Mary Moultrie, interview by Jean-Claude Bouffard, July 28, 1982; Rosetta Simmons, interview by author, June 25, 2008; Mary Moultrie, William Saunders, and Rosetta Simmons, interview by Kerry Taylor, March 5, 2009, digital voice recording, Charleston, SC, Charleston and the Long Civil Rights Movement series, The Citadel Oral History Program, The Citadel, Charleston, SC.

16. Foner and North, *Not for Bread Alone*, 68; Mary Moultrie, interview by Jean-Claude Bouffard, July 28, 1982; Rosetta Simmons, interview by author, June 25, 2008; Mary Moultrie, William Saunders, and Rosetta Simmons, interview by Kerry Taylor, March 5, 2009.

17. William Saunders, interview by author, June 23, 2008; Isaiah Bennett, interview by Leon Fink, February 29, 1980; Richard L. Black, Charleston County Manager, "The Charleston Hospital Workers' Strike—A Case or a Cause," August 26, 1969, William M. McCord Papers, Waring Historical Library, Medical University of South Carolina, Charleston; Rosetta Simmons, interview by author, June 25, 2008, digital voice recording, Charleston, SC.

18. Rosetta Simmons, interview by author, June 25, 2008; Rosetta Simmons, interview by author, August 26, 2009, digital voice recording, Charleston, SC; Patricia Hill Collins, *Black Feminist Thought: Knowledge, Consciousness, and the Politics of Empowerment*, 2nd ed. (New York: Routledge, 2000), 45.

19. Mary Moultrie, interview by Jean-Claude Bouffard, July 28, 1982; Mary Moultrie, William Saunders, and Rosetta Simmons, interview by Kerry Taylor, March 5, 2009; David White, interview by Leon Fink, June 5, 1979.

20. Mary Moultrie, interview by Jean-Claude Bouffard, July 28, 1982; Mary Moultrie, William Saunders, and Rosetta Simmons, interview by Kerry Taylor, March 5, 2009; Rosetta Simmons, interview by author, June 25, 2008; David White, interview by Leon Fink, June 5, 1979.

21. Lillie Doster, interview by author, June 25, 2008; Waugh, "Charleston's Cigar Factory Strike, 1945–1946."

22. Lillie Doster, interview by author, June 25, 2008; Mary Moultrie, interview by Jean-Claude Bouffard, July 28, 1982; Auxiliary Workers of Medical College Hospital, "List of Grievances" from the Septima Clark Papers, Avery Research Center for African American

History and Culture, Charleston, SC (This is a handwritten document that is mostly likely a draft of the final product. It is unclear whether this list of grievances could have been the "letter" that Mary Moultrie and Lillie Doster penned to Dr. William McCord or if it could be a second document that was sent to the administrator. The document includes a space for the date, but it has been left blank. The document is clearly a communication from the group of organizing workers prior to unionization because the workers are referred to as "Auxillary Workers of Medical College Hospital"); Rosetta Simmons, interview by author, June 25, 2008; Mary Moultrie, interview by author, June 26, 2009.

23. Auxiliary Workers of Medical College Hospital, "List of Grievances"; Mary Moultrie, March 28, 1969, telegram addressee unknown, Isaiah Bennett Papers, Avery Research Center for African American History and Culture, Charleston, SC.

24. Mary Moultrie, interview by author, June 23, 2008; Mary Moultrie, interview by Jean-Claude Bouffard, July 28, 1982; Auxiliary Workers of Medical College Hospital, "List of Grievances."

25. Mary Moultrie, interview by Jean-Claude Bouffard, July 28, 1982; Mary Moultrie, interview by author, June 23, 2008; William McCord, letter to Medical College employees, October 14, 1968, National Union of Hospital and Health Care Employees (Local 1199) Records, 1938-1972, Catherwood Library Kheel Center, Cornell University, Ithaca, NY; William McCord, letter to John Cummings, president of Retail, Wholesale, and Tobacco Workers Local 15A, October 14, 1968, National Union of Hospital and Health Care Employees (Local 1199) Records, 1938–1972, Catherwood Library Kheel Center, Cornell University, Ithaca, NY; John E. Wise, vice president of Medical College, letter to John Cummings, November 12, 1968, National Union of Hospital and Health Care Employees (Local 1199) Records, 1938–1972, Catherwood Library Kheel Center, Cornell University, Ithaca, NY; Mary Moultrie, William Saunders and Rosetta Simmons, interview by Kerry Taylor, March 5, 2009; Fink and Greenberg, *Upheaval in the Quiet Zone*, 135.

26. Isaiah Bennett, interview by Leon Fink, February 29, 1980; Fink and Greenberg, *Upheaval in the Quiet Zone*, 135; William Saunders, interview by Kieran Taylor and author, June 17, 2008, digital voice recording, Charleston, SC; William Saunders, interview by author, June 23, 2008; Otis Robinson led the "Hospital Workers' Defense Team" along with Saunders during the strike.

Chapter 3: "Union Power"

1. Fink and Greenberg, *Upheaval in the Quiet Zone*, 19–20; Foner and North, *Not for Bread Alone*, 32–33.

2. Fink and Greenberg, *Upheaval in the Quiet Zone*, 19–27; Foner and North, *Not for Bread Alone*, 32–33; Leon Fink, "Union Power, Soul Power: The Story of 1199B and Labor's Search for a Southern Strategy," *Southern Changes*, March/April 1983, 9–10, Steve Estes Papers, Avery Research Center for African American History and Culture, Charleston, SC; Fink and Greenberg, *Upheaval in the Quiet Zone*, 129, 134; Philip S. Foner, *Women and the American Labor Movement: From the First Trade Unions to the Present* (Chicago: Haymarket Books, 2018), 403–5; Henry Nicholas, interview by Brian Greenberg, January

11, 1978, audio recording, Local 1199 offices in New York, NY; Grose, *South Carolina at the Brink*, 249; "Charleston," from the National Union of Hospital and Health Care Employees (Local 1199) Records, 1938-1972, Catherwood Library Kheel Center, Cornell University, Ithaca. This document lays out how the union planned to approach the situation in Charleston and ultimately charter a local union.

    3. P. S. Foner, *Women and the American Labor Movement*, 388-403.

    4. Fink and Greenberg, *Upheaval in the Quiet Zone*, 17-18. M. Foner and North, *Not for Bread Alone*, 38-40.

    5. Fink and Greenberg, *Upheaval in the Quiet Zone*, 16-19.

    6. Isaiah Bennett, interview by Leon Fink, February 29, 1980; Fink and Greenberg, *Upheaval in the Quiet Zone*, 135; Mary Moultrie, interview by author, June 23, 2008; David White, interview by Leon Fink, June 5, 1979.

    7. Fink and Greenberg, *Upheaval in the Quiet Zone*, 129, 135; Mary Moultrie, interview by author, June 23, 2008; David White, interview by Leon Fink, June 5, 1979; David White, report to Local 1199 on Charleston, SC, National Union of Hospital and Health Care Employees (Local 1199) Records, 1938-1972, Catherwood Library Kheel Center, Cornell University, Ithaca, NY; Fink, "Union Power, Soul Power," 9-10; Henry Nicholas, interview by Brian Greenberg, January 11, 1978; Grose, *South Carolina at the Brink*, 249; "Charleston," from the National Union of Hospital and Health Care Employees (Local 1199) Records, 1938-1972, Catherwood Library Kheel Center, Cornell University, Ithaca.

    8. Mary Moultrie, interview by author, June 23, 2008.

    9. Mary Moultrie, interview by author, June 23, 2008; Charles Payne, "Men Led, but Women Organized: Movement Participation of Women in the Mississippi Delta," in *Women in the Civil Rights Movement: Trailblazers & Torchbearers, 1941-1965*, ed. Vicki L. Crawford, Jacqueline Anne Rouse, and Barbara Woods (Bloomington: Indiana University Press, 1990), 1.

    10. Sally Ward Maggard, "'We're Fighting Millionaires!': The Clash of Gender and Class in Appalachian Women's Union Organizing," in *No Middle Ground: Women and Radical Protest*, ed. Kathleen M. Blee (New York: New York University Press, 1998), 289-91, 294-95.

    11. Mary Moultrie, interview by author, June 23, 2008; P. S. Foner, *Women and the American Labor Movement*, 388-403; Payne, "Men Led, but Women Organized," 1-2, 8-9, 11; Meeting Minutes of a December 11, 1968 meeting with the following attendees: Reginald Barrett, Bishop Rembert, Rev. Blake, members of the NAACP compliance survey team, Mr. Coaxum, Jack Bradford, Mrs. Frazier, Claire Brown, Mrs. Alston, Mary Moultrie, Charles Fennessy, John Wise, Mr. Porter, and Mr. Huff, William M. McCord Papers, Waring Historical Library, Medical University of South Carolina, Charleston, SC; Minutes of President's Meeting with Employees of the Medical College of South Carolina, March 7, 1969, William M. McCord Papers, Waring Historical Library, Medical University of South Carolina, Charleston, SC.

    12. Fink and Greenberg, *Upheaval in the Quiet Zone*, 134; Isaiah Bennett, interview by Leon Fink, February 29, 1980; Isaiah Bennett, November 29, 1968, letter to Reginald Barrett, Retail, Wholesale, and Department Store Union, Local 1199 Drug and Hospital Employee Union Records, Kheel Center for Labor-Management Documentation and Archives, Cornell University Library.

13. F. W. Kinard, M.D., December 2, 1968, letter to William McCord, Governor Robert E. McNair Papers, South Carolina Political Collections, University of South Carolina; John C. Hawk Jr., M.D., December 5, 1968, letter to William McCord, Governor Robert E. McNair Papers, South Carolina Political Collections, University of South Carolina; Isaiah Bennett, March 23, 1969, telegram to Delbert L. Woods, Vice President of South Carolina NAACP, Isaiah Bennett Papers, Avery Research Center for African American History and Culture, Charleston, South Carolina; Isaiah Bennett, February 28, 1969, telegram to Representative Robert Turner, Isaiah Bennett Papers, Avery Research Center for African American History and Culture, Charleston, South Carolina Isaiah Bennett, March 17, 1969, telegram to J. Palmer Gaillard, Mayor of Charleston in 1969, Isaiah Bennett Papers, Avery Research Center for African American History and Culture, Charleston, South Carolina; Isaiah Bennett, March 24, 1969, telegram to Shirley Chisholm, Isaiah Bennett Papers, Avery Research Center for African American History and Culture, Charleston, SC.

14. William McCord, October 18, 1968 letter to Daniel R. McLeod, South Carolina State Attorney General, William M. McCord Papers, Waring Historical Library, Medical University of South Carolina, Charleston; F. M. Ball, M.D., December 2, 1968, letter to William McCord, William M. McCord Papers, Waring Historical Library, Medical University of South Carolina, Charleston; Laurie L. Brown, M.D., December 13, 1968, letter to Isaiah Bennett, William M. McCord Papers, Waring Historical Library, Medical University of South Carolina, Charleston, SC; William D. McDonald, "Hospital Employees Charge Racial Bias," *The State*, February 27, 1969; "Medical College Still Refuses to Negotiate," *The State*, February 28, 1969; Barbara Williams, "There's Trouble at the Medical College," *Charleston News and Courier*, March 2, 1969; "Hospital Workers Ask HEW Probe," *Charleston News and Courier*, March 3, 1969.

15. McDonald, "Hospital Employees Charge Racial Bias"; "Medical College Still Refuses to Negotiate"; Williams, "There's Trouble at the Medical College"; Barbara Williams, "Hospital Sets Monthly Sessions on Grievances," *Charleston News and Courier*, March 4, 1969.

16. Williams, "There's Trouble at the Medical College"; "Hospital Workers Denied Hearing," *Charleston News and Courier*, March 13, 1969.

17. Father Henry Grant, interview by Leon Fink, February 27, 1980, voice recording, Charleston, SC, National Union of Hospital and Health Care Employees (Local 1199) Records, 1938–1972, Catherwood Library Kheel Center, Cornell University, Ithaca, NY.

18. Father Henry Grant, interview by Leon Fink, February 27, 1980; William Saunders, interview by Kerry Taylor and author, June 17, 2008; William Saunders, interview by Kerry Taylor, June 9, 2011; Mary Moultrie, William Saunders and Rosetta Simmons, interview by Kerry Taylor, March 5, 2009.

19. Father Henry Grant, interview by Leon Fink, February 27, 1980; Abstract of Henry Grant Papers, Avery Research Center for African American History and Culture, College of Charleston, Charleston, SC.

20. Father Henry Grant, interview by Leon Fink, February 27, 1980.

21. "Hospital Workers Ask HEW Probe"; Williams, "Hospital Sets Monthly Sessions on Grievances"; Milla Sanes and John Schmitt, *Regulation of Public Sector Collective*

Bargaining in the States (Washington: Center for Economic and Policy Research, 2014), 57; Ashley Byrd, "SC Senate Bill Officially Bars Union for Government Employees," *Palmetto Primary*, December 23, 2013.

22. Williams, "Hospital Sets Monthly Sessions on Grievances."

23. Williams, "Hospital Sets Monthly Sessions on Grievances."

24. "Union Workers Dislike Dr. McCord's Proposal," *Charleston News and Courier*, March 5, 1969; "Dr. McCord Meets with Employees," *Charleston News and Courier*, March 7, 1969.

25. Mary Moultrie, interview by Jean-Claude Bouffard, July 28, 1982; Statement from Medical College of South Carolina regarding the details of March 17, 1969, stamped as received on March 19, 1969, Governor Robert E. McNair Papers, South Carolina Political Collections, University of South Carolina; Isaiah Bennett, telegram to Mayor J. Palmer Gaillard, March 17, 1969, Isaiah Bennett Papers, Avery Research Center for African American History and Culture, Charleston, SC; Isaiah Bennett, telegram to Governor Robert E. McNair, March 17, 1969, Isaiah Bennett Papers, Avery Research Center for African American History and Culture, Charleston, SC. The twelve workers that were terminated are referred to as the "magic" twelve and the "famous" twelve. There are two documents that list the workers: Mary Moultrie, Virginia Stanley, Daniel Andrew, Margaret Kelley, Rosalee Fields, Vera Smalls, Mary Grimes, Louise Brown, Annie Lee, Priscilla Gladden, Hazel White, and Helen Husser. "Magic Twelve," Governor Robert E. McNair Papers, South Carolina Political Collections, University of South Carolina; this document lists the twelve who were terminated on March 17, 1969, their positions, and their hourly wage; Mary Moultrie, interview by author, June 23, 2008; "The Famous 12 That Was Drove from the Hospital," Isaiah Bennett Papers, Avery Research Center for African American History and Culture, Charleston, SC; Board of Trustees of the Medical College of South Carolina, Regular Meeting Minutes, August 9, 1968, William M. McCord Papers, Waring Historical Library, Medical University of South Carolina, Charleston, SC.

26. Elaine S. Stanford, "Workers Picket Medical College: Injunction Granted to Halt Strike," *Charleston News and Courier*, March 21, 1969; Judge Clarence Singletary, interview by Leon Fink, voice recording, February 27, 1980, National Union of Hospital and Health Care Employees (Local 1199) Records, 1938–1972, Catherwood Library Kheel Center, Cornell University, Ithaca, NY; Grose, *South Carolina at the Brink*, 252.

27. Judge Clarence Singletary, interview by Leon Fink, February 27, 1980. Judge Clarence Singletary mistakenly placed the event in 1963.

28. Judge Clarence Singletary, interview by Leon Fink, February 27, 1980; Elaine S. Stanford, "Workers Picket Medical College: Injunction Granted to Halt Strike," *Charleston News and Courier*, March 21, 1969.

29. Stewart R. King and Elaine S. Stanford, "Judge Orders Halt to Port Walkout," *Charleston News and Courier*, March 4, 1969.

30. David White, interview by Leon Fink, June 5, 1979; Father Henry Grant, interview by Leon Fink, February 27, 1980; Reverend Thomas Duffy, interview by Leon Fink, February 28, 1980; Henry Nicholas, interview by Brian Greenberg, January 11, 1978.

31. Elaine S. Stanford and William Walker Jr., "Medical College Injunction Violated," *Charleston News and Courier*, March 22, 1969; Reverend Thomas Duffy, interview by Leon

Fink, February 28, 1980; Concerned Clergy Committee, "Peace with Justice Proposal," Governor Robert E. McNair Papers, South Carolina Political Collections, University of South Carolina, Columbia, SC.

32. Stanford and Walker, "Medical College Injunction Violated"; Reverend Thomas Duffy, interview by Leon Fink, February 28, 1980; Concerned Clergy Committee, "Peace with Justice Proposal"; Leo M. Croghan, letter to Governor McNair from the Liaison Committee of the Concerned Clergy Committee, March 29, 1969, Governor Robert E. McNair Papers, South Carolina Political Collections, University of South Carolina, Columbia, SC.

33. Elaine S. Stanford, "McCord Rejects Clergy Committee's Peace Proposal," *Charleston News and Courier*, April 3, 1969. Document has no title, but it was stamped as received in the governor's office on April 7, 1969. The use of personal pronouncs and language that refers to the hospital indicates that it is a document submitted by the hospital. The language also indicates that it may have been a press release that they shared a copy of with the governor's office. This document is from Governor Robert E. McNair Papers, South Carolina Political Collections, University of South Carolina, Columbia, SC.

34. Elaine S. Stanford, "McCord Rejects Clergy Committee's Peace Proposal."

35. Father Henry Grant, interview by Leon Fink, February 27, 1980, voice recording, Charleston, SC; Concerned Clergy Committee, "Peace with Justice Proposal"; Kathryn L. Nasstrom, "Down to Now: Memory, Narrative, and Women's Leadership in the Civil Rights Movement in Atlanta, Georgia," *Gender & History* 11, no. 1 (April 1999): 22; Collins, *Black Feminist Thought*, 203–4.

36. Stewart King, "More than 50 Pickets Arrested at Hospital," *Charleston News and Courier*, March 24, 1969.

37. Document from "GE" to "File" regarding "Local 1199-B—Medical College of South Carolina Hospital and County Hospital of Charleston" and the timeline of events regarding their early phase of their legal battles with the state and hospital, South Carolina," April 16, 1969, National Union of Hospital and Health Care Employees (Local 1199) Records, 1938–1972, Catherwood Library Kheel Center, Cornell University, Ithaca, NY; King, "More than 50 Pickets Arrested at Hospital"; Judge Clarence Singletary, interview by Leon Fink, February 27, 1980.

38. Stanford and Walker, "Medical College Injunction Violated"; File document drafted by "GE" regarding "Local 1199-B—Medical College of South Carolina Hospital and County Hospital of Charleston" and the timeline of events regarding their early phase of their legal battles with the state and hospital, South Carolina," April 16, 1969; Elaine Stanford, "Negotiators Meet in Hospital Strike," *Charleston News and Courier*, March 23, 1969; Grose, *South Carolina at the Brink*, 248–49; Eugene G. Eisner and I. Philip Sipser, "The Charleston Hospital Dispute: Organizing Public Employees and the Right to Strike," *St. John's Law Review* 45, no. 2 (December 1970): 260–61. The authors of this article provided Local 1199 with legal representation during the hospital workers strike. King, "More than 50 Pickets Arrested at Hospital"; Elaine Stanford, "Hospital Strikers Ordered to Obey Limiting Injunction," *Charleston News and Courier*, March 25, 1969.

39. Moe Foner, interview by Robert Master, August 29, 1985, voice recording, New York, NY, National Union of Hospital and Health Care Employees (Local 1199) Records,

1938–1972, Catherwood Library Kheel Center, Cornell University, Ithaca, NY; Isaiah Bennett, telegram to Sister Maria administrator at Saint Francis Xavier Hospital, March 24, 1969, Isaiah Bennett Papers, Avery Research Center for African American History and Culture, Charleston, SC; Sister Maria, telegram to Isaiah Bennett, March 27, 1969, Isaiah Bennett Papers, Avery Research Center for African American History and Culture, Charleston, SC; Elaine Stanford, "Federal Judge Remands Hospital Case to State," *Charleston News and Courier*, March 26, 1969; Jack Roach, "McNair to Name Strike Study Panel," *Charleston News and Courier*, March 28, 1969; Elaine Stanford, "Picket Lines Established at Second Local Hospital," *Charleston News and Courier*, March 29, 1969.

Chapter 4: "Soul Power"

1. P. S. Foner, *Women and the American Labor Movement*, 412–14; Mary Moultrie, interview by author, June 23, 2008.

2. Fink and Greenberg, *Upheaval in the Quiet Zone*, 102–3.

3. Ralph David Abernathy, *And the Walls Came Tumbling Down* (New York: Harper and Row, 1989), 494–500; Martin Luther King Jr., "Speech to AFL-CIO" (speech at the Fourth Constitutional Convention of the AFL-CIO, Miami Beach, FL, December 11, 1961), Southern Christian Leadership Conference records, 1963–1968, Rubenstein Library, Duke University, Durham, NC.

4. Philip S. Foner, *Organized Labor and the Black Worker* (New York: International Publishers, 1981), 177–78, 334; A. Philip Randolph to "Dear Friend," July 19, 1963, National Union of Hospital and Health Care Employees (Local 1199) Records, 1938–1972, Catherwood Library Kheel Center, Cornell University, Ithaca, NY.

5. David J. Garrow, *Bearing the Cross: Martin Luther King, Jr., and the Southern Christian Leadership Conference* (New York: Open Road Integrated Media, Inc., 2015), 535, 548, 578.

6. Garrow, *Bearing the Cross*, 534, 548, 578–79; Abernathy, *And the Walls Came Tumbling Down*, 414–16; Andrew Young, interview by Leon Fink, January 31, 1980, voice recording, Chapel Hill, NC; John Reynolds, interview by author, April 24, 2021, digital voice recording, Seabrook Island, SC.

7. Abernathy, *And the Walls Came Tumbling Down*, 414–16; Green, *Battling the Planation Mentality*, 1–2, 251, 276–77.

8. Abernathy, *And the Walls Came Tumbling Down*, 494, 499–500, 501–5; John Reynolds, interview by author, April 24, 2021; Southern Christian Leadership Conference, "PPC in High Gear," *Soul Force: Official Journal of SCLC* 1, no. 2 (May 1, 1968) from the "Hospital Strike" folder, Avery Research Center for African American History and Culture, Charleston, SC.

9. Abernathy, *And the Walls Came Tumbling Down*, 502–3, 522, 526, 529–39. The Southern Christian Leadership Conference set forth the following goals as the outcome of Resurrection City: free food stamps rather than commodities, job-training programs, increased jobs, housing for low-income families.

10. Abernathy, *And the Walls Came Tumbling Down*, 541–44; Fink and Greenberg, *Upheaval in the Quiet Zone*, 138–39.

11. Abernathy, *And the Walls Came Tumbling Down*, 541–44; Fink and Greenberg, *Upheaval in the Quiet Zone*, 139–40; David White, interview by Leon Fink, June 5, 1979, no location provided.

12. Stewart King, "Strike Rally Set," *Charleston News and Courier*, March 31, 1969; Stewart King, "Abernathy Pledges Support to Strikers," *Charleston News and Courier*, April 1, 1969; James T. Wooten, "Racial Overtones Mark Strike of Charleston Hospital Workers," *New York Times*, April 5, 1969; Abernathy, *And the Walls Came Tumbling Down*, 547; John Reynolds, interview by author, April 24, 2021; "500 Expected to March to Hospitals Today," *Charleston News and Courier*, April 4, 1969; Elaine Stanford and William Walker Jr., "Peaceful March Staged by Strikers," *Charleston News and Courier*, April 5, 1969; "Strikers to Seek Support from Area Churches Today," *Charleston News and Courier*, April 6, 1969; Stewart King, "Striking Workers to Seek Statewide Support Today," *Charleston News and Courier*, April 7, 1969; William Walker Jr., "King Street Merchants Warned of 'Blacklist,'" *Charleston News and Courier*, April 19, 1969.

13. Jack Roach, "McNair to Name Strike Study Panel," *Charleston News and Courier*, March 28, 1969; Governor McNair, letter to Leo Croghan, April 15, 1969, Governor Robert E. McNair Papers, South Carolina Political Collections, University of South Carolina, Columbia, SC; Jack Roach, "McNair Agrees to Meet with Striking Workers," *Charleston News and Courier*, April 8, 1969.

14. Roach, "McNair to Name Strike Study Panel"; Governor McNair, letter to Leo Croghan, April 15, 1969; Roach, "McNair Agrees to Meet with Striking Workers."

15. William Walker Jr., "Court Orders Limit to Hospital Pickets," *Charleston News and Courier*, April 11, 1969; "31 Hospital Workers Arrested for Disobeying Injunction," *Charleston News and Courier*, April 12, 1969.

16. Walker, "Court Orders Limit to Hospital Pickets"; "31 Hospital Workers Arrested for Disobeying Injunction."

17. Mary Moultrie, "Speech by Mary Ann Moultrie, President, Local 1199B, National Organizing Committee of Hospital and Nursing Home Employee" (speech, Burke High School Stoney Field Stadium, Charleston, SC, May 29, 1969), National Union of Hospital and Health Care Employees (Local 1199) Records, 1938–1972, Catherwood Library Kheel Center, Cornell University, Ithaca, NY.

18. Moe Foner, interview by Robert Master, August 29, 1985; Moe Foner, interview by Leon Fink, March 9, 1979; Henry Nicholas, interview by Brian Greenberg, January 11, 1978; Fink and Greenberg, *Upheaval in the Quiet Zone*, 138–39; Andrew Young, interview by Leon Fink, January 31, 1980; Morris, *The Origins of the Civil Rights Movement*, 250–51; Stewart King, "Abernathy to Lead Rally Here," *Charleston News and Courier*, April 21, 1969; Stewart King, "Abernathy Sets Mass March Against Struck Hospitals," *Charleston News and Courier*, April 22, 1969; Abernathy, *And the Walls Came Tumbling Down*, 547.

19. David White, interview by Leon Fink, June 5, 1979; Fink and Greenberg, *Upheaval in the Quiet Zone*, 140–41; Moe Foner, interview by Robert Master, August 29, 1985.

20. Abernathy, *And the Walls Came Tumbling Down*, 547–48; William Walker Jr., "Mr. Abernathy Leads 800 on Medical Center March," *Charleston News and Courier*, April 23, 1969; James T. Wooten, "Abernathy Leads March of Strikers," *New York Times*, April 23, 1969; "Charleston Cool to March," *The Atlanta Constitution*, April 23, 1969;

William Saunders, interview by Kerry Taylor and author, June 17, 2008; William Saunders, interview by Kerry Taylor, June 9, 2011; Mary Moultrie, William Saunders and Rosetta Simmons, interview by Kerry Taylor, March 5, 2009; William Saunders, interview by Leon Fink, March 1, 1980.

21. King, "Abernathy Sets Mass March Against Struck Hospitals"; Walker, "Mr. Abernathy Leads 800 on Medical Center March"; Wooten, "Abernathy Leads March of Strikers"; Stanford and Walker, "Peaceful March Staged by Strikers"; "400 Youths Urged to Join March," *Charleston News and Courier*, April 24, 1969; William Walker Jr. and Stewart R. King, "Guardsmen Ordered into Tense Charleston," *Charleston News and Courier*, April 26, 1969; "Abernathy and 101 Others Arrested in S. Carolina Strike," *Los Angeles Times*, April 26, 1969; "Abernathy Held in Strike Action: 101 More in South Carolina Also Seized at Hospital," *The Sun*, April 26, 1969; "Jail Abernathy, 101 Others for Picketing," *Chicago Tribune*, April 25, 1969.

22. "Abernathy Backs S.C. Strike," *The Washington Post, Times Herald*, April 22, 1969; Wooten, "Abernathy Leads March of Strikers"; Moe Foner, interview by Robert Master, August 29, 1985; Moe Foner, interview by Leon Fink, March 9, 1979. Charleston did not have a major Black newspaper during the period of the strike.

23. Stewart King, "Abernathy Leads March, Hits at Acts of Violence," *Charleston News and Courier*, May 5, 1969; "Violence in Hospital Strike Is Disowned by Abernathy," *The Sun*, May 5, 1969; Mary Moultrie, interview by Steve Estes, October 20, 1994, voice recording, Charleston, SC, Steve Estes Papers, Avery Research Center for African American History and Culture, College of Charleston, Charleston, SC; Naomi White, interview by Steve Estes, October 21, 1994, voice recording, Charleston, SC, Steve Estes Papers, Avery Research Center for African American History and Culture, College of Charleston, Charleston, SC; Jessie Jefferson, interview by Steve Estes, October 22, 1994, voice recording, Charleston, SC, Steve Estes Papers, Avery Research Center for African American History and Culture, College of Charleston, Charleston, SC.

24. Mary Moultrie, interview by Steve Estes, October 20, 1994; Naomi White, interview by Steve Estes, October 21, 1994; Jessie Jefferson, interview by Steve Estes, October 22, 1994.

25. Abernathy, *And the Walls Came Tumbling Down*, 555–56, 560; King, "Abernathy Leads March, Hits at Acts of Violence."

26. Mary Moultrie, interview by Steve Estes, October 20, 1994; Naomi White, interview by Steve Estes, October 21, 1994; Jessie Jefferson, interview by Steve Estes, October 22, 1994; Carrie Mitchell, interview by author, June 25, 2008, digital voice recording, Charleston, SC.

27. Beverly Kennedy, nurse's aide at Medical College, "My Feelings About the Strike," National Union of Hospital and Health Care Employees (Local 1199) Records, 1938–1972, Catherwood Library Kheel Center, Cornell University, Ithaca, NY; Hosea Williams, interview by Steve Estes, February 9, 1996, voice recording, Atlanta, GA, Steve Estes Papers, Avery Research Center for African American History and Culture, College of Charleston, Charleston, SC; Naomi White, interview by Steve Estes, October 21, 1994.

28. "A Charleston Student Speaks," *Soul Force*, June 1969; "Students Speak Out During 1969 Hospital Strike," *The Chronicle*, March 14, 1981; "400 Youths Urged to Join March," *Charleston News and Courier*, April 24, 1969; Joseph Preston Strom, Chief of the South

Carolina Law Enforcement Division, "11:25am report to McNair," April 28, 1969, Governor Robert E. McNair Papers, South Carolina Political Collections, University of South Carolina, Columbia, SC.

29. "A Charleston Student Speaks"; "Students Speak Out During 1969 Hospital Strike"; "400 Youths Urged to Join March"; Strom, "11:25am report to McNair"; William Walker Jr., "Arrest of 30 by Police Ends 4-Hour Protest Here," *Charleston News and Courier*, April 27, 1969; James T. Wooten, "100 Negroes Seized in Charleston Protest March," *New York Times*, April 27, 1969; David White, interview by Leon Fink, June 5, 1979; Deirdre Mays, "Remembering 'The Militant Clergy' 30 Years Later," *The Catholic Miscellany: Good News from the Diocese of Charleston*, July 1, 1999; James Wooten, "Charleston Is Armed Camp as 142 More are Held," *New York Times*, April 29, 1969; *I Am Somebody*, streaming video, directed by Madeline Anderson (Icarus Films, 1970), accessed March 2, 2017, http://docuseek2.com.libproxy.lib.unc.edu/if-iams.

30. Father Henry Grant, interview by Leon Fink, February 27, 1980; *I Am Somebody*, streaming video.

31. Bruce Golphin, "Mrs. King to Lead Charleston March," *The Washington Post, Times Herald*, April 30, 1969; "King's Widow Leads March in Charleston: Tells Striking Hospital Workers of Support," *Chicago Tribune*, May 1, 1969; *I Am Somebody*, streaming video; Moe Foner, interview by Robert Master, August 29, 1985; Abernathy, *And the Walls Came Tumbling Down*, 551.

32. Golphin, "Mrs. King to Lead Charleston March"; "King's Widow Leads March in Charleston"; Stewart King, "Widow of Dr. King Leads 1,500 on Hospital March," *Charleston News and Courier*, May 1, 1969; Joseph Preston Strom, Chief of the South Carolina Law Enforcement Division, "9:45am report to McNair," April 28, 1969, Governor Robert E. McNair Papers, South Carolina Political Collections, University of South Carolina, Columbia, SC.

Chapter 5: Respectable and Disorderly

1. Kali Nicole Gross, *Hannah Mary Tabbs and the Disembodied Torso: A Tale of Race, Sex, and Violence in America* (New York: Oxford University Press, 2016), 4–5.

2. Beverly Kennedy, "My Feelings About the Strike!," National Union of Hospital and Health Care Employees (Local 1199) Records, 1938–1972, Catherwood Library Kheel Center, Cornell University, Ithaca, NY; Mary Moultrie, interview by Jean-Claude Bouffard, 28 July 1982, voice recording, unknown location; Elaine S. Stanford, "Strikers Seek Food Stamps, Appeal Ruling by Simons," *Charleston New and Courier*, April 2, 1969; "Striking Workers Seek Welfare Aid," *Charleston News and Courier*, May 8, 1969; Margaret Rose, "From the Fields to the Picket Line: Huelga Women and the Boycott, 1965–1975, in *No Middle Ground: Women and Radical Protest*, ed. Kathleen M. Blee (New York: New York University Press, 1998), 225–27.

3. Mary Moultrie, William Saunders, and Rosetta Simmons, interview by Kerry Taylor, March 5, 2009; Mary Moultrie, interview by Jean-Claude Bouffard, July 28, 1982; *I Am Somebody*, streaming video.

4. Rosetta Simmons, interview by author, June 25, 2008; Mary Moultrie, William Saunders, and Rosetta Simmons, interview by Kerry Taylor, March 5, 2009.

5. Mary Moultrie, William Saunders, and Rosetta Simmons, interview by Kerry Taylor, March 5, 2009; Naomi White, interview by author, June 25, 2008.

6. "Students Speak Out During 1969 Hospital Strike," *The Charleston Chronicle*, March 14, 1981. The schools did not actually close, but they did experience major increases in student absences.

7. Joseph Preston Strom, Chief of the South Carolina Law Enforcement Division, "1:45pm report to McNair," April 28, 1969, Governor Robert E. McNair Papers, South Carolina Political Collections, University of South Carolina, Columbia, SC; Clifford B. Smith, Transcript of his tape-recorded statement to James A. Martin and Johnnie T. Epting, March 27, 1969, William M. McCord Papers, Waring Historical Library, Medical University of South Carolina, Charleston, SC; "Students Stage Protests at 4 Colleges," *The Atlanta Constitution*, April 29, 1969; "Unrest Spreads on U.S. Campuses: 30 at Voorhees Held, ROTC Sit-In Staged at Dartmouth," *The Sun*, April 30, 1969; "What's Happening on the Campuses," *New York Amsterdam News*, May 3, 1969.

8. Strom, "1:45pm report to McNair, April 28, 1969"; The *Times and Democrat* reported thirty-one armed students, while other sources like the *Chicago Daily Defender* reported seventy-five. Based on the information, it seems that approximately two hundred students were involved in various capacities; William Cotterell, "Campus is Without Food as Armed Students Takeover Voorhees College Building," *Chicago Daily Defender*, April 29, 1969; "Armed Students Seize Control of Negro School," *Los Angeles Times*, April 29, 1969; "What's Happening on the Campuses," *New York Amsterdam News*, May 3, 1969; Richard Reid, "Black History Month: Armed Voorhees Students Took Over Administration Building in 1969," *The Times and Democrat*, February 22, 2017. For further discussion on the Orangeburg incident see the following: Jack Bass, "Documenting the Orangeburg Massacre: Campus Killings of Black Students Received Little News Coverage in 1968, but a Book About Them Keeps Their Memory Alive," *Nieman Reports*, Fall, 2003, 8–9; Cleveland Sellers, "Thirty-Five Years Ago: An African-American Professor Recalls the Orangeburg Massacre at South Carolina State College," *Journal of Blacks in Higher Education* 41 (Autumn, 2003): 67; Grose, *South Carolina at the Brink*, 215–24; Mike Davis, "3 Dead, 50 Shot on S.C. Campus: Mike Davis Pinned Down by Gunfire," *Afro-American*, February 10, 1968.

9. Strom, "1:45pm report to McNair," April 28, 1969; "Armed Black Students Surrender Building at S. Carolina College," *Washington Post, Times Herald*, April 30, 1969; Adam Raphael, "Quiet End to College Siege," *The Guardian*, April 30, 1969; Richard Reid, "Black History Month: Armed Voorhees Students Took Over Administration Building in 1969," *The Times and Democrat*, February 22, 2017; "Voorhees Reopens," *New York Times*, May 13, 1969.

10. Hugh E. Gibson, "McNair Squares Off Against SCLC, Insurrectionists," *Charleston News and Courier*, May 2, 1969; "One Governor Is Not Afraid," *Chicago Tribune*, May 8, 1969; W. K. Pillow Jr. and Betty Walker, "Economy Feeling Pangs of Violence," *Charleston News and Courier*, May 4, 1969; King, "Widow of Dr. King Leads 1,500 on Hospital March"; "King's Widow Leads March in Charleston: Tells Striking Hospital Workers of Support," *Chicago Tribune*, May 1, 1969.

11. Gibson, "McNair Squares Off Against SCLC, Insurrectionists"; "One Governor Is Not Afraid."

12. Executive Order and Proclamation, Office of the Governor, State of South Carolina (Columbia, 1969), Governor Robert E. McNair Papers, South Carolina Political Collections, University of South Carolina, Columbia, SC; Robert E. McNair, statement on curfew, May 1, 1969, Governor Robert E. McNair Papers, South Carolina Political Collections, University of South Carolina, Columbia, SC; Stewart R. King, "Curfew Imposed to 'Cool Down' Tense Charleston: Guardsmen, Police Busy Checking Violence, Arson," *Charleston News and Courier*, May 2, 1969; "McNair Issues Executive Order," *Charleston News and Courier*, May 2, 1969; "Curfew Imposed for Charleston: South Carolina's Governor Acts in Hospital Strike," *New York Times*, May 2, 1969; "Charleston Curfew Ordered," *The Sun*, May 2, 1969; "S.C. Clamps Lid on City; Mrs. King Sparks Fight," *Chicago Daily Defender*, May 3, 1969.

13. "Police Car, Fire Truck Fired On in Charleston," *The Washington Post, Times Herald*, May 2, 1969; "Gunfire in Charleston Despite a Curfew," *Chicago Tribune*, May 2, 1969; Betty Walker, "Curfew Fails to Halt Violence," *Charleston News and Courier*, May 2, 1969; Betty Walker, "Scattered Violence Hits County, City," *Charleston News and Courier*, May 3, 1969.

14. Sacks, *Caring by the Hour*, 13–14; A. Philip Randolph, form letter to announce launch of March on Washington for Jobs and Freedom, July 19, 1963, National Union of Hospital and Health Care Employees (Local 1199) Records, 1938–1972, Catherwood Library Kheel Center, Cornell University, Ithaca, NY; March on Washington for Jobs and Freedom Administrative Committee, *Organizing Manual no. 2: Final Plans for March on Washington for Jobs and Freedom* (New York: Trades Council, date unknown), 1–11; Fink and Greenberg, *Upheaval in the Quiet Zone*, 129; Auxiliary Workers of Medical College Hospital, "List of Grievances" from the Septima Clark Papers, Avery Research Center for African American History and Culture, Charleston, South Carolina (This is a handwritten document that is mostly likely a draft of the final product. It is unclear whether this list of grievances could have been the "letter" that Mary Moultrie and Lillie Doster penned to Dr. William McCord or if it could be a second document that was sent to the administrator. The document includes a space for the date, but it has been left blank. The document is clearly a communication from the group of organizing workers prior to them being unionized because the workers are referred to as "Auxillary Workers of Medical College Hospital"); Akinyele Omowale Umoja, *We Will Shoot Back: Armed Resistance in the Mississippi Freedom Movement* (New York: New York University Press, 2013), 7–8.

15. Naomi White, interview by author, June 25, 2008; Elaine S. Stanford, "Workers Picket Medical College: Injunction Granted to Halt Strike," *Charleston News and Courier*, March 21, 1969; Herb Frazier, "Workers Fought for Respect," *The Post and Courier*, April 17, 1994.

16. Naomi White, interview by author, June 25, 2008; P. S. Foner, *Women and the American Labor Movement*, 408; Stanford, "Workers Picket Medical College"; White's mention of the autoclave is in reference to the equipment used sterilize medical tools.

17. Rosetta Simmons, interview by author, June 25, 2008; Lillie Doster, interview by author, June 25, 2008.

18. Naomi White, interview by author, June 25, 2008.

19. Naomi White, interview by author, June 25, 2008.

20. Rosetta Simmons, interview by author, June 25, 2008; Naomi White, interview by author, June 25, 2008.

21. William Saunders, interview by Kerry Taylor and author, June 17, 2008; William Saunders, interview by Kerry Taylor, June 9, 2011; Mary Moultrie, William Saunders, and Rosetta Simmons, interview by Kerry Taylor, March 5, 2009; William Saunders, interview by author, June 23, 2008; William Saunders, "Local Organizing: South Carolina," *Social Policy* 21, no. 3 (Winter 1991): 58. Interviews with Andrew Young and Hosea Williams, members of SCLC, mention William Saunders but offer no indication that they knew anything about his militant activity.

22. Mary Moultrie, William Saunders, and Rosetta Simmons, interview by Kerry Taylor, March 5, 2009; Rosetta Simmons, interview by author, June 25, 2008.

23. Carol Mueller, "Ella Baker and the Origins of 'Participatory Democracy,'" in *Women in the Civil Rights Movement*, ed. Crawford, Rouse, and Woods, 53; Grace Jordan McFadden, "Septima P. Clark and the Struggle for Human Rights," in *Women in the Civil Rights Movement*, ed. Crawford, Rouse, and Woods, 85.

24. Elaine S. Stanford, "Injunction Granted to Halt Strike," *Charleston News and Courier*, April 3, 1969; Associated Press, "Widow Becoming Symbol of Rights Leaders' Dream," *Charleston News and Courier*, March 21, 1969. For a discussion on how Coretta Scott King has been perceived see Jeanne Theoharis, "Accidental Matriarchs and Beautiful Helpmates: Rosa Parks, Coretta Scott King, and the Memorialization of the Civil Rights Movement," in *Civil Rights History from the Ground Up: Local Struggles, a National Movement*, ed. Emilye Crosby (Athens: University of Georgia Press, 2011), 385–418.

25. Taylor Branch, *Parting the Waters: America in the King Years, 1954–63* (New York: Simon & Schuster Paperbacks, 1988), 95, 100–101; Naomi White, interview by author, June 25, 2008; Associated Press, "Widow Becoming Symbol of Rights Leaders' Dream," *Charleston News and Courier*, March 21, 1969.

26. Associated Press, "Widow Becoming Symbol of Rights Leaders' Dream"; Jacquelyn D. Hall, "Disorderly Women: Gender and Labor Militancy in the Appalachian South," *The Journal of American History* 73, no. 2 (September 1986): 372–74; Stanford, "Injunction Granted to Halt Strike."

27. Stanford, "Workers Picket Medical College." Most subsequent articles identify the cause of the strike as a demand for union recognition and the reinstatement of the twelve discharged workers or for union recognition.

Chapter 6: "McNair Fiddles While Rome Burns"

1. F. E. Ellis, letter to Robert E. McNair, May 12, 1969, Governor Robert E. McNair Papers, South Carolina Political Collections, University of South Carolina, Columbia, SC.

2. F. E. Ellis, letter to Governor Robert E. McNair, May 12, 1969; Ellis does not provide names for all of the meeting attendees. For the April 28, 1969, meeting, he does not provide the name of Abernathy's administrative assistant. For the April 29, 1969, meeting, in addition to the names he provided, he identified another attendee affiliated with

Local 1199 as "the white organizer, also from New York." He identified the other two as "Negroes": "one other female believed to be from the County Hospital" and "one other whose name I did not get"; "Demands of Union Officials," April 29, 1969, Governor Robert E. McNair Papers, South Carolina Political Collections, University of South Carolina, Columbia, SC.

3. Meeting between Governor Robert E. McNair and the Charleston County Legislative Delegation, memorandum for the record, April 29, 1969, Governor Robert E. McNair Papers, South Carolina Political Collections, University of South Carolina, Columbia, SC; "Demands of Union Officials," April 29, 1969, Governor Robert E. McNair Papers, South Carolina Political Collections, University of South Carolina, Columbia, SC. There are two copies of the list of demands. One copy is a part of F. E. Ellis's report to Governor McNair. The other copy is the list of demands that Attorney General McLeod presented to Governor, which includes handwritten notes rejecting some of the demands and dollar amounts associated with wage adjustments.

4. J. Gregory Prior, "Citizens Unit to Tackle Hospital Row," *Charleston News and Courier*, May 1, 1969; Strom, "1:45pm report to McNair, April 28, 1969."

5. Citizens' Committee appointed by Mayor Palmer Gaillard, "Summary of Position of Committee Appointed by Mayor of Charleston," May 1, 1969, Governor Robert E. McNair Papers, South Carolina Political Collections, University of South Carolina, Columbia, SC; *I Am Somebody*, streaming video.

6. Citizens' Committee appointed by Mayor Palmer Gaillard, "Summary of Position of Committee Appointed by Mayor of Charleston," May 1, 1969; Gibson, "McNair Squares Off Against SCLC, Insurrectionists."

7. Barbara Williams, "Negro Leaders Petition Politicians on Strike," *Charleston News and Courier*, May 1, 1969; Political Action Committee of Charleston County, South Carolina, *Constitution and By-Laws*, January 19, 1966, Bernice Robinson Papers, Avery Research Center for African American History and Culture, College of Charleston, Charleston, SC. The PAC aimed at "securing political justice" for Charleston citizens. More often than not, it focused its efforts on the underserved and underrepresented in an effort to ensure that local citizens got fair treatment in regard to local and state politics.

8. Williams, "Negro Leaders Petition Politicians on Strike"; Robert E. McNair, letter to Reverend Leo M. Croghan, April 15, 1969, Governor Robert E. McNair Papers, South Carolina Political Collections, University of South Carolina, Columbia, SC; Robert E. McNair, letter to Archibald Rutledge, April 17, 1969, Governor Robert E. McNair Papers, South Carolina Political Collections, University of South Carolina, Columbia, SC; These letters are examples of the governor's stance against collective bargaining or recognizing the union.

9. Meeting held by Governor Robert McNair with eighteen attendees, memorandum for record, April 29, 1969, Governor Robert E. McNair Papers, South Carolina Political Collections, University of South Carolina, Columbia, SC; "Solomon Blatt, 91, Legislator in South Carolina Since 1933, Obituary of Solomon Blatt, *New York Times*, May 15, 1986; Solomon Blatt, as of his death in 1986, was credited with being the nation's longest-serving state legislator. He served as House Speaker of South Carolina from 1937 to 1947 and from 1951 to 1973.

10. House Military, Municipal and Public Affairs Committee, *A Concurrent Resolution Affirming the Public Policy Regarding Collective Bargaining with Certain Employees, as Pronounced by His Excellency, the Governor*, Military, Public and Municipal Affairs Committee, HR, South Carolina General Assembly (April 29, 1969), Governor Robert E. McNair Papers, South Carolina Political Collections, University of South Carolina, Columbia, SC; "Legislature Reaffirms State's Stand on Strike," *Charleston News and Courier*, May 1, 1969.

11. "Legislature Reaffirms State's Stand on Strike."

12. Caroline H. Rugheimer, Clerk of Council, letter to Governor Robert E. McNair, May 22, 1969, Governor Robert E. McNair Papers, South Carolina Political Collections, University of South Carolina, Columbia, SC; *Resolution*, Charleston County Council, South Carolina (May 20, 1969), Governor Robert E. McNair Papers, South Carolina Political Collections, University of South Carolina, Columbia, SC.

13. "Union President Critical of Stand on Negotiations," *Charleston News and Courier*, May 5, 1969.

14. Stewart R. King, "Abernathy Released from County Jail: SCLC Official Out on $500 Bond," *Charleston News and Courier*, May 3, 1969; "Nixon Rejects Abernathy Plea," *Chicago Tribune*, May 3, 1969; "Nixon Visits State Today," *Charleston News and Courier*, May 3, 1969; "Memorandum for the Record," April 30, 1969, Governor Robert E. McNair Papers, South Carolina Political Collections, University of South Carolina, Columbia, SC; Barbara S. Williams, "Committee Members Silent," *Charleston News and Courier*, May 6, 1969.

15. King, "Abernathy Released from County Jail"; "Nixon Rejects Abernathy Plea"; "Nixon Visits State Today"; "Memorandum for the Record," April 30, 1969; Williams, "Committee Members Silent."

16. Barbara S. Williams, "Possibility of Solution in Hospital Strike Cited," *Charleston News and Courier*, May 3, 1969.

17. Williams, "Committee Members Silent"; William Huff, "Report from Mr. Huff, Medical College," May 8, 1969, Governor Robert E. McNair Papers, South Carolina Political Collections, University of South Carolina, Columbia, SC; William Huff was the vice president for development at Medical College of South Carolina; Barbara S. Williams, "Hospital Strike Talk Ends in Walkout," *Charleston News and Courier*, May 9, 1969. The Local 1199 attorney is not mentioned by name in the sources, but it was most likely Eugene G. Eisner who had been providing legal representation for the union throughout the dispute.

18. "Graham Is Standing Firm on Rejecting Union Talks," *Charleston News and Courier*, May 7, 1969; Barbara S. Williams, "Hospital Workers to Be Included in Classification Study," *Charleston News and Courier*, May 9, 1969.

19. Ralph D. Abernathy, speech at Mother's Day Poor People's March, Southern Christian Leadership Conference, Charleston, SC, May 11, 1969; William Cotterell, "10,000 March in S. C. Hospital Demonstration," *Chicago Daily Defender*, May 12, 1969; "7,000 March in Charleston Labor Protest," *Chicago Tribune*, May 12, 1969; "10,000 Join Abernathy in Charleston March: Protesters Include Reuther, Congressmen in 'Phase Two of the Poor People's Campaign,'" *Los Angeles Times*, May 12, 1969; W. K. Pillow Jr. and Stewart King, "Thousands March in Support of Strike," *Charleston News and Courier*, May

12, 1969. Each source has a different estimation of the number of marchers there were that day, ranging from five to ten thousand; however, most of the sources agree that it was the largest march since the strike began.

20. Lawrence H. Geller, "Local PCLC Head Says Bus Load Leaves Sunday to Assist SCLC Marchers in Charleston," *Philadelphia Tribune*, May 6, 1969; Cotterell, "10,000 March in S. C. Hospital Demonstration"; "7,000 March in Charleston Labor Protest"; "10,000 Join Abernathy in Charleston March"; Pillow and King, "Thousands March in Support of Strike"; Garrow, *Bearing the Cross*, 331.

21. Ralph D. Abernathy, speech at Mother's Day Poor People's March, Southern Christian Leadership Conference, Charleston, South Carolina, May 11, 1969; Cotterell, "10,000 March in S. C. Hospital Demonstration"; "7,000 March in Charleston Labor Protest"; "10,000 Join Abernathy in Charleston March"; Pillow and King, "Thousands March in Support of Strike."

22. "McNair Stands Firm on Hospital Strike," *Charleston News and Courier*, May 12, 1969; Billy E. Bowles, "Nixon to Send Observers to Strike Scene," *Charleston News and Courier*, May 10, 1969.

23. "McNair Stands Firm on Hospital Strike"; Bowles, "Nixon to Send Observers to Strike Scene."

24. Bowles, "Nixon to Send Observers to Strike Scene."

25. Michael K. Honey, *Black Workers Remember: An Oral History of Segregation, Unionism, and the Freedom Struggle* (Berkeley: University of California Press, 1999), 286–89; Senator Jacob Javits and Senator Walter F. Mondale, letter to President Richard M. Nixon, May 15, 1969, National Union of Hospital and Health Care Employees (Local 1199) Records, 1938–1972, Catherwood Library Kheel Center, Cornell University, Ithaca, NY; "Senators Ask Nixon's Aid in S.C. Strike," *Observer* (the first part of the newspaper's name is cut off), May 16, 1969, Governor Robert E. McNair Papers, South Carolina Political Collections, University of South Carolina, Columbia, SC; "Senators Ask Nixon's Help," *New York Times*, May 16, 1969; "Another Memphis," *The Sun*, May 3, 1969; "Two Strikes Termed Similar," *Charleston News and Courier*, May 6, 1969; "U. S. Mediator Urged for Charleston: Congressional Report Gas Delay Asked 53 back S.S. Rise," *The Washington Post, Times Herald*, May 16, 1969.

26. Honey, *Black Workers Remember*, 286–89; Senator Jacob Javits and Senator Walter F. Mondale, letter to President Richard M. Nixon, May 15, 1969; "Senators Ask Nixon's Aid in S.C. Strike"; "Senators Ask Nixon's Help"; "Another Memphis"; "Two Strikes Termed Similar"; "U. S. Mediator Urged for Charleston"; *I Am Somebody*, streaming video. For a comprehensive discussion on the Memphis sanitation workers strike see Green, *Battling the Planation Mentality*. For a discussion on African American-centered labor movements undergirded by civil rights, see R. Korstad, *Civil Rights Unionism*, 1–40, and R. Korstad and Lichtenstein, "Opportunities Found and Lost," 786–811. For a discussion on African American labor as a civil rights issue, see Nancy MacLean, *Freedom Is Not Enough: The Opening of the American Workplace* (New York: Russell Sage Foundation, 2006), 76–113.

27. Hugh E. Gibson, "McNair Denounces Senators' Appeal," *Charleston News and Courier*, May 17, 1969.

28. National Organizing Committee of Hospital and Nursing Home Employees, "Text of Statement Signed by National Civil Rights Leaders on Charleston, South Carolina Hospital Strikes Issued by Mrs. Coretta S. King for Release Monday A.M.," April 21, 1969 (the document was signed by: Coretta Scott King, National Organizing Committee of Local 1199; Ralph D. Abernathy, SCLC; Roy Wilkins, NAACP; A. Philip Randolph, Negro American Labor Council; Whitney Young, National Urban League; Roy Innis, CORE; Bayard Rustin, A. Philip Randolph Institute; Dorothy Height, National Council of Negro Women; George A. Wiley, National Welfare Rights Organization; Representative Shirley Chisholm; Representative John M. Conyers; Mayor Richard G. Hatcher, Gary, Indiana; May Carl B. Stokes, Cleveland, Ohio; and Julian Bond, Georgia House of Representatives) South Carolina Council on Human Relations Collection, The South Caroliniana Library, University of South Carolina, Columbia, SC; National Organizing Committee of Hospital and Nursing Home Employees, "All National Civil Rights Leaders, Five Black Elected Officials Announce Support for Charleston, S.C. Hospital Strikers," Press Release, April 21, 1969, South Carolina Council on Human Relations Collection, The South Caroliniana Library, University of South Carolina, Columbia, SC.

29. Matthew D. McCollom and Paul Matthias, South Carolina Council on Human Relations, "A Crisis in Charleston," April 23, 1969, South Carolina Council on Human Relations Records, 1934–1976, The South Caroliniana Library, University of South Carolina, Columbia, SC; "Background" and "Beginnings," South Carolina Council on Human Relations Records, 1934–1976, The South Caroliniana Library, University of South Carolina, Columbia, SC.

30. W. K. Pillow Jr., "Thousands March in Support of Strike," *Charleston News and Courier*, May 12, 1969; "The Charleston Coalition," *New York Times*, May 14, 1969; "AFL-CIO Gives Union $25,000; Curfew," newspaper source unknown, May 15, 1969, Isaiah Bennett Papers, Avery Research Center for African American History and Culture, College of Charleston, Charleston, SC; "Strike Aided by Donations: 400 Charleston Workers Get Union Funds," *The Sun*, May 17, 1969; Contributions from National Unions Received by Charleston Office as of July 31, 1969; Report on All Contributions Received by Our Office for the Charleston Strike as of August 1, 1969; Report on Contributions from Members of #1199, August 1, 1969; Contributions to the Charleston Strike from Local Unions of New York City as of August 1, 1969; Contributions to the Charleston Strike from Newspaper Ad-Public Individuals and Organizations $100 and Over, no date; Contributions to the Charleston Strike from Nation Unions Received by NY Office as of August 1, 1969, all financial reports are from the National Union of Hospital and Health Care Employees (Local 1199) Records, 1938–1972, Catherwood Library Kheel Center, Cornell University, Ithaca, NY. During the Mother's Day March on May 11, 1969, Walter Reuther, president of the United Auto Workers of America, presented Moultrie with a ten-thousand-dollar check and another to Abernathy for five hundred dollars, pledging to provide their ongoing support in the form of a weekly five-hundred-dollar payment to SCLC for as long as they remained in the city. Cleveland Robinson, president of the Negro American Labor Council, a check for one thousand dollars.

31. W. K. Pillow Jr. and Betty Walker, "Economy Feeling Pangs of Violence," *Charleston News and Courier*, May 4, 1969.

32. *I Am Somebody*, streaming video; David White, interview by Leon Fink, June 5, 1979; Mary Moultrie, interview by Steve Estes, October 20, 1994; Carrie Mitchell, interview by author, June 25, 2008; William F. Kelly, Charleston County Sheriff, letter to Joseph P. Strom with leaflet regarding boycott of local businesses attached, May 16, 1969, Governor Robert E. McNair Papers, South Carolina Political Collections, University of South Carolina, Columbia, SC; William Walker Jr., "King Street Merchants Warned of 'Blacklist,'" *Charleston News and Courier*, April 19, 1969; Pillow and Walker, "Economy Feeling Pangs of Violence"; William Walker Jr., "Curfew Hurting Business," *Charleston News and Courier*, May 9, 1969. King Street was and is Charleston's main thoroughfare. The boycott was barely mentioned in news sources, so the impact is unclear.

33. Pillow and Walker, "Economy Feeling Pangs of Violence"; Walker, "Curfew Hurting Business"; Small Business Men, letter to Governor Robert E. McNair, May 21, 1969, Governor Robert E. McNair Papers, South Carolina Political Collections, University of South Carolina, Columbia, SC.

34. Pillow and Walker, "Economy Feeling Pangs of Violence"; Walker, "Curfew Hurting Business"; Small Business Men, letter to Governor Robert E. McNair, May 21, 1969.

35. "Race Panel Set Up in South Carolina: Group Seeking Community Uplift and State Harmony," *New York Times*, November 12, 1967; "Carolina Clerics Back Race Group: New Task Force for Uplift of Community Endorsed," *New York Times*, November 26, 1967; South Carolina Task Force for Community Uplift, petition to South Carolina General Assembly, May 16, 1969, South Carolina Council on Human Relations Collection, The South Caroliniana Library, University of South Carolina, Columbia, SC.

36. South Carolina Task Force for Community Uplift, petition to South Carolina General Assembly, May 16, 1969.

37. Katherine Elder, "Civil Rights Act of 1964," *The SAGE Encyclopedia of Economics and Society*, ed. Frederick F. Wherry and Juliet B. Schor, accessed March 8, 2017, http://dx.doi.org.libproxy.lib.unc.edu/10.4135/9781452206905.n153; National Archives and Records Administration, "The Civil Rights Act of 1964 and the Equal Employment Opportunity Commission," accessed March 8, 2017, https://www.archives.gov/education/lessons/civil-rights-act; Henry S. Commager, *Documents of American History*, 9th ed. (Englewood Cliffs: Prentice-Hall, 1973), 687–88; Murray Seeger, "Racial Inquiry Starts in Strike at Hospital: Office of HEW Will Study Charges by Negroes Discharged in Charleston, S.C.," *Los Angeles Times*, May 20, 1969; "U.S. Probes Bias Charge at Charleston Hospital," *The Washington Post, Times Herald*, May 20, 1969.

38. William Saunders, interview by Leon Fink, March 1, 1980; William Saunders, interview by Kerry Taylor and author, June 17, 2008; William Saunders, interview by Kerry Taylor, June 9, 2011; William Saunders, interview by author, June 23, 2008; J. Edwin Schachte Jr., confidential memorandum to Governor Robert E. McNair, May 27, 1969, Governor Robert E. McNair Papers, South Carolina Political Collections, University of South Carolina, Columbia, SC.

39. J. Edwin Schachte Jr., confidential memorandum to Governor Robert E. McNair, May 27, 1969; Grose, *South Carolina at the Brink*, 256–57; Mary Moultrie, William Saunders, and Rosetta Simmons, interview by Kerry Taylor, March 5, 2009; William

Saunders, interview by Leon Fink, March 1, 1980; Mary Moultrie, William Saunders and Rosetta Simmons, interview by Kerry Taylor, March 5, 2009.

40. J. Edwin Schachte Jr., confidential memorandum to Governor Robert E. McNair, May 27, 1969; Grose, *South Carolina at the Brink*, 256–57; Mary Moultrie, William Saunders and Rosetta Simmons, interview by Kerry Taylor, March 5, 2009; William Saunders, interview by Leon Fink, March 1, 1980; Mary Moultrie, William Saunders and Rosetta Simmons, interview by Kerry Taylor, March 5, 2009.

41. William M. McCord, statement at press conference, June 19, 1969, Governor Robert E. McNair Papers, South Carolina Political Collections, University of South Carolina, Columbia, SC; Fred Rigsbee, "HEW Recommends Rehiring Workers," *Charleston Evening Post*, June 10, 1969; Jack Nelson, "U. S. May Stop Funds for Charleston Hospital: Government Demands that Facility Hit by Strike Rehire Workers, Eliminate Bias," *Los Angeles Times*, June 12, 1969; Bruce Galphin, "HEW Orders 12 Rehired in Charleston," *The Washington Post, Times Herald*, June 12, 1969; Rudolph Pyatt, "Hospital Strike Now Political Football," *Charleston News and Courier*, June 15, 1969; "Secretary Robe and the Charleston Strike," *The Washington Post, Times Herald*, June 18, 1969; Office of Federal Contract Compliance Programs, "Executive Order 11246—Equal Employment Opportunity, 1965," United States Department of Labor, accessed March 9, 2017, https://www.dol.gov/ofccp/regs/compliance/ca_11246.htm.

42. Rigsbee, "HEW Recommends Rehiring Workers"; Robert E. McNair, "Notes for Speech to General Faculty of Medical College," June 10, 1969, Governor Robert E. McNair Papers, South Carolina Political Collections, University of South Carolina, Columbia, SC; Medical College of South Carolina Out-Patient Department Nurses, letter to Robert E. McNair, May 1, 1969, Governor Robert E. McNair Papers, South Carolina Political Collections, University of South Carolina, Columbia, SC.

43. William McCord, letter to Robert E. McNair, June 17, 1969, Governor Robert E. McNair Papers, South Carolina Political Collections, University of South Carolina, Columbia, SC; William M. McCord, statement at press conference, June 19, 1969, Governor Robert E. McNair Papers, South Carolina Political Collections, University of South Carolina, Columbia, SC; Moe Foner, interview by Robert Master, August 29, 1985; Fink and Greenberg, *Upheaval in the Quiet Zone*, 153; Bruce Galphin, "Political Infighting Balks Charleston Hospital Pact: Hospital Strike Accord Balked in Charleston," *The Washington Post*, June 16, 1969; "The Charleston Strike," *New York Times*, June 18, 1969.

44. "Accord Fails in Charleston and Protestors Blame Thurmond," *New York Times*, June 14, 1969; Rudolph A. Pyatt, "Hospital Strike Now Political Football," *Charleston News and Courier*, June 15, 1969, National Union of Hospital and Health Care Employees (Local 1199) Records, 1938–1972, Catherwood Library Kheel Center, Cornell University, Ithaca, NY; "The Charleston Strike," *New York Times*, June 18, 1969, National Union of Hospital and Health Care Employees (Local 1199) Records, 1938–1972, Catherwood Library Kheel Center, Cornell University, Ithaca, NY; "Secretary Finch and the Charleston Strike," *The Washington Post, Times Herald*, June, 18, 1969; "James Strom Thurmond, R.I.P 1902–2003," *The Journal of Blacks in Higher Education*, no. 40 (Summer 2003): 24–25, http://www.jstor.org/stable/3134007 (accessed March 12, 2017); John W. Chambers, ed., *The Oxford Companion to American Military History* (Oxford: Oxford University Press, 2004),

accessed March 10, 2017, http://www.oxfordreference.com.libproxy.lib.unc.edu/view/10.1093/acref/9780195071986.001.0001/acref-9780195071986-e-0783; Neil Maxwell, "Dixie Negroes: South Carolina's Sen. Hollings Courts Them with Care," *Wall Street Journal*, October 30, 1968; Don Oberdorfer, "Hollings' Candor on Hunger Brings Praise, Jabs from S.C.: Problem Covered Up Strong Reactions New Coalition Seen Feeding the Lions Too Much for State Former NAACP Foe 'The Truth Hurts,'" *The Washington Post, Times Herald*, February 23, 1969; Mary Moultrie, interview by author, June 23, 2008; "Dixie Shows Power in Charleston," *Afro-American*, June 21, 1969.

 45. Moe Foner, interview by Robert Master, August 29, 1985; "Negroes, Cops Clash in Charleston March," *Chicago Tribune*, June 21, 1969; "Abernathy Is Jailed in Carolina March," *New York Times*, June 21, 1969; "Curfew Covers Charleston," *Chicago Tribune*, June 22, 1969; "Curfew in Charleston; Abernathy Bail $50,000: Police, National Guardsmen Turn Back New March by Hospital Strike Supporters," *Los Angeles Times*, June 22, 1969.

 46. "Violence Feared in Hospital Strike: 'Fringe Element' Cited by SCLC Aides in Charleston," *The Sun*, June 23, 1969; William Saunders, interview by Kerry Taylor and author, June 17, 2008; William Saunders, interview by Leon Fink, March 1, 1980; Mary Moultrie, William Saunders, and Rosetta Simmons, interview by Kerry Taylor, March 5, 2009; Grose, *South Carolina at the Brink*, 259.

Chapter 7: Resolution and Disillusion

 1. James T. Wooten, "Negroes Visit White Churches and March in Calm Charleston," *New York Times*, June 23, 1969; "2 Marches Held in Charleston," *Chicago Tribune*, June 23, 1969; "Violence Feared in Hospital Strike: 'Fringe Element' Cited by SCLC Aides in Charleston," *The Sun*, June 23, 1969; Andrew Young, interview by Leon Fink, January 31, 1980. The sources do not pinpoint exactly when the Andrew Young met with William McCord. After meeting with William McCord, Andrew Young states that they began making calls to New York in order to connect with the governor's office. It is unclear whom they contacted in New York. It could have been his contact Jay Islan.

 2. Moe Foner, interview by Leon Fink, March 9, 1979; Moe Foner, interview by Robert Master, August 29, 1985. The sources do not pinpoint exactly when Andrew Young met with the nurses.

 3. Moe Foner, interview by Leon Fink, March 9, 1979; Moe Foner, interview by Robert Master, August 29, 1985; Grose, *South Carolina at the Brink*, 258–59; "The Behind the Scenes of the Charleston Strike Settlement Is Revealed in the Following Chapter from a New Book by Leon E. Panetta and Peter Gall," document disseminated by Local 1199 that included an excerpt of chapter 12 from *Bring Us Together: The Nixon Team and the Civil Rights Retreat* (Philadelphia: Lippincott, 1971), no page numbers included, National Union of Hospital and Health Care Employees (Local 1199) Records, 1938–1972, Catherwood Library Kheel Center, Cornell University, Ithaca, NY. The timeline is unclear at this point. It is clear that meetings between Local 1199 and SCLC representatives, the meeting between SCLC and McCord, the meeting with the nurses, the phone call to Moynihan, and the subsequent arrival of federal government agents happened between June 12 and June 28, 1969.

4. James T. Wooten, "Charleston Port May Face Strike: Labor Threatens a Walkout in Support of Negroes," *New York Times*, June 26, 1969; Paul Valentine, "Fauntroy Leads Protest at HEW to Support Charleston Strikers: Patient Abandonment Charged to Strikers," *The Washington Post, Time Herald*, June 20, 1969; Paul Valentine, "30 Picket at HEW on Hospital Strike: Federal Judge to Hear Abernathy Release Plea," *The Washington Post, Times Herald*, June 27, 1969.

5. Fink and Greenberg, *Upheaval in the Quiet Zone*,154–55; Grose, *South Carolina at the Brink*, 258–59; "The Behind the Scenes of the Charleston Strike Settlement Is Revealed in the Following Chapter from a New Book by Leon E. Panetta and Peter Gall," no page numbers included; William L. Walker, "Medical College Strike Ends After 100 Days: McCord Breaks News," *Charleston News and Courier*, June 28, 1969; Elaine S. Stanford, "It Took 100 Days to End Strike at Medical College," *Charleston News and Courier*, June 28, 1969; "13-Week South Carolina Hospital Strike Ends: Negro Workers Reach Agreement With Institution; Talks Under Way at Second," *Los Angeles Times*, June 28, 1969; "Hospital Strike in Carolina Ends: Abernathy Refuses to Leave Jail Till Charleston County Accord is Also Reached," *New York Times*, June 28, 1969; "Major Strike Settled in Charleston: One Hospital Strike in Charleston Ends," *The Washington Post, Times Herald*, June 28, 1969; C. L. Fennessy, Director of Medical College Personnel Department, letter to Martha Grant, June 30, 1969, National Union of Hospital and Health Care Employees (Local 1199) Records, 1938–1972, Catherwood Library Kheel Center, Cornell University, Ithaca, NY. This is a copy of the packet sent to reinstated workers, which included the official letter of reinstatement, a breakdown of the details of the settlement, a notice regarding the implementation of the new state job classification and compensation plan, and information on the grievance procedure.

6. "Cheers, Sighs of Relief Greet News of Settlement: Governor Hopes for Peace in City," *Charleston News and Courier*, June 28, 1969, William Saunders Personal papers; "13-Week South Carolina Hospital Strike Ends: Negro Workers Reach Agreement with Institution; Talks Under Way at Second," *Los Angeles Times*, June 28, 1969.

7. "Hospital Won't Rehire All Striking Employees," *Los Angeles Times*, June 29, 1969; "Hospital Strike Sides in Bargain in Charleston," *The Atlanta Constitution*, June 29, 1969; "Workers Rejoining Carolina Hospital," *New York Times*, July 2, 1969; "Hospital Ultimatum Stirs More Protest Threat," *The Atlanta Constitution*, July 13, 1969; "Charleston Strikers Reject Hospital's Ultimatum: Around the Nation," *The Washington Post, Times Herald*, July 13, 1969; "Charleston Council Gives Strikers Friday Deadline," *Afro-American*, July 19, 1969. The number of workers attempting to be rehired varies depending on the source. It seems that there were approximately ninety Charleston County Hospital workers left on strike after the Medical College strike settled. Out of that number, approximately sixty-five were actually seeking reinstatement.

8. "Rehiring All Is Issue in Charleston," *The Sun*, June 29, 1969; James T. Wooten, "Abernathy Waits in Carolina Jail: Refuses to Leave Until 2d Hospital Pact Is Gained," *New York Times*, June 29, 1969; Leon J. Davis, President of Local 1199, letter to Reverend Ralph E. Abernathy, July 2, 1969, National Union of Hospital and Health Care Employees (Local 1199) Records, 1938–1972, Catherwood Library Kheel Center, Cornell University, Ithaca, NY; James T. Wooten, "Abernathy Leaves Jail, Hopeful of an Imminent Hospital

Accord," *New York Times*, July 4, 1969; Leon J. Davis, letter to Local 1199 Hospital Division Delegates, July 15, 1969, National Union of Hospital and Health Care Employees (Local 1199) Records, 1938–1972, Catherwood Library Kheel Center, Cornell University, Ithaca, NY; "Pickets March at Charleston," *The Atlanta Constitution*, July 3, 1969; Barbara Williams, "High Hopes for Normalcy Evaporate," *Charleston News and Courier*, July 3, 1969, William Saunders Personal papers.

9. "Rehiring All Is Issue in Charleston"; Wooten, "Abernathy Waits in Carolina Jail"; Leon J. Davis, President of Local 1199, letter to Reverend Ralph E. Abernathy, July 2, 1969; Wooten, "Abernathy Leaves Jail, Hopeful of an Imminent Hospital Accord"; Leon J. Davis, letter to Local 1199 Hospital Division Delegates, July 15, 1969; "Pickets March at Charleston"; Williams, "High Hopes for Normalcy Evaporate."

10. "Hospital Strike Ultimatum Stirs More Protest Threat," *The Atlanta Constitution*, July 13, 1969; "2D Hospital Ends Carolina Strike: 113-Day Walkout Marked by Turmoil in Charleston," *New York Times*, July 19, 1969; "Charleston's Long Strike Settled," *The Washington Post, Times Herald*, July 19, 1969; "End Strike in S.C.," *New York Amsterdam News*, July 26, 1969; "A Charleston Victory," *Chicago Daily Defender*, August 2, 1969; *I Am Somebody*, streaming video.

11. Mary Moultrie, interview by Leon Fink, February 28, 1980; Mary Moultrie, interview by Jean-Claude Bouffard, July 28, 1982; Mary Moultrie, "Reflections: 1969 Hospital Workers Strike," 1994, National Union of Hospital and Health Care Employees (Local 1199) Records, 1938–1972, Catherwood Library Kheel Center, Cornell University, Ithaca, NY; Mary Moultrie, William Saunders, and Rosetta Simmons, interview by Kerry Taylor, March 5, 2009.

12. Mary Moultrie, interview by Leon Fink, February 29, 1980; Mary Moultrie, "Reflections: 1969 Hospital Workers Strike,"; Mary Moultrie, interview by Jean-Claude Bouffard, July 28, 1982; Isaiah Bennett, interview by Steve Estes, October 21, 1994; Mary Moultrie, "What the Strike Meant to Me," National Union of Hospital and Health Care Employees (Local 1199) Records, 1938–1972, Catherwood Library Kheel Center, Cornell University, Ithaca, NY.

13. Isaiah Bennett, interview by Steve Estes, October 21, 1994.

14. Isaiah Bennett, interview by Steve Estes, October 21, 1994; Rosetta Simmons, interview by author, June 25, 2008; Mary Moultrie, William Saunders, and Rosetta Simmons, interview by Kerry Taylor, March 5, 2009.

15. Mary Moultrie, interview by Jean-Claude Bouffard, July 28, 1982; Mary Moultrie, interview by Leon Fink, February 28, 1980; Mary Moultrie, William Saunders, and Rosetta Simmons, interview by Kerry Taylor, March 5, 2009.

16. Mary Moultrie, interview by Jean-Claude Bouffard, July 28, 1982; Rosetta Simmons, interview by author, 25 June 2008; Naomi White, interview by Steve Estes, 21 October 1994; Carrie Mitchell, interview by author, June 25, 2008.

17. Naomi White, interview by Steve Estes, October 21, 1994; Naomi White, interview by author, June 25, 2008; Jessie Jefferson, interview by Steve Estes, October 22, 1994.

18. Carrie Mitchell, interview by author, June 25, 2008.

19. Rosetta Simmons, interview by author, June 25, 2008; Mary Moultrie, William Saunders, and Rosetta Simmons, interview by Kerry Taylor, March 5, 2009.

20. Mary Moultrie, interview by author, June 23, 2008; Mary Moultrie, interview by Leon Fink, February 28, 1980; Mary Moultrie, William Saunders, and Rosetta Simmons, interview by Kerry Taylor, March 5, 2009; Sharon J. Stagg, Daniel J. Sheridan, Ruth A. Jones, and Karen G. Speroni, "Workplace Bullying: The Effectiveness of a Workplace Program," *Workplace Health and Safety* 61, no. 8 (2013): 333–38; Sharon J. Stagg, Ruth A. Jones, and Karen G. Speroni, "Evaluation of a Workplace Bullying Cognitive Rehearsal Program in a Hospital Setting," *The Journal of Continuing Education in Nursing* 42, no. 9 (2011): 395–401. Stagg, Jones, and Speroni defined workplace mobbing, also referred to as workplace bullying, as "repetitive inappropriate behavior, direct and indirect, whether verbal, physical, or otherwise, carried out by one or more persons against another or others, at the workplace and/or in the course of employment, which undermines the individual's right to dignity at work."

21. Mary Moultrie, "Reflections: 1969 Hospital Workers Strike," 1994; Claire G. Brown, "My Thoughts About the Charleston Hospital Workers Strike," National Union of Hospital and Health Care Employees (Local 1199) Records, 1938–1972, Catherwood Library Kheel Center, Cornell University, Ithaca, NY; Donna M. Whack, "What the Strike Meant," National Union of Hospital and Health Care Employees (Local 1199) Records, 1938–1972, Catherwood Library Kheel Center, Cornell University, Ithaca, NY.

22. Mary Moultrie, interview by author, June 23, 2008; Local 1199-B roster and dues record, National Union of Hospital and Health Care Employees (Local 1199) Records, 1938–1972, Catherwood Library Kheel Center, Cornell University, Ithaca, NY; Jessie Jefferson, interview by Steve Estes, October 22, 1994; Mary Moultrie, interview by Jean-Claude Bouffard, July 28, 1982; Andrew Young, interview by Leon Fink, January 31, 1980.

23. Mary Moultrie, interview by Steve Estes, October 20, 1994; Leon Davis, letter to Mary Moultrie, December 22, 1969, National Union of Hospital and Health Care Employees (Local 1199) Records, 1938–1972, Catherwood Library Kheel Center, Cornell University, Ithaca, NY; Elliott Godoff, National Director, letter to Isaiah Bennet, February 10, 1970, National Union of Hospital and Health Care Employees (Local 1199) Records, 1938–1972, Catherwood Library Kheel Center, Cornell University, Ithaca, NY; Elliott Godoff, letter to Mary Moultrie, February 10, 1970, National Union of Hospital and Health Care Employees (Local 1199) Records, 1938–1972, Catherwood Library Kheel Center, Cornell University, Ithaca, NY; Author unknown, letter to Doris Turner, February 12, 1970, February 10, 1970, National Union of Hospital and Health Care Employees (Local 1199) Records, 1938–1972, Catherwood Library Kheel Center, Cornell University, Ithaca, NY.

24. David White, interview by Leon Fink, June 5, 1979; Henry Nicholas, interview by Brian Greenberg, 11 January 1980; Horace Small, letter to Elliott Godoff, June 25, 1970; Claire G. Brown, letter to Leon Davis, August 31, 1970; all of the sources above are located in National Union of Hospital and Health Care Employees (Local 1199) Records, 1938–1972, Catherwood Library Kheel Center, Cornell University, Ithaca, NY; Isaiah Bennett, interview by Steve Estes, October 21, 1994; Fink and Greenberg, *Upheaval in the Quiet Zone*, 156–57; Mary Moultrie, interview by Jean-Claude Bouffard, July 28, 1982; Naomi White, interview by Steve Estes, October 21, 1994. None of these sources give definitive information on when Local 1199B voted Mary Moultrie out or when the local dissolved.

25. "'Decent Salaries' Garbage Workers Strike Charleston: Prisoners Used to Collect Trash," newspaper unknown, August 16, 1969, South Carolina Council on Human

Relations Collection, The South Caroliniana Library, University of South Carolina, Columbia, SC; "Strikers Threaten 'Mass Marches,'" newspaper referred to as *"Record,"* August 23, 1969, South Carolina Council on Human Relations Collection, The South Caroliniana Library, University of South Carolina, Columbia, SC; "Charleston Garbage Collectors Settle Strike Without Winning Recognition," *Afro-American*, November 8, 1969; "Charleston's Striking Garbagemen March," *The Charlotte Observer*, September 2, 1969.

26. "Charleston Garbage Collectors Settle Strike Without Winning Recognition"; "Garbage Strike Talks Set," *The Charlotte Observer*, August 19, 1969, South Carolina Council on Human Relations Collection, The South Caroliniana Library, University of South Carolina, Columbia, SC; "Charleston Strike Talks Kept Quiet," *The Charlotte Observer*, August 21, 1969, South Carolina Council on Human Relations Collection, The South Caroliniana Library, University of South Carolina, Columbia, SC; "Charleston Mayor Meets with Strikers in Dispute," newspaper referred to as *"Record,"* August 21, 1969, South Carolina Council on Human Relations Collection, The South Caroliniana Library, University of South Carolina, Columbia, SC; Mary Moultrie, interview by Jean-Claude Bouffard, July 28, 1982; Naomi White, interview by Steve Estes, October 21, 1994.

27. Max Greenberg, president of RWDSU, letter to Leon Davis, letter is not dated, National Union of Hospital and Health Care Employees (Local 1199) Records, 1938–1972, Catherwood Library Kheel Center, Cornell University, Ithaca, NY; Moe Foner, "Progress Report—Charleston Hospital Strike Film," December 30, 1969, National Union of Hospital and Health Care Employees (Local 1199) Records, 1938–1972, Catherwood Library Kheel Center, Cornell University, Ithaca, NY.

28. Moe Foner, letter to Harry Watchel, October 8, 1969, National Union of Hospital and Health Care Employees (Local 1199) Records, 1938–1972, Catherwood Library Kheel Center, Cornell University, Ithaca, NY; Moe Foner, "Progress Report—Charleston Hospital Strike Film," December 30, 1969; *I Am Somebody*, streaming video.

29. Fink and Greenberg, *Upheaval in the Quiet Zone*, 158–80; Naomi White, interview by Steve Estes, October 21, 1994; Haynes Johnson and Nick Kotz, "Union Ratio of Workers falls as Economy Rises: Dispute Over Organizing: How Much Have Unions Lost?," *The Washington Post, Times Herald*, April 17, 1972; "Facts About District 1199: Membership," *New York Amsterdam News*, September 1, 1979.

30. Fink and Greenberg, *Upheaval in the Quiet Zone*, 157; "SCLC Promotes Williams, Makes Other Staff Changes," *Afro-American*, March 20, 1971; Ralph Abernathy, "Media Ignored SCLC Drive," *Afro-American*, March 27, 1971; "Robinson Bucks Abernathy, Won't Change Group's Name," *Chicago Daily Defender*, August 2, 1971; "Jackson, Relieved by S.C.L.C., Vows to Keep Helping the Poor," *New York Times*, December 1971.

Conclusion

1. Robert E. McNair, "Summary of Position on Committee Appointed by Mayor of Charleston," May 1, 1969, Governor Robert E. McNair Papers, South Carolina Political Collections, University of South Carolina, Columbia, SC; Isaiah Bennett, interview by Steve Estes, October 21, 1995; Linda Meggett, "The Workers 'Stood Up for What Was

Right,'" *The Post and Courier*, April 17, 1994, Steve Estes Papers, Avery Research Center for African American History and Culture, College of Charleston, Charleston, SC; John E. Rosen, "We Shall Overcome," *Charleston City Paper*, February 3, 1999, Avery Research Center for African American History and Culture, College of Charleston, Charleston, SC; Theoharis, "Accidental Matriarchs and Beautiful Helpmates: Rosa Parks, Coretta Scott King, and the Memorialization of the Civil Rights Movement," in *Civil Rights History from the Ground Up: Local Struggles, a National Movement*, ed. Emilye Crosby (Athens: University of Georgia Press, 2011), 389–95.

2. Mary Moultrie, interview by author, June 23, 2008; Henry Nicholas, interview by Brian Greenberg, January 11, 1980; Fink and Greenberg, *Upheaval in the Quiet Zone*, 156–57.

3. Adam Parker, "Local Hospital Workers' Courage Changed Workplaces Forever," *The Charleston Post and Courier*, September 30, 2013; Statehouse Report, "History: Charleston Hospital Workers' Strike," January 20, 2015, accessed March 23, 2017, http://www.statehousereport.com/2015/01/20/history-charleston-hospital-workers-strike/.

4. Parker, "Local Hospital Workers' Courage Changed Workplaces Forever."

5. Reis Thebault, "In D.C. the Poor People's Campaign Hits 50 and Looks Ahead," *The Washington Post*, June 23, 2018; North Carolina National Association for the Advancement of Colored People, "Our Leadership," accessed March 12, 2019, https://naacpnc.org/leadership/; Repairers of the Breach, https://www.breachrepairers.org; Kairos: The Center for Religions, Rights, and Social Justice, accessed March 12, 2019, https://kairoscenter.org/staff/; Kenrya Rankin, "Poor People's Campaign Launches with March on Capitol Hill," *Colorlines*, May 14, 2018.

6. Rosetta Simmons, interview by author, June 26, 2009.

BIBLIOGRAPHY

Manuscript Collections

Avery Research Center Oral History Collection. Avery Research Center for African American History and Culture, College of Charleston, Charleston, South Carolina.

Bernice Robinson Papers. Avery Research Center for African American History and Culture, College of Charleston, Charleston, South Carolina.

Charleston and the Long Civil Rights Movement Series, The Citadel Oral History Program, The Citadel, Charleston, SC

Esau Jenkins Papers. Avery Research Center for African American History and Culture, College of Charleston, Charleston, South Carolina.

Governor Robert McNair Papers. South Carolina Political Collection, University of South Carolina, Columbia, South Carolina.

Henry Grant Papers. Avery Research Center for African American History and Culture, College of Charleston, Charleston, South Carolina.

Hospital Strike Collection. Avery Research Center for African American History and Culture, College of Charleston, Charleston, South Carolina.

Isaiah Bennett Papers. Avery Research Center for African American History and Culture, College of Charleston, Charleston, South Carolina.

National Union of Hospital and Health Care Employees (Local 1199) Records, 1938–1972. Catherwood Library Kheel Center, Cornell University, Ithaca, New York.

Septima Clark Papers. Avery Research Center for African American History and Culture, College of Charleston, Charleston, South Carolina.

South Carolina Council on Human Relations Records, 1934–1976. The South Caroliniana Library, University of South Carolina, Columbia, South Carolina.

Southern Christian Leadership Conference records, 1963–1968. Rubenstein Library, Duke University, Durham, North Carolina.

Steve Estes Papers. Avery Research Center for African American History and Culture, College of Charleston, Charleston, South Carolina.

William M. McCord Papers. Waring Historical Library, Medical University of South Carolina, Charleston, South Carolina.

Newspapers and Journals

Afro-American
The Atlanta Constitution
Bulletin of the History of Medicine
The Catholic Miscellany: Good News from the Diocese of Charleston
The Charleston Chronicle
Charleston City Paper
Charleston Evening Post
Charleston News and Courier
The Charleston Post and Courier
The Charlotte Observer
Chicago Daily Defender
Chicago Tribune
Gender and History
The Guardian
The Journal of African American History
The Journal of American History
Journal of the History of Medicine and Allied Sciences
Journal of Postcolonial Writing
The Journal of Southern History
Journal of Urban History
Los Angeles Times
New Masses
New York Amsterdam News
The New York Times
Palmetto Primary
Poverty and Race
Soul Force: Official Journal of SCLC
South Carolina Historical Association
Southern Medical Journal
St. John's Law Review
The State
The Sun
The Times and Democrat
The Wall Street Journal
The Washington Post, Times Herald

Film

I Am Somebody. Directed by Madeline Anderson. Icarus Films, 1970, http://docuseek2.com
.libproxy.lib.unc.edu/if-iams.

Oral Histories by Author

Marjorie Amos-Frazier, June 17, 2008, and June 24, 2008, Charleston, South Carolina.
Thaddeus J. Bell, April 23, 2021, Charleston, South Carolina
Lillie Doster, June 25, 2008, Charleston, South Carolina.
Robert Ford, June 25, 2008, Charleston, South Carolina.
Carrie Mitchell, June 25, 2008, Charleston, South Carolina.
Mary Moultrie, June 23, 2008, and August 26, 2009, Charleston, South Carolina.
Carolyn Murray, June 2, 2021, Rock Hill, South Carolina.
John Reynolds, April 24, 2021, Seabrook Island, South Carolina.
William Saunders, June 17, 2008, June 23, 2008, and July 7, 2010, Charleston, South Carolina.
Rosetta Simmons, June 25, 2008, and August 26, 2009, Charleston, South Carolina.
Naomi White, June 25, 2008, and August 26, 2009, Charleston South Carolina.
Cecil Williams, April 25, 2021, Seabrook Island, South Carolina.

Other Oral Histories

Isaiah Bennett, interview by Leon Fink, February 29, 1980. National Union of Hospital and Health Care Employees (Local 1199) Records, 1938–1972, Catherwood Library Kheel Center, Cornell University.
Isaiah Bennett, interview by Steve Estes, October 21, 1994. Steve Estes Papers, Avery Research Center for African American History and Culture, College of Charleston.
Louise Brown, interview by Kerry Taylor, February 23, 2018. Charleston, South Carolina.
Reverend Thomas Duffy, interview by Leon Fink, February 28, 1980. National Union of Hospital and Health Care Employees (Local 1199) Records, 1938–1972, Catherwood Library Kheel Center, Cornell University.
Moe Foner, interview by Leon Fink, March 9, 1979. National Union of Hospital and Health Care Employees (Local 1199) Records, 1938–1972, Catherwood Library Kheel Center, Cornell University.
Moe Foner, interview by Robert Master, August 29, 1985. National Union of Hospital and Health Care Employees (Local 1199) Records, 1938–1972, Catherwood Library Kheel Center, Cornell University.
Father Henry Grant, interview by Leon Fink, February 27, 1980. National Union of Hospital and Health Care Employees (Local 1199) Records, 1938–1972, Catherwood Library Kheel Center, Cornell University.
Jessie Jefferson, interview by Steve Estes, October 22, 1994. Steve Estes Papers, Avery Research Center for African American History and Culture, College of Charleston.
Mary Moultrie, interview by Jean-Claude Bouffard, July 28, 1982. Avery Research Center Oral History Collection, Avery Research Center for African American History and Culture, College of Charleston.
Mary Moultrie, interview by Leon Fink, February 28, 1980. National Union of Hospital and Health Care Employees (Local 1199) Records, 1938–1972, Catherwood Library Kheel Center, Cornell University.

Mary Moultrie, interview by Steve Estes, October 20, 1994. Steve Estes Papers, Avery Research Center for African American History and Culture, College of Charleston.

Mary Moultrie, William Saunders and Rosetta Simmons, interview by Kerry Taylor, March 5, 2009. Charleston and the Long Civil Rights Movement series, The Citadel Oral History Program, The Citadel.

Henry Nicholas, interview by Brian Greenberg, January 11, 1978. National Union of Hospital and Health Care Employees (Local 1199) Records, 1938–1972, Catherwood Library Kheel Center, Cornell University.

William Saunders, interview by Leon Fink, March 1, 1980. National Union of Hospital and Health Care Employees (Local 1199) Records, 1938–1972, Catherwood Library Kheel Center, Cornell University.

William Saunders, interview by Kerry Taylor, June 9, 2011. Civil Rights Project, Library of Congress, https://www.loc.gov/item/afc2010039_crhp0027/.

Judge Clarence Singletary, interview by Leon Fink, February 27, 1980. National Union of Hospital and Health Care Employees (Local 1199) Records, 1938–1972, Catherwood Library Kheel Center, Cornell University.

David White, interview by Leon Fink, June 5, 1979. National Union of Hospital and Health Care Employees (Local 1199) Records, 1938–1972, Catherwood Library Kheel Center, Cornell University.

Naomi White, interview by Steve Estes, October 21, 1994. Steve Estes Papers, Avery Research Center for African American History and Culture, College of Charleston.

Hosea Williams, interview by Steve Estes, February 9, 1996. Steve Estes Papers, Avery Research Center for African American History and Culture, College of Charleston.

John E. Wise, interview by Leon Fink, February 28, 1980. National Union of Hospital and Health Care Employees (Local 1199) Records, 1938–1972, Catherwood Library Kheel Center, Cornell University.

Andrew Young, interview by Leon Fink, January 31, 1980. National Union of Hospital and Health Care Employees (Local 1199) Records, 1938–1972, Catherwood Library Kheel Center, Cornell University.

Online Sources

Brown, Millicent, Clerc Cooper, and John Hale. *Somebody Had to Do It: First Children in School Desegregation*. Lowcountry Digital History Initiative. College of Charleston, Charleston, South Carolina. http://ldhi.library.cofc.edu/exhibits/show/somebody_had_to_do_it.

National Park Service. "Gullah/Geechee Cultural Heritage Corridor: North Carolina, South Carolina, Georgia, Florida." National Park Service, United States Department of the Interior. http://www.nps.gov/history/nr/travel/cultural_diversity/Gullah_Geechee_Cultural_Heritage_Corridor.html.

Waugh, Dwana. *Charleston's Cigar Factory Strike, 1945–1946*. Lowcountry Digital History Initiative, College of Charleston, Charleston, South Carolina. http://ldhi.library.cofc.edu/exhibits/show/cigar_factory.

Documents, Reports, Publications, and Government Publications

The City of Charleston. "Centennial Celebration of the Incorporation of the City of Charleston," August 13, 1883. In the University of North Carolina-Chapel Hill Digital Library, https://babel-hathitrust-org.libproxy.lib.unc.edu/cgi/pt?id=loc.ark:/13960/t54f2jh7c;view=1up;seq=175.

House Military, Municipal and Public Affairs Committee, HR. *A Concurrent Resolution Affirming the Public Policy Regarding Collective Bargaining with Certain Employees, as Pronounced by His Excellency, the Governor*, South Carolina General Assembly, April 29, 1969. Governor Robert E. McNair Papers, South Carolina Political Collections, University of South Carolina.

March on Washington for Jobs and Freedom Administrative Committee. *Organizing Manual no. 2: Final Plans for March on Washington for Jobs and Freedom*. New York: Trades Council, date unknown.

Medical Society of South Carolina. Rules and Regulations for the Government of the Trustees and Officers of Roper Hospital. Charleston: Evans & Cogswell, 1861. In Rare Books Collection, Perkins Library, Duke University, Durham, North Carolina.

Political Action Committee of Charleston County, South Carolina. *Constitution and By-Laws*, January 19, 1966. Bernice Robinson Papers, Avery Research Center for African American History and Culture, College of Charleston.

Sanes, Milla, and John Schmitt. *Regulation of Public Sector Collective Bargaining in the States*. Washington: Center for Economic and Policy Research, 2014.

U.S. Bureau of the Census. "24 Million Americans: Poverty in the United States, 1969." In *Current Population Reports*, series P-60, no. 76, https://www2.census.gov/prod2/popscan/p60-076.pdf.

U.S. Commission on Civil Rights. *Equal Opportunity in Hospitals and Health Facilities: Civil Rights Policies Under the Hill-Burton Program*. Commission on Civil Rights Special Publication, no. 2 (March 1965), https://www.nlm.nih.gov/exhibition/forallthepeople/img/1706.pdf.

U.S. Congress. *Hospital Survey and Construction Act with Amendments*. August 13, 1946. Public Law 725. 79th Cong., 2d sess.

Books and Articles

Abernathy, Ralph David. *And the Walls Came Tumbling Down*. New York: Harper and Row, 1989.

Beardsley, E. H. "Good-Bye to Jim Crow: The Desegregation of Southern Hospitals, 1945–70." *Bulletin of the History of Medicine* 60, no. 3 (Fall 1986): 367–86.

Branch, Taylor. *Parting the Waters: America in the King Years, 1954–63*. New York: Simon & Schuster Paperbacks, 1988.

Charron, Katherine M. *Freedom's Teacher: The Life of Septima Clark*. Chapel Hill: University of North Carolina Press, 2009.

Collins, John W., III, and Nancy P. O'Brien, eds. *Missouri ex rel. Gaines vs. Canada*, 305 U.S. 337 (1938). In *The Greenwood Dictionary of Education*. Santa Barbara: ABC-CLIO, 2011.

Collins, Patricia Hill. *Black Feminist Thought: Knowledge, Consciousness, and the Politics of Empowerment*. 2nd ed. New York: Routledge, 2000.

Commager, Henry S. *Documents of American History*. 9th ed. Englewood Cliffs: Prentice-Hall Inc., 1973.

Conner, Catherine. "'The University That Ate Birmingham': The Healthcare Industry, Urban Development, and Neoliberalism." *Journal of Urban History* 42, no. 2 (January 29, 2016): 284–305.

Debnam, Jewell. "Black Women and the Charleston Hospital Workers' Strike of 1969." Doctor of Philosophy dissertation, Michigan State University, 2016.

Dittmer, John. *The Good Doctors: The Medical Committee for Human Rights and the Struggle for Social Justice in Health Care*. New York: Bloomsbury Press, 2009.

Eisner, Eugene G., and I. Philip Sipser. "The Charleston Hospital Dispute: Organizing Public Employees and the Right to Strike." *St. John's Law Review* 45, no. 2 (December 1970): 254–73.

Fink, Leon, and Brian Greenberg. *Upheaval in the Quiet Zone: 1199SEIU and the Politics of Healthcare Unionism*. 2nd ed. Urbana: University of Illinois Press, 2009.

Fink, Leon, and Brian Greenberg. "Union Power, Soul Power: The Story of 1199B and Labor's Search for a Southern Strategy." *Southern Changes*, March/April 1983, 9–20.

Foner, Moe, and Dan North. *Not for Bread Alone: A Memoir*. Ithaca: Cornell University Press, 2022.

Foner, Philip S. *Organized Labor and the Black Worker*. New York: International Publishers, 1981.

Foner, Philip S. *Women and the American Labor Movement: From the First Trade Unions to the Present*. 2nd ed. Chicago: Haymarket Books, 2018.

Garrow, David J. *Bearing the Cross: Martin Luther King, Jr., and the Southern Christian Leadership Conference*. New York: Open Road Integrated Media Inc., 2015.

Green, Laurie B. *Battling the Plantation Mentality: Memphis and the Black Freedom Struggle*. Chapel Hill: University of North Carolina Press, 2007.

Greene, Christina. *Our Separate Ways: Women and the Black Freedom Movement in Durham, North Carolina*. Chapel Hill: University of North Carolina Press, 2005.

Grose, Philip G. *South Carolina at the Brink: Robert McNair and the Politics of Civil Rights*. Columbia: University of South Carolina Press, 2006.

Gross, Kali Nicole. *Hannah Mary Tabbs and the Disembodied Torso: A Tale of Race, Sex, and Violence in America*. New York: Oxford University Press, 2016.

Hall, Jacquelyn D. "Disorderly Women: Gender and Labor Militancy in the Appalachian South." *The Journey of American History* 73, no. 2 (September 1986): 354–82.

Hall, Jacquelyn D. "The Long Civil Rights Movement and the Political Uses of the Past." *The Journal of American History* 91, no. 4 (March 2005): 1233–1263.

Hennen, John. *A Union for Appalachian Healthcare Workers: The Radical Roots and Hard Fights of Local 1199*. Morgantown: West Virginia University Press, 2021.

Hoffius, Steve "Charleston Hospital Workers Strike, 1969." In *Working Lives: The Southern Exposure History of Labor in the South*, edited by Marc Miller, 244–58. New York: Pantheon Books, 1980.

Honey, Michael K. *Black Workers Remember: An Oral History of Segregation, Unionism, and the Feedom Struggle*. Berkeley: University of California Press, 1999.

Hunter, Tera W. *To 'Joy My Freedom: Southern Black Women's Lives and Labor after the Civil War*. Cambridge: Harvard University Press, 1997.

"James Strom Thurmond, R.I.P 1902–2003." *The Journal of Blacks in Higher Education 40* (Summer 2003), 24–25.

Knight, Felice F. "Portrait of a Community Activist: William 'Bill' Saunders and the Black Freedom Struggle in Charleston, SC, 1951–2004." Master of Arts thesis, The College of Charleston, 2006.

Korstad, Karl. "Tobacco Road, Union Style." *New Masses*, May 1946, 13–15.

Korstad, Robert. *Civil Rights Unionism: Tobacco Workers and the Struggle for Democracy in the Mid-Twentieth-Century South*. Chapel Hill: University of North Carolina Press, 2003.

Korstad, Robert, and Nelson Lichtenstein. "Opportunities Found and Lost: Labor, Radicals, and the Early Civil Rights Movement." *The Journal of American History* 75, no. 3 (December 1988): 786–811.

Lau, Peter F. *Democracy Rising: South Carolina and the Fight for Black Equality since 1865*. Lexington: University of Kentucky Press, 2006.

Lennon, Linda A., and Ruth M. Miller. *The Angel Oak*. Charleston: Tradd Street Press, 1989.

Lewis, Simon. "Slavery, Memory, and the History of the 'Atlantic Now': Charleston, South Carolina and Global Racial/Economic Hierarchy." *Journal of Postcolonial Writing* 45, no. 2 (2009): 125–35.

Maggard, Sally Ward. "'We're Fighting Millionaires!': The Clash of Gender and Class in Appalachian Women's Union Organizing." In *No Middle Ground: Women and Radical Protest*. Edited by Kathleen M. Blee. New York: New York University Press, 1998.

McFadden, Grace Jordan. "Septima P. Clark and the Struggle for Human Rights." In *Women in the Civil Rights Movement: Trailblazers & Torchbearers, 1941–1965*. Edited by Vicki L. Crawford, Jacqueline A. Rouse, and Barbara Woods. Bloomington, Indiana University Press, 1990.

Meffert, John, Sherman E. Pyatt, and the Avery Research Center. *Charleston, South Carolina*. Charleston: Arcadia Publishing, 2000.

Mueller, Carol. "Ella Baker and the Origins of 'Participatory Democracy.'" In *Women in the Civil Rights Movement: Trailblazers & Torchbearers, 1941–1965*. Edited by Vicki L. Crawford, Jacqueline A. Rouse, and Barbara Woods. Bloomington, Indiana University Press, 1990.

Nasstrom, Kathryn L. "Down to Now: Memory, Narrative, and Women's Leadership in the Civil Rights Movement in Atlanta, Georgia." *Gender & History* 11, no. 1 (April 1999): 113–44.

Oceanic Linguistics Special Publications. "Gullah." In *A Bibliography of Pidgin and Creole Languages*. Honolulu: University of Hawaii Press, 1975.

Omowale, Akinyele. *We Will Shoot Back: Armed Resistance in the Mississippi Freedom Movement*. New York: New York University Press, 2013.

O'Neill, Stephen. "The Struggle for Black Equality Comes to Charleston: The Hospital Strike of 1969." *South Carolina Historical Association* (1986): 82–91.

Payne, Charles. "Men Led, but Women Organized: Movement Participation of Women in the Mississippi Delta." In *Women in the Civil Rights Movement: Trailblazers and Torchbearers, 1941–1965*. Edited by Vicki L. Crawford, Jacqueline Anne Rouse, and Barbara Woods. Bloomington: Indiana University Press, 1990.

Roberts, Blain, and Ethan Kytle. "Looking the Thing in the Face: Slavery, Race, and the Commemorative Landscape of Charleston, South Carolina, 1865–2010." *The Journal of Southern History* 78, no. 3 (August 2012): 639–84.

Robnett, Belinda. *How Long? How Long?: African-American Women in the Struggle for Civil Rights*. New York: Oxford University Press, 1997.

Rose, Margaret. "From the Fields to the Picket Line: Huelga Women and the Boycott, 1965–1975." In *No Middle Ground: Women and Radical Protest*. Edited by Kathleen M. Blee. New York: New York University Press, 1998.

Rouse, Jacqueline A. "'We Seek to Know . . . in Order to Speak the Truth': Nurturing the Seeds of Discontent—Septima P. Clark and Participatory Leadership" In *Sisters in the Struggle: African American Women in the Civil Rights-Black Power Movement*. Edited by Bettye Collier-Thomas and V. P. Franklin. New York: New York University Press, 2001.

Sacks, Karen B. *Caring by the Hour: Women, Work, and Organizing at Duke Medical Center*. Urbana: University of Illinois Press, 1988.

Sanford, Ezelle, III. "Civil Rights and Healthcare: Remembering Simkins v. Cone (1963)." *Black Perspectives*, February 4, 2017, https://www.aaihs.org/civil-rights-and-healthcare-remembering-simkins-v-cone-1963/#:~:text=Cone%20Health%20commemorated%20the%20legacy,of%20the%20Guilford%20County%20Courthouse;

Sellers, Cleveland. "Thirty-Five Years Ago: An African-American Professor Recalls the Orangeburg Massacre at South Carolina State College." *The Journal of Blacks in Higher Education* 41 (Autumn 2003): 67.

Smith, David B. "Stealth Capture: The Civil Rights Movement and the Implementation of Medicare." *Poverty and Race* 25, no. 2 (April–June 2016): 1–14.

Stagg, Sharon J., Daniel J. Sheridan, Ruth A. Jones, and Karen G. Speroni. "Workplace Bullying: The Effectiveness of a Workplace Program." *Workplace Health and Safety* 61, no. 8 (2013): 333–38.

Stagg, Sharon J., Daniel J. Sheridan, Ruth A. Jones, and Karen G. Speroni. "Evaluation of a Workplace Bullying Cognitive Rehearsal Program in a Hospital Setting." *The Journal of Continuing Education in Nursing* 42, no. 9 (2011): 395–401.

Theoharris, Jeanne. "Accidental Matriarchs and Beautiful Helpmates: Rosa Parks, Coretta Scott King, and the Memorialization of the Civil Rights Movement." In *Civil Rights History from the Ground Up: Local Struggles, a National Movement*. Edited by Emilye Crosby. Athens: University of Georgia Press, 2011.

Thomas, Karen K. *Deluxe Jim Crow: Civil Rights and American Health Policy, 1935–1954*. Athens: University of Georgia Press, 2011.

Thomas, Karen K. "Dr. Jim Crow: The University of North Carolina, The Regional Medical School for Negroes, and the Desegregation of South Medical Education, 1945–1960." *The Journal of African American History* 88, no. 3 (Summer 2003): 223–44.

Thomas, Karen K. "Simkins v. Cone." *Encyclopedia of North Carolina*, ed. William S. Powell. Chapel Hill: University of North Carolina Press, 2006. https://www.ncpedia.org/simkins-v-cone.

Waring, Joseph I. "Charleston Medicine 1800–1860." *Journal of the History of Medicine and Allied Sciences* 31, no. 3 (1976): 320–42.

Waring, Joseph I. "History of Medical University of South Carolina." *Southern Medical Journal* 67, no. 8 (1974): 888–95.

Waring, Joseph I. *A History of Medicine in South Carolina*. Columbia: The South Carolina Medical Association, 1964.

INDEX

Abernathy, Ralph David, 59–62, 65–69, 71, 88, 94, 96, 101, 105–6, 110–11. *See also* Southern Christian Leadership Conference (SCLC)
activism, 3–6, 8, 9–12, 16–17, 32, 41–42, 61, 64, 71, 73, 84, 87, 88, 120, 123; church-based, 10; grassroots, 10, 13, 17, 37, 55, 76, 88, 116, 120; health-care, 22–36; student, 26; women's, 3–4, 7, 12, 37, 42, 56, 72, 73–75, 80, 87
affirmative action, 28–29, 104
Alston, Eva, 84
American Federation of Labor and Congress of Industrial Organizations (AFL-CIO), 14, 39, 59, 99–100, 109, 119
American Federation of State, County and Municipal Employees (AFSCME) Local 1733, 60
American Glanzstoff, 86
American Journal of Nursing, The, 108
American Medical Association, 26
American Tobacco Company, 19–21
arrests, 61, 64, 66, 68–71, 75, 76, 78, 81, 85, 94, 106, 110, 122

Baker, Ella, 85, 86
Baltimore, MD, 119
Bamberg County Jail, 78
Barber, William, II, 122–23
Barrett, Reginald, 43–44
Bennett, Isaiah, 6, 19, 31, 33, 36, 43, 45, 46, 50, 81, 89–90, 117
Beth-El Hospital, 58

Birmingham, AL, 65
Black Freedom Movement, 80
Black Power Movement, 10, 60–61, 69, 97
Blatt, Solomon, 46, 92
boycotts, 20, 49, 63, 65, 76, 100–101, 106
Bradford, Jack, 33, 41–42, 63
Brimm, Hugh A., 28–29, 102, 104
Broome, F. William, 100
Brotherhood of Sleeping Car Porters, 58, 59
Brown, Claire, 15, 42, 119
Brown, Louise, 123
Brown, Sadie, 33
Budget and Control Board, 63
Buncum, Thelma, 69
Burke High School, 14, 17, 70

Campbell, V. W. H., 55
Charleston, SC, 3–8, 11, 16–17, 19, 21, 24–25, 36, 37, 40–41, 44–46, 48, 50, 52, 54–56, 57, 61–63, 65–69, 71–72, 73, 77–79, 81–82, 86, 88–92, 94, 96–102, 106, 108–12, 116–20, 121–23; Citizens' Committee, 11, 13–14, 91–95; curfew, 78–79, 89, 96, 98, 100–101, 106, 111; Johns Island, 10–13, 16–17, 66; Mother's Day March, 96–97; protest tradition, 9–21; tourism, 100, 106
Charleston Cigar Factory Strike, 19–21, 34, 36
Charleston County Council, 93, 110
Charleston County Hospital, 3, 6–8, 21, 23, 31–32, 55, 57, 66, 75, 93, 95, 96, 99, 102, 110–11, 113, 122

Charleston County Legislative Delegation, 44, 89
Charleston County Library, 121
Charleston County Welfare Department, 74
Charleston hospital workers' campaign, 3–8, 9–10, 12, 14, 19, 21, 22–36, 37–38, 41–44, 47–56, 57–58, 61–66, 69, 71–72, 73–85, 87, 88–106, 107–20, 121–23
Charleston News and Courier, 47, 67, 85, 87
Charleston Post and Courier, 80
Charleston Trident Chamber of Commerce, 100
Chicago Public Schools, 27
Chicago Tribune, 72
Chisholm, Shirley, 44
churches and the clergy, 51–53, 56, 57–58, 62–63, 66, 70, 86, 107, 120. *See also* Concerned Clergy Committee
City Hospital, 23
Civil Rights Act of 1964, 29; Title VI, 27, 29, 102; Title VII, 102
civil rights movement and campaigns, 4–8, 9–10, 12, 16, 18, 21, 22–23, 26–28, 31, 34, 36, 37–42, 50–52, 55–56, 57–62, 64, 66, 70–72, 73, 76, 79–81, 85, 88–89, 94, 98–99, 108, 112, 118, 120, 121–23
Clark, Septima P., 12–13, 85, 86
collective bargaining, 31, 39, 41, 47–48, 54–55, 59, 63, 78, 91–92, 94, 99, 112, 119
College of Charleston, 86
Columbia, SC, 44, 46, 48, 63, 66, 94
Committee for Justice to Hospital Workers, 58
Communications Workers of America (CWA), 42
Communist Party, 39–40
Community Relations Committee, 46, 71
Concerned Citizens of Charleston, 62
Concerned Clergy Committee, 52–53, 63, 66
Congress of Industrial Organizations (CIO), 20. *See also* American Federation of Labor and Congress of Industrial Organizations
Congress of Racial Equality (CORE), 58

Conroy, John E., 49–50, 70, 72, 108
Conyers, John, Jr., 96
Cooks, Sydney, 107–8
Crawcheck, Leonard, 89
Croghan, Leo, 71

Davis, Leon, 38–41, 57–58, 110–11, 116–17. *See also* Local 1199 Hospital and Nursing Home Employees Union
Delano Grape strike, 74
Dennis, Rembert C., 91
Department of Health, Education, and Welfare (HEW), 27–29, 43, 45, 102, 104–5, 109
Diggs, Charles C., 96
discrimination, 11–13, 15–16, 20–21, 22, 25, 27–28, 30–32, 34–36, 43–44, 47–48, 53, 55–56, 57, 76, 81, 87, 92, 96, 99, 102, 123. *See also* racism
disrespect, 5–6, 16, 21, 31–35, 43–44, 46, 47, 53, 55, 57, 63, 70, 80–83, 98, 107, 116, 122–23
Dittmer, John, 25
Doster, Lillie, 34, 82
Duke Medical Center, 79

Edisto, SC, 66
education, 10–13, 17, 25–28, 40, 71, 86, 92, 123
Eisner, Eugene, 89
Ellis, Earl, 63
Ellis, F. E., 88–89, 103
Emanuel AME Church, 71
Enwright, John T., 48
equal employment opportunities, 28–29, 104
equality, 5–6, 13, 16, 21, 25–26, 34–36, 57, 59–61, 87, 123; gender, 8; in health care, 22–23, 26, 30–31, 36; racial, 5, 8, 16, 22, 25, 45, 60, 79; within the workplace, 34, 60
Evans, Grace, 45
exclusion, 22, 29, 36, 39, 87
Executive Order 11246, 28, 104

Farber Brothers, 30
Farris, Carl, 62, 70, 88

Fauntroy, Walter, 109
Federal Bureau of Investigation (FBI), 106
Fennessy, Charles, 103
Fielding, Herber U., 48, 91
Finch, Robert F., 105, 109
Florida, 169
Foner, Moe, 31, 67, 108–9, 119. *See also* Local 1199 Hospital and Nursing Home Employees Union
Food, Tobacco, Agriculture and Allied Workers and Congress of Industrial Organizations (FTA-CIO), 19, 34
For Freedom's Sake (Lee), 3
Fourteenth Amendment, 26
Fourth Baptist Church, 62
Freedom Rides, 58, 76
Freedom Summer, 76

Gaillard, J. Palmer, 49–50, 52, 90, 108, 118
Gaines v. Missouri (1938), 25
gender, 3, 8, 19, 39, 41–42, 56, 73, 85–87. *See also* women
Georgia, 16
Godoff, Elliott, 40, 46–47, 89–90, 95, 108. *See also* Local 1199 Hospital and Nursing Home Employees Union
Goolsby, Bert, 94
Grady, Z. L., 51
Graham, J. Mitchell, 95–96, 110
Grant, Henry, 46–47, 71
Grant, Sammy, 11
Green, Laurie, 29
Greenberg, Jack, 94
Greensboro, NC, 26
grievances, 6, 16, 20, 31, 33–35, 43–49, 52–53, 55, 89, 92, 94–96, 98–99, 102, 103, 107, 109–11, 113–14, 118
Grimes, Ernestine, 33
Gross, Kali Nicole, 73
Gullah language and culture, 16–17

Hannah Mary Tabbs and the Disembodied Torso (Gross), 73
Harding Inn, 47
Harper's Magazine, 108

Hartnett, Thomas F., 93
Harvard University, 100
Harvey, Linda, 76
health care and health-care systems, 4, 6, 13, 22–26, 28, 31–32, 36, 73, 77, 87, 98, 102
Hell's Angels, 68, 83. *See also* White, Naomi
Highlander Folk School, 13
Hill-Burton Act, 6, 25–27
Holiday Inn, 101
Hollings, Ernest F., 105
Hospital Survey and Construction Act. *See* Hill-Burton Act
Hospital Workers Defense Team, 68, 84, 103. *See also* Saunders, William
Howe, Johnny, 101
Huff, William, 103
human dignity, 15, 33, 55, 80, 123
Hunter, Tera, 3

I Am Somebody, 75, 119
integration, 16, 20, 24–25. *See also* segregation
International Longshoreman's Association Local 1422-A, 6, 51, 55, 109
interracialism, 38–39
Islan, Jay, 108

Japan, 18
Jefferson, Jessie, 68–69
Jenkins, Esau, 10–13, 17, 48
Jenkins, Janie B., 11
Johns Hopkins Hospital, 119
Johnson, Lyndon B., 27, 98
Jones, James, 76
Jordan, Barbara, 117
Joyce, William, 66, 71
justice, 16, 26, 36, 63, 66–67, 70, 91–92, 99, 102; economic, 3–5, 8, 21–22, 31, 36, 39, 41, 55, 60–61, 79, 87, 88, 96, 106, 120, 122–23; racial, 4, 8, 10, 22, 25, 106, 120, 122; social, 3, 31, 36, 87, 88; vigilante, 85

Kennedy, Beverly, 69, 74
Kennedy, Jacqueline, 100
Kiely, Owen, 102

King, Coretta Scott, 40–41, 67, 71–72, 79, 85–86, 88, 90
King, Martin Luther, Jr., 7, 35, 58–62, 67, 69, 72, 85–86, 98–99, 122
King, Martin Luther, Sr., 72
Kircher, William F., 100, 109
Koch, Edward I., 96
Korea, 18

labor movements, 4–8, 9–10, 14, 19, 21, 23, 31, 34, 36, 37, 41, 51, 55–56, 59, 62, 66, 72, 73, 79–80, 85, 88, 94, 98–100, 118, 120, 121, 123
labor organizing, 8, 10, 13, 17, 21, 30, 32, 39, 62, 64, 74, 79, 82, 85–86, 88, 100, 105, 108, 116, 120, 121, 123. See also unions and unionization
leadership, 6, 8, 10, 76; African American, 10, 16, 43, 47–48, 57; political, 92; white, 46
Lee, Chana Kai, 3
Local 1199 Hospital and Nursing Home Employees Union, 6–7, 31, 36, 37, 38, 40–43, 46–47, 51, 53–56, 57–58, 62, 65–67, 71–72, 74, 76, 88–89, 94–95, 100, 103, 107, 110, 112, 117, 119–20, 121–22
Local 1199B Hospital and Nursing Home Employees Union, 41, 43, 51, 55–56, 65–66, 68, 75–76, 88, 111–13, 115–18, 121–22
Local 1199 Hospital Division Delegates Assembly, 111
Local 1199 Retail Drug Employees Union, 38–39
Lowenstein, Allard K., 96
L. Richardson Hospital, 26
Lutheran Hospital, 119

Maggard, Sally Ward, 42
Malcolm X, 18, 77
Manhattan Eye, Ear and Throat Hospital, 58
March on Washington for Jobs and Freedom, 59–60, 122
Matthias, Paul W., 99
McCollom, Matthew D., 99

McCord, William, 27–28, 30, 34–36, 43–45, 47–49, 51–53, 55, 58, 102–5, 107–9
McGinnis, Harold F., 20
McLeod, Daniel R., 28, 54, 88–90, 95
McNair, Robert E., 46, 50, 63–65, 67, 77–79, 89–93, 97, 98–104, 106, 110–11
Meany, George, 100
Medical College Hospital, 3, 5–8, 13–15, 21, 23, 28–30, 32–35, 43–49, 53–54, 57–58, 64, 67, 69, 72, 74–75, 81, 84–85, 89–90, 92, 94–96, 99, 101–5, 108–11, 113, 116, 119, 122–23; employee credit union, 103, 110, 114, 116; injunction, 50–51, 53–54, 64, 67, 72, 98; retaliation against strikers, 114; settlement, 21, 90, 104–5, 108–10, 112; termination and rehiring of twelve unionized workers, 50–53, 64, 87, 89, 102, 103–5, 108–11, 113–15, 118; termination of five hospital workers, 6, 16, 27–28, 31; union acknowledgment, 21, 54–55, 64, 110, 112
Medical College of South Carolina, 23–24
Medical College of the State of South Carolina, 24–25, 27–28
Medical Committee for Human Rights (MCHR), 26–27
Medical Society of South Carolina, 23–24
Medical University of South Carolina (MUSC), 122–23. See also Medical College Hospital
Memphis, TN, 29–30, 60, 72, 98–99
Memphis garbage workers' strike, 60, 97–99
Memphis State University, 77
Methodist Hospital Workers Strike, 42
Michigan, 96
Mississippi, 96
Mitchell, Carrie, 115
Mitchell, John N., 97
Moncks Corner, SC, 103
Monserrat, Joseph, 58
Moore, Fred Henderson, 63, 95, 103
Morris, Aldon, 10
Morris Brown African Methodist Episcopal Church, 53, 66–67, 72

mortality rates, 24
Moses H. Cone Memorial Hospital, 26
mothering, 74–76, 86–87
Moultrie, Mary, 3, 6, 13–17, 19, 30–36, 38, 41–43, 46, 49, 53, 63–69, 84, 89, 93, 95, 112–18, 121–22
Mount Sinai Hospital, 81
Moynihan, Daniel, 108–9
Muhammad, Elijah, 18

National Association for the Advancement of Colored People (NAACP), 11–14, 25–27, 44, 58, 94, 100, 101
National Association of Colored Women (NACW), 9
National Council of Distributive Workers of America, 118
National Guard, 65, 67, 70, 72, 77–78, 89, 92, 96, 102. *See also* police and law enforcement
National Labor Relations Board, 45
National Maritime Union, 20
National Urban League, 58
National War Labor Relations Board, 19
Negro American Labor Council, 59. *See also* Randolph, A. Philip
New York, 14, 16, 38–40, 58, 77, 96, 100, 108, 111, 112, 117, 122
New York Drug Clerks Association (NYDCA), 38–39
New York Times, The, 58, 67
Nicholas, Henry, 40–41, 51, 76, 89, 121–22
Nixon, Richard, 94, 97, 98, 108
North Carolina, 16, 96
North Charleston General Hospital, 119
Nunez, Emilio, 58

O'Neill, Stephen, 15
Orangeburg, SC, 76–77
Origins of the Civil Rights Movement, The (Morris), 10
Osman, Arthur, 36

Payne, Charles, 42
Payton, George, 63

Pennsylvania, 20, 47, 96
Perry, Trixie, 86
Pharmacists Union of Greater New York, 38–39
Philadelphia, PA, 20, 47
picketing and picket lines, 21, 26, 34, 41, 50–51, 53–55, 63–64, 67, 69, 71–72, 74–77, 80–83, 86, 106, 111, 116, 122
Pickney, William, 17
Pikesville, KY, 42
plantation mentality, 29–30
police and law enforcement, 18, 49–51, 61, 64, 69–72, 76–77, 79–81, 85, 89, 92, 95–96, 106, 107. *See also* National Guard; South Carolina Law Enforcement Division (SCLED)
Political Action Committee (PAC) of Charleston County, South Carolina, 91
politics, 13, 40, 88, 92, 96, 99, 105, 118, 120
Poor People's Campaign (PPC), 7, 60–61, 122–23. *See also* Southern Christian Leadership Conference (SCLC)
Poor People's Campaign: A National Call for Moral Revival (PPC), 122–23
Potts, John F., 77–78
poverty, 5, 17–18, 35, 53, 58, 60–61, 64, 99, 105, 123
power, 3, 5, 16, 21, 30, 33, 36, 38–42, 45–46, 52, 54, 56, 59, 65, 69, 81, 84–86, 88–89, 91–92, 100, 116–17, 119
Preservation Society of Charleston, 122
Progressive Club, 11, 17
protest community, 4, 9–10, 12–13, 15, 17, 31, 43, 120
protests, 6, 41, 50, 59, 64–68, 72, 76–80, 109–10; antiwar, 10; armed resistance, 79–81, 84; direct-action approach, 9, 62, 79; marches, 36, 59–60, 62, 65–67, 69–72, 75–76, 79, 88, 90, 96–97, 105–6, 109, 122; militant approach, 9–10, 38, 73, 77, 79–82, 84, 87, 97, 119; nonviolent approach, 9, 61–62, 68–69, 73, 79–81, 97–98, 106, 107, 119–20; self-defense approach, 9, 97; sit-ins, 5, 20, 26, 36, 49–50, 59; students and youth, 10, 65, 67, 69–71,

75–79; tradition, 6, 9–21, 123; walkouts, 55, 76, 81, 86, 109
Public Health Service, 27

Queens College, 77

race, 3, 5, 8, 14, 18, 21, 23, 29–30, 35, 38–39, 41, 45, 50, 79, 94, 96, 98, 101, 118; Black, 3–5, 7–8, 9–21, 22–26, 28–36, 37, 42–45, 47–48, 52–53, 55–56, 57–59, 62, 66–67, 69–72, 73–74, 77, 79–81, 85–87, 95, 98–100, 102, 105–6, 107, 113, 118, 120, 121–23; white, 11, 15, 17, 19–21, 24, 28–30, 32–35, 45–46, 69, 81, 107, 108, 113
racism, 6, 14, 16, 18, 29–31, 36, 56, 60, 76, 96. *See also* discrimination
Randolph, A. Philip, 58–59
Republican Party, 40, 105
resistance, 10, 19, 22, 25, 50, 55, 64–66, 72, 73, 79–81, 84–85, 87, 99, 104, 120
Resurrection City, 7, 61, 122
Retail, Wholesale, and Department Store Union (RWDSU), 36, 43, 119
Reuther, Walter, 100
Reynolds, James, 98
Reynolds, John, 60
Riley, Joseph P., Jr., 93
Rivers, Mendel, 105
Robinson, Otis, 84. *See also* Hospital Workers Defense Team
Robnett, Belinda, 13
Rockefeller, Nelson, 58
Roper, Thomas, 24
Roper Hospital, 24–25, 32
Rose, Margaret, 74
Ruffin, Josephine St. Pierre, 9
Ryan, William Fitz, 96

Sacks, Karen Brodkin, 42, 79
Saunders, William, 6, 16–19, 31–33, 36, 46, 57, 68, 84, 103–4, 106, 116, 122
scabs, 68, 70, 80, 82–83, 85, 114
Scarborough, Robert B., 89–90, 92
Schachte, J. Edwin, 64, 90
Schlitt, Jacob, 94

Schultz, George, 109
Schutt, Barbara, 108
segregation, 5–6, 12, 14, 20, 22, 25–29, 99, 105. *See also* integration
Selma, AL, 65, 72
Senate Select Committee on Nutrition and Human Needs, 105
separate but equal doctrine, 23, 25–27
sexism, 56
Sheraton-Fort Sumter Hotel, 100
Simkins, George, Jr., 26
Simmons, Rosetta, 31–34, 41, 55, 75, 83–85, 111, 113, 115, 117, 121, 123
Simons, Charles E., 54
Singletary, Clarence E., 50–51, 54, 64
slavery, 12, 16, 30, 58, 66
Small, Horace, 117
Smalls, Jerome, 70, 76
Smith, Clifford B., 76
social class, 3, 85, 98; poor, 17, 23, 60–61, 96, 105, 123; working class, 3–5, 8, 9–10, 13–14, 16, 21, 35, 37, 42, 56, 73, 86, 118, 120, 123
Solidarity Day, 61
South, 3, 5, 21, 22, 25–26, 30, 40, 42, 56, 66, 72, 86; hospitals, 27; medical schools, 23; racial etiquette, 18
South Carolina, 9, 34, 48, 51, 62, 76, 78, 90–91, 96–97, 102, 104–5, 108, 120, 121–23; dealing with unions, 53–55, 63, 65, 89, 93
South Carolina Council on Human Relations (SCCHR), 99
South Carolina General Assembly, 23, 44–45, 92–93, 95, 101, 102
South Carolina Law Enforcement Division (SCLED), 77–78. *See also* police and law enforcement
South Carolina Nurses Association, 108
South Carolina State College, 76
South Carolina Task Force for Community Uplift, 101–2
Southern Christian Leadership Conference (SCLC), 7, 56, 57–62, 65–72, 78, 84, 88–91, 94, 96, 97–98, 100, 103, 105–6, 107, 109–10, 112, 118, 120, 121

spying, 83–84
Stanfield, Reuel, 20
St. Francis Hospital, 32
St. Louis University, 77
St. Philip's Hospital, 23
Strom, Joseph, 77–79
St. Stephen's Episcopal Church, 46, 71
Students for a Democratic Society (SDS), 26

Teamsters Union, 14, 40. *See also* Moultrie, Mary
Theoharis, Liz, 122–23
Thurmond, Strom, 105
tobacco workers' strike of 1945, 6, 55, 82–83
Tobacco Worker's Union Local 15A, 19–20, 36, 43, 55, 117
To 'Joy My Freedom (Hunter), 3
Trade Union Unity League (TUUL), 39
Travis, Jason C., 101
Trenton, NJ, 20
tribal recognition and sovereignty, 123
Turner, Doris, 117
Turner, James, 94
Turner, Robert N., 45, 48
Turner, Robert W., 92
Turner, Sally, 30

Umoja, Akinyele Omowale, 80
union dues, 31, 35, 89, 103, 110, 114, 116, 121
unions and unionization, 5–7, 20–21, 30–31, 34–36, 37–56, 57–60, 63–65, 67, 72, 73–80, 83, 87, 88–91, 93–95, 97–99, 101–4, 107–8, 110, 112–14, 116–19, 121–23. *See also* labor organizing
United Auto Workers (UAW), 100
United Public Workers of America (UPWA), 40
University of South Carolina School of Medicine, 25
University of South Carolina system, 45–46
US Army, 17–19
US Commission on Civil Rights (USCCR), 94
US Department of Justice, 26, 94, 97
US Department of Labor, 28, 98

Van Arsdale, Harry, Jr., 99
vandalism, 78–79, 101
Veterans Affairs Hospital, 33
Veterans and Naval Hospital, 110
Vietnam, 69
violence, 10–12, 52–53, 68–70, 78–80, 82, 84–85, 96, 98, 106, 107, 111
Voorhees College, 77–78, 92
voter registration and voting, 11–13, 16, 25–26, 123

wages and pay, 5–6, 15–16, 21, 29, 31, 34–35, 43, 44–45, 47–49, 53, 57–60, 63, 73–74, 77, 80, 87, 89, 91, 94, 98–99, 103, 107, 118, 122; living, 25, 40, 63, 73, 123; minimum, 5, 15, 29, 39, 89, 96, 103, 109; poverty, 35, 44, 58, 105
Wainwright, John T., 51
Washington, DC, 61, 96
Washington Post, The, 67
"We Shall Overcome," 63, 108, 166
White, David, 41, 62, 66
White, Naomi, 15, 68–70, 75–76, 80–86, 114–15, 121
White House, 65, 97, 108–9
Wilbur, George W., 77
Williams, Hosea, 69, 106
Wise, John E., 15, 29
women, 5–6, 9, 21, 33–34, 39–42, 63, 73–75, 84–87, 103, 107; African American, 3–4, 6–8, 9–10, 12, 14–15, 19–21, 25, 30–33, 35, 37, 39–40, 42, 55–56, 72, 73–74, 79–81, 85–87, 120, 122–23; Filipino, 74; Hispanic, 40, 79; Puerto Rican, 39; white, 19, 20, 33; working-class, 3–4, 8, 9–10, 31, 35, 37, 42, 56, 73, 120, 123
working conditions, 6, 32, 39, 47, 49, 60, 73, 94, 98, 113

Young, Andrew, 66, 71, 88–90, 100, 107–8, 110, 120

ABOUT THE AUTHOR

Photo courtesy of the author

O. Jennifer Dixon-McKnight is an associate professor of history and African American studies and serves as program coordinator for the African American Studies minor at Winthrop University. She is also the director of Project 2020: A Collaborative Oral History, which is an oral history project that explores various aspects of the pivotal year 2020 and its impact on American society. Dr. Dixon-McKnight teaches courses in African American history, African American studies, and United States history. As faculty advisor to the Association of Ebonites, Winthrop's oldest African American student organization, and Gamma Beta Phi National Honor Society, she demonstrates a commitment to a student-centered approach to campus engagement that stretches beyond the classroom.

Her research interests include African American history, United States history, and women's and gender history, with a particular focus on using oral history to examine social movements forged by African American women. Dr. Dixon-McKnight was recognized as the Winthrop University 2023 Outstanding Junior Professor. She was awarded the Winthrop University Division of Student Affairs Faculty Student Life Award in Spring 2023. She was also recognized as the 2024 National Advisor of the Year for the Gamma Beta Phi National Honor Society.

www.ingramcontent.com/pod-product-compliance
Lightning Source LLC
Chambersburg PA
CBHW022023220426
43663CB00007B/1184